Uncle John's

BATHROOM READER

Takes a swing at **Baseball**

By the
Bathroom Readers' Institute

Bathroom Readers' Press
Ashland, Oregon

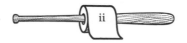

UNCLE JOHN'S BATHROOM READER®
TAKES A SWING AT BASEBALL

For information, write:
The Bathroom Readers' Institute, P.O. Box 1117,
Ashland, OR 97520
www.bathroomreader.com • 888-488-4642

Cover design by Michael Brunsfeld, San Rafael, CA
(Brunsfeldo@comcast.net)

Uncle John's Bathroom Reader® Takes a Swing at Baseball
by the Bathroom Readers' Institute

ISBN-13: 978-1-59223-882-3   ISBN-10: 1-59223-882-8

Library of Congress Cataloging-in-Publication Data
Uncle John's bathroom reader takes a swing at baseball.
p. cm.
ISBN 978-1-59223-882-8 (pbk.)
1. Baseball—Miscellanea. 2. Baseball—Humor.
GV873.U63 2008
796.357092—dc22
[B]
                                    2008004019

Printed in the United States of America
1 2 3 4 5   12 11 10 09 08

iii

THANK YOU!

The Bathroom Readers' Institute sincerely thanks the people whose advice and assistance made this book possible.

Gordon Javna	Lisa Meyers
Jay Newman	Eddie Deezen
Brian Boone	Sydney Stanley
John Dollison	Scarab Media
Amy Miller	Laurel Graziano
Thom Little	Ginger Winters
Julia Papps	Monica Maestas
JoAnn Padgett	David Calder
Melinda Allman	Karen Malchow
Michael Brunsfeld	(Mr.) Mustard Press
Claudia Bauer	Steven Style Group
Angela Kern	Publishers Group West
Judy Plapinger	Sarah, Kent & Mary
Dan Mansfield	Raincoast Books
Jef Fretwell	Porter the Wonder Dog
Lorraine Bodger	Thomas Crapper

✳   ✳   ✳

THE BIGGEST TRADE THAT NEVER WAS

Dan Topping, owner of the Yankees, and Tom Yawkey, owner of the Red Sox, got a little tipsy at a New York City bar one night in 1946. How tipsy? They decided to trade their respective teams' best hitters: the Red Sox's Ted Williams for the Yankees' Joe DiMaggio. They even shook hands on the deal. The next morning, however, cooler heads prevailed and they decided to call the deal off. But Yawkey said he'd still be interested if the Yankees threw in one of their younger players—"that little left fielder," Yogi Berra. Topping thought about it…and said no.

Hi Brendan! Hi Willa! (Future Hall of Famers.)

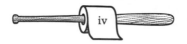

CONTENTS

Because the BRI understands your reading needs, we've divided the contents by length as well as subject.

Short—a quick read
Medium—2 to 3 pages
Long—for those extended visits, when something a little more involved is required
* Extended—for those leg-numbing experiences

v

❄   ❄   ❄

DICKEY PEARCE: BASEBALL INNOVATOR

Pearce's 22-year career began in 1856 during the heyday of the amateur era and ended two years after the National League rose to prominence. Along the way, the 5'3" player became a big star and revolutionized two important aspects of the game.

• **Shortstop:** Originally, the shortstop's duty was to stand in the outfield and relay short throws from outfielders into the infield. Pearce was the first to move to the spot between second and third base in an effort to stop groundballs *before* they reached the outfield.

• **The "tricky hit":** Always looking for an edge at the plate, sometime around 1866 Pearce decided not to swing at a pitch, but instead put his bat out front with both hands to "deaden" the ball so it only rolled a few feet. Soon after, other batters copied the technique, and the *bunt* became a new offensive tool.

INTRODUCTION

HEY BATTA BATTA! SWWWING, BATTA!
Welcome to our first all-baseball edition of the *Bathroom Reader*! We've wanted to do one of these for years. And now that we have, it's made us love the game even more: Baseball is loaded with heroes and goats, kings and jesters, and more than a few loons (our kind of people). And even though the game is usually celebrated for its spectacular moments, we found that it's the everyday events that illustrate what a truly unique sport it is. And that's what we've tried to capture.

With nearly two centuries' worth of stories to tell, we were only able to cram in a fraction of what we discovered (we're already planning another all-baseball edition), but this book will give you a lush picture of where the game came from, what kind of people play it (and watch it), and what goes on behind the scenes to make it happen. Some highlights:

• **Origins:** How are Medieval milkmaids linked to the birth of baseball? How did a man who never played the game get credited with inventing it? How did umpires survive the lawless 1890s?

• **The Greats:** Branch Rickey's struggles to innovate baseball, the original Cleveland Indian, and the courage of Lou Gehrig.

• **Records and Milestones:** History's most lopsided routs, things that only happened once, and how a famous play-by-play call might have been lost forever were it not for an overconfident fan.

• **The Fundamentals:** Does the tie go the runner? What exactly was the reserve clause? What's the ruling if a ball rolls into an empty beer cup?

• **The Bizarre:** Learn about "magic mud," the pitcher who performed cartwheels when leaving the mound, and *blernsball*.

Now it's time to step up to the plate and swing away. As we say at the Bathroom Readers' Institute:

Go with the Flow!

—Uncle John, the BRI Staff, and Porter the Wonder Dog

OPENING DAY!

*For the first page of this book, we celebrate the first day of a new
baseball season! Optimism runs high, but things can get
weird. So in that spirit, we say, "Play ball!"*

NO BUSINESS LIKE SNOW BUSINESS

April brings thoughts of sunshine and flowers. But neither showed up at New York's Polo Grounds on April 11,
1907, for the Giants' home opener: A storm the previous day had
buried the field under several inches of snow. When game time
arrived, the groundskeepers had barely finished shoveling the
snow off the field and into huge piles along the foul lines.

From the first pitch, the Giants couldn't get anything going
against the Phillies. And with the home team down 3–0 in the
late innings, their freezing fans grew restless. One man—noticing
how convenient it was that the huge pile of snow was within
reach of the front-row seats—made a snowball and threw it onto
the field. Then another fan did, then another, and another. Soon it
was a melee. Fans ran onto the field and pelted the players,
umpires, and each other with snowballs. As most of the players
retreated into their clubhouses (a few stayed out to throw snowballs), umpire Bill Klem was forced to call the game. The Giants
had to forfeit the first game of the season, on their way to a
fourth-place finish.

PAINT THE TOWN RED

Fans arrived at the first game of the Boston Braves' 1946 season
to find the outfield seats covered in a fresh new coat of red paint...
that hadn't completely dried yet. Immediately after the game,
several hundred fans with new red stripes on their pants stormed
into the team's offices and demanded that the Braves pay their
cleaning bills, which the team (eventually) did.

SEEN ONE DIAMOND, SEEN THEM ALL

The 1982 Opening Day ceremonies at the minor league Little
Falls Mets Field in New York were supposed to feature four parachuters descending onto the mound to throw out the first pitch.

Mr. April: Ted Williams batted .449 in Opening Day games, and hit safely in all 14 he played.

When the time came, the public-address announcer told the eager fans to look up and wait for them. The fans looked up and waited. And waited. Meanwhile, the plane's pilot had flown over a softball field about 10 miles away and mistakenly told the jumpers, "There's your field!" Back at the ballpark, the fans were still waiting. Eventually, the umpire told the teams to just start the game. About 20 minutes later, the four parachuters arrived at the ballpark…in a car.

PRESIDENTIAL STYLE

The first U.S. president to attend an Opening Day game was William Howard Taft in 1911. Clark Griffith, the owner of the Washington Senators, wanted the publicity, and Taft, who weighed 300 lbs., wanted to prove to the country that he was fit enough to throw a ball. From his grandstand seat, Taft threw a weak pitch to the Senators' star pitcher, Walter Johnson, but Johnson scooped up the ball before it hit the ground, saving the president from certain ridicule in the papers. Since then, every president except Jimmy Carter has thrown out a first pitch of the season. President Truman actually threw two first pitches on Opening Day, 1950—one with his right arm and the other with his left. Both were strikes.

QUICK WORK

Hank Aaron ended the 1973 season with 713 career homers—one behind Babe Ruth. Over the off-season, the 39-year-old slugger had to deal with death threats from people who didn't want a black player to break Ruth's record. Aaron, playing with the Atlanta Braves, opened the 1974 campaign in Cincinnati. He hit the very first ball thrown to him over the fence. Two games later, at the Braves' home opener, Aaron broke Ruth's record.

* * *

"Baseball is a game where a curve is an optical illusion, a screwball can be a pitch or a person, stealing is legal, and you can spit anywhere you like except in the umpire's eye or on the ball."

—Jim Murray

Pitcher with the most Opening Day starts: Tom Seaver (16).

MR. BASEBALL

The contributions and ideas of 19th-century sportswriter Henry
Chadwick made him one of baseball's most important pioneers.

WICKET TO RIDE
As late as the 1850s, Americans still played cricket, the
English bat-and-ball game. There were professional
cricket leagues on the East Coast and the *New York Times* hired an
English cricket fan and sportswriter named Henry Chadwick to
cover the games. But in 1854, while at a cricket park in Hoboken,
New Jersey, Chadwick witnessed a new and different bat-and-ball
game being played: baseball. Chadwick was immediately hooked
and became the game's champion. He believed the sport had the
potential to be, as he called it, "America's national game," so he
stopped writing about cricket and started writing about baseball for
several New York newspapers. He was such a passionate authority
on the game that he even came up with many rules and innovations that remain part of the game today. Here are a few of them.

• **RULES.** In 1864 Chadwick served on the Rules Committee at
the Eighth Annual Base-Ball Convention, where the official rules
for organized baseball were finalized. Among his contributions: He
called for the elimination of underhand pitching, he established
the distance between the pitcher's mound and home plate at 60.5
feet, and eliminated the rule that a hitter was out if a fielder
caught a hit on the first bounce.

• **STATISTICS.** Chadwick came up with the idea of the statistical
batting average—the three-digit number that represents a player's
percentage of hits per at-bat. (Thirty hits in 100 at-bats = a .300
average.) He also devised the earned-run average, the fundamental
statistical indicator of a pitcher's performance. ERA calculates the
average number of runs a pitcher gives up over the course of pitching a nine-inning game. The formula: the total number of runs the
pitcher has given up, divided by the number of innings pitched,
multiplied by nine. The lower the ERA, the better the pitcher.

• **KEEPING SCORE.** He also created the box score so he could
record all the events of a baseball game in a small amount of
space, which allowed more newspapers to cover baseball games.

Whitey Ford nicknamed Pete Rose "Charlie Hustle" in 1963, after Rose ran to first on a walk.

LITTLE-KNOWN FIRSTS

This is the first page of baseball firsts we've ever done.

• First baseball film: *The Ball Game*, a short documentary produced in 1898 by the Edison Manufacturing Company.

• First feature-length baseball film: 1915's *Right Off the Bat*. It starred former Giants outfielder Mike Donlin.

• First major league team to purchase its own airplane: the Brooklyn Dodgers, in 1957.

• First season that batting-average statistics were printed in newspapers: 1874

• What's so special about March 31, 1996? It was the first day that a regular-season major league game was played before April 1st.

• First former Little Leaguer to play in the majors: a 17-year-old pitcher named Joey Jay, who made his debut with the Milwaukee Braves on July 21, 1953.

• On October 17, 1987, the home-team Twins beat the Cardinals 10–1...in the first World Series game played indoors (at the Minneapolis Metrodome).

• First season in which there were no player-managers in the majors: 1956

• First rookie to hit a grand slam in the World Series: Yankees' infielder Gil McDougald, against the Giants in 1951. (The Yankees won the Series.)

• First former major leaguer to be inducted into the Radio Hall of Fame: "Mr. Baseball," Bob Uecker.

• First Canadian pitcher to start a World Series game: Reggie Cleveland, a native of Swift Current, Saskatchewan. In 1975 he pitched Game 5 for the Red Sox (but lost to the Reds).

• First intercollegiate "base ball" game: Amherst vs. Williams, on July 1, 1859. (Amherst won, 66–32.)

• First baseball journalist: William Cauldwell. He covered the New York Mutuals in 1853.

• In his first Little League at-bat in 1971, seven-year-old Mark McGwire hit a home run.

The first permanent concession stand in baseball was built at Wrigley Field in 1914.

TEAM NAME ORIGINS

*Here are the stories of how major league teams got their colorful
nicknames (although Uncle John would one day like to
see an actual pirate fight an actual bear cub).*

PITTSBURGH PIRATES. In 1882 they were known as the
Alleghenys, named after the nearby Allegheny River. But in the
1890s, they earned a new nickname—the Pirates—after they lured
(or stole) a few players from a rival club.

LOS ANGELES DODGERS. When the team was formed in
Brooklyn, New York, in 1890, the city had hundreds of trolley cars
zigzagging through its streets, and pedestrians were constantly
scurrying out of their way. That's why their team was called the
Brooklyn Trolley Dodgers (later shortened to Dodgers).

SEATTLE MARINERS. Seattle is one of the country's most
important seaports, so the name of the team reflects the city's
association with the maritime industry.

DETROIT TIGERS. Legend says that the Detroit Creams (the
cream of the baseball crop) became the Tigers in 1896, when Phil
Reid of the *Detroit Free Press* remarked that the team's striped uniforms looked like those of the Princeton Tigers.

CHICAGO CUBS. In 1902 the team was without a name
(abandoning tries with the Colts and the Orphans). That's when
a sportswriter named them "the Cubs." Why? Because it was short
enough to fit into a newspaper headline.

PHILADELPHIA PHILLIES. In case it's not obvious, a "philly"
is someone from the city of Philadelphia.

SAN FRANCISCO GIANTS. The New York Gothams baseball
club was fighting for a National League championship in 1886.
After one particularly stunning victory, manager Jim Mutrie
proudly addressed them as "my big fellows, my giants." The name
stuck. The New York Giants moved to San Francisco in 1958.

KANSAS CITY ROYALS. Kansas City already had a long baseball tradition when the American League expanded in 1969. The
Kansas City Monarchs of the Negro National League played there
from 1920 until the franchise folded in 1965. The Athletics were
there from 1955 until they moved to Oakland in 1968. So the city
was a natural choice for a new expansion franchise, which they
named after the "American Royal," one of the biggest livestock
shows in the United States, held annually in Kansas City.

TORONTO BLUE JAYS. When Toronto was awarded an expansion team in 1976, the new owners, Labatt Breweries, were trying to
come up with a name. At a meeting, Labatt board member (and
former Ontario Premier) John Robarts was talking about his morning routine: "I was shaving, and I saw a blue jay out my window."
One of the other members said, "Now, that's an interesting name."

FLORIDA MARLINS. Named after the minor league team it
replaced, the Miami Marlins, which was named after the large fish
found in the waters off the coast of Florida.

LOS ANGELES ANGELS. *Los Angeles* is Spanish for "the angels."
It was also the name of an old minor league team in Los Angeles.

MINNESOTA TWINS. The team represents the Twin Cities of
Minneapolis and St. Paul. It's also the first team named for an
entire state.

WASHINGTON NATIONALS. The District of Columbia had
two major league teams from 1901 until 1971: one known officially
as the Senators—then the Nationals, and then the Senators
again—that played from 1901 to 1961 (they became the Minnesota
Twins); and another team called the Senators that played from
1961 until 1971 (they became the Texas Rangers). When Washington, D.C., got another team in 2005, the choice for a name was
between those two, and the Nationals won out. Why? Mayor
Anthony Williams wanted to protest the District's lack of representation: He said it would be an outrage to name the team the
"Senators"—because D.C. has no senators in Congress.

For more team-name stories, turn to page 206.

GROUND RULE DOUBLE

*A freak play, a bad bounce, or a ballpark's particular quirks can
sometimes make a ball go where it's not supposed to go. When it does,
umpires may call it a ground rule double. The most common: when a
ball hits the ground in the outfield and bounces into the stands. Here
are some of the more bizarre ground rule doubles in history.*

• In 2001 Oakland's Johnny Damon hit a line drive into right
field. The ball hit the ground in fair territory...and then rolled
into an empty beer cup that had fallen out of the stands. Umpires
called it a ground rule double. (If the the ball hadn't landed in the
cup, Damon probably would have made it to second anyway.)

• In August 1982, Bill Buckner of the Chicago Cubs hit a long
drive into the outfield of Wrigley Field. If it had gone a few feet
higher, it would have cleared the wall for a home run. But it didn't.
Instead, it landed in the famous ivy that covers Wrigley's outfield
wall...and stayed there. The umpires gave Buckner a ground rule
double.

• The Minnesota Twins' Metrodome has a relatively low roof—it's
only 172 feet high—so there are some special rules for the stadium.
If the ball hits the roof and then lands in foul territory, it's a foul
ball. If it hits the roof and lands fair, it's a fair ball. If it gets caught
in the roof over fair territory, it's a ground rule double, and that's
happened only once—in 2004, to Corey Koskie of the Twins. But
in 1984, Dave Kingman of Oakland hit a pop fly that went up...
and disappeared. What happened? It was later discovered that
Kingman's ball had flown through a tiny drainage hole in the
roof—and out of the stadium. Kingman got a ground rule double.

• In 2007 Melky Cabrera of the New York Yankees hit a line
drive into the middle of the infield. The ball hit Kansas City
pitcher Ryan Braun in the leg so hard that it flew into the air (the
ball, not Braun's leg), bounced once on the Yankees' dugout roof
(along the first base line), and went into the stands. Cabrera got a
ground rule double (and Braun wasn't hurt).

Richie Ashburn once hit the same fan twice with foul balls—in the same at-bat.

DUH!

Baseball may be the "thinking man's game," but even great thinkers can have occasional lapses of...thinking.

"Man, it was tough out there. The wind was blowing about 100 degrees."
—Mickey Rivers

"We're not the brightest tools in the shed."
—Doug Mientkiewicz, on his Red Sox teammates

"The secret to keeping winning streaks going is to maximize the victories while at the same time minimizing the defeats."
—John Lowenstein

"Two weeks—maybe three. You never know with psychosomatic injuries."
—Jim Palmer, on how long he'd be on the DL

"It's a good thing I stayed in Cincinnati for four years. It took me that long to learn how to spell it."
—Rocky Bridges

"Slow thinkers are part of the game, too. And some of these slow thinkers can hit a ball a long way."
—Alvin Dark

"That's why I don't talk. Because I talk too much."
—Joaquin Andujar

"Not true at all. Vaseline is manufactured right here in the United States."
—Don Sutton, when accused of using foreign substances

"All I'm asking for is what I want."
—Rickey Henderson

"Sometimes they write what I say and not what I mean."
—Pedro Guerrero

"I'm a four-wheel-drive-pickup type of guy, and so is my wife."
—Mike Greenwell

"The only problem I have in the outfield is with fly balls."
—Carmelo Martinez

Steve Balboni: Hitting your first grand slam is a thrill. I'll always remember this.
Reporter: You hit one two years ago.
Balboni: (*Pause*) You're right. I guess I forgot about that one.

Any player named on at least 75% of ballots cast is elected to the Hall of Fame.

SCREWBALL PROMOTIONS

By design, some days at the ball park are much stranger than others.

THE POLITICALLY CORRECT GAME

In July 2007, the Lowell (Mass.) Spinners, the Class A minor league club for the Red Sox, announced that for their game against the Brooklyn Cyclones, they would try not to offend anyone in attendance. The basemen were renamed "base persons"; the bat boy became the "bat person"; and the shortstop was the "vertically challenged stop." When an error was committed, it wasn't announced (it might have made the player who committed the error feel bad). Sadly, the home team had a "run differential" of four runs, and lost 9–5. This wasn't the Spinners' only unusual promotion. After their former player, 5'7" David Eckstein, was named 2006 World Series MVP, the Spinners honored the short shortstop with "David Eckstein's Step Stool Night." (Said Eckstein, "If you're short like me, it's useful.")

MUSTACHE NIGHT

Among New York Mets fans, what's even more popular than Keith Hernandez? Keith Hernandez's mustache. He's been sporting it since his 1970s heyday with the Mets, and it was recently named "Top Sports Mustache of All Time" by the American Mustache Institute. Hernandez, now a Mets broadcaster (and spokesman for Just for Men Beard and Mustache dye), was honored during a 2007 home game against the Phillies: The first 20,000 fans were given fake mustaches. One fan, who called himself Sal, didn't need the fake: "I grew my mustache because of Keith's and I've kept it ever since!"

PRE-PLANNED FUNERAL NIGHT

In August 2003, the minor league Hagerstown (Maryland) Suns held a drawing. More than 2,000 fans entered, but only one could win the grand prize: an all-expenses-paid funeral, including a death certificate, embalming, and a casket—a combined value of over $6,500. (Hopefully the winning fan will have to wait many years to use it.)

Tom Brokaw and Kiss's Gene Simmons have both been honored by bobblehead nights.

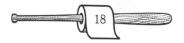

GRANDSTAND MANAGERS DAY

By August 1951, the St. Louis Browns were out of the pennant race. Unhappy fans were grumbling that they could do a better job of managing than Zack Taylor was doing, so owner Bill Veeck decided to let them give it a try. A week prior to a game against the Philadelphia Athletics, Veeck ran a press release in the St. Louis *Globe–Dispatch* announcing the challenge, along with a ballot that allowed readers to choose the starting lineup. The fans responded enthusiastically, benching two starters and starting two backup players, Sherm Lollar and Hank Arft. When game time arrived, Taylor sat in the stands smoking his pipe. He and 1,100 other fans all held large signs that said "YES" on one side and "NO" on the other. When a tactical decision came up in the game, such as whether to bring in a relief pitcher or to play the infielders back for the double play, the "grandstand managers" were asked what to do. They held up their signs while a local judge tallied up the majority and then relayed the results to the dugout. So how did the fans do? Not bad. The Browns won the game 5–3, and Lollar and Arft combined for three runs and four RBIs. "Never has a game been called better," boasted Veeck.

SILENT NIGHT

Bill Veeck's son, minor league owner Mike Veeck, is continuing his father's tradition of odd promotions. In July 2003, Veeck held "Silent Night," so his Charleston Riverdogs could claim the record for "Quietest Game Ever." Fans were given duct tape to wear over their mouths, along with signs saying "YAY," "BOO," and "HEY BEER MAN." After the fifth inning—thus making it an official game—relieved fans were allowed to remove the duct tape and express themselves verbally. (In 2002 the Riverdogs held "Nobody Night," in which the gates remained locked until after the fifth inning, guaranteeing the team the lowest attendance in professional baseball history: zero.)

TED WILLIAMS POPSICLE NIGHT

In 2003, after the legendary hitter's body was cryogenically frozen, the Bisbee-Douglas Copper Kings celebrated the…um…event by giving each of the first 500 fans a popsicle.

WHY DO BASEBALL GAMES START AT 5:05?

Vitally important questions about all things baseball.

Q: *Why do baseball managers, unlike coaches of other professional sports teams, wear uniforms?*

A: This goes back to the early days of baseball—when managers were often also players, and had to wear uniforms to play. That was not the case for early basketball coaches, or for most early hockey and football coaches. And though player-managers had become scarce by the mid-1900s (Pete Rose of the 1986 Reds was the last), the tradition of wearing the uniform remained. Only two managers, Connie Mack of the Philadelphia Athletics from 1901 to 1950, and Burt Shotton of the Brooklyn Dodgers in the late 1940s, have ever gone against tradition by wearing suits during the games. The official rules say that "coaches" must wear uniforms. But although they are the equivalent of coaches in other sports…baseball managers are *managers*, and, therefore, not held to the rule.

Q: *Why do baseball games begin at five minutes after the hour or half-hour, at times like 1:05 or 7:35, instead of exactly on the hour?*

A: It's believed to have begun when radio stations started broadcasting games. Radio shows were already timed to start and end on the hour or half hour, so having the games start at five minutes after gave stations time for ads, for the announcers to talk about the game to be played, and, since 1941, for the national anthem to be played. But not *all* games start at five after: Toronto starts games at seven minutes after, other teams start games at 10 or even 15 after, and afternoon games often start at five minutes *before* the hour. And in 2006, the Chicago White Sox signed a three-year, half-million-dollar deal to change the times of their 7:05 games to…7:11. (Guess who they made the deal with.)

Q: *Why do players pound home plate with their bats?*

A: It's not as silly a question as you might first think. Many play-

---

Kids, stay in school! You must be a high-school graduate to play for a big-league baseball team.

ers do it for a specific reason—to gauge their position relative to the plate, so they will stand in their exactly "right" spot. (The rest of them probably just do it to look tough.)

Q: *Why aren't there any women in Major League Baseball?*
A: Probably because a woman good enough to make a big-league team hasn't tried yet. Currently there is no rule that says women can't play, and although it's fair to say that the "men-only" tradition of the game would die hard, baseball is a business, and the first team to have a successful female player would undoubtedly be rewarded financially. So maybe there's one coming soon. There have been female players in the *minor* leagues. The first, and most famous, was Jackie Mitchell, who was signed to the Southern Association's Double-A Chattanooga Lookouts in 1931 when she was 17 years old. On April 2 of that year, she braved the boos and taunts of the fans at her first game, an exhibition game against the New York Yankees in Chattanooga…and struck the first batter out on five pitches. She needed only three pitches for the next strikeout. Who were the batters? Babe Ruth and Lou Gehrig. Mitchell was pulled from the game after she walked the next batter, and women were banned from minor and major league baseball by Commissioner Kenesaw Mountain Landis just days later, on the grounds that it was "too strenuous" for them. The truth was, it was too embarrassing for the men to get struck out by a woman. Mitchell played in exhibition games for the next few years and retired when she was 23. She died in 1987, five years before the ban on women in professional baseball was officially lifted.

*   *   *

HE PITCHED A NO-PITCHER

On July 15, 2005, Mike Stanton came in to pitch for the Nationals against the Brewers in the bottom of the 9th. The bases were loaded. Before he threw a pitch, he balked, walking the hitter, and sending the man on third base across the plate. Stanton was credited with the loss, despite not having thrown a single pitch.

There was only one Canadian on the 1993 Blue Jays World Series team. (Outfielder Rob Butler.)

CONFERENCE CALL

When the manager goes out to the mound, or the batter and the umpire exchange words, only the lip-readers in the crowd know what they're saying. Thankfully, some players love to play and tell. (Warning for the faint-of-heart: Baseball players sometimes use strong language...so proceed with caution.)

AIR CONDITIONING

During a very hot spring training game in Florida, Phillies veteran Lenny Dykstra made several derogatory comments to home plate umpire Eric Gregg, arguing every call. Finally, Gregg had heard enough: "Lenny, I know exactly what you want me to do. You want me to run you out of this game. If I got to stay in this heat, you got to stay in this heat, so it doesn't matter what you call me, how many times you call me, I'm not running you out of this game." Dykstra stayed in...and kept his mouth shut.

WHEN YOU GOTTA GO

Philadelphia A's manager Connie Mack was known as much for his class and civility as he was for his managerial prowess. Mack almost never cursed...almost. One day, though, he wasn't at all happy with the performance of his best pitcher, Robert "Lefty" Grove. Mack walked out to the mound and held his hand out for the ball. Grove scowled at him and said, "Go take a sh*t." Mack calmly replied, "No, you go take a sh*t, Robert."

DON'T ASK ME

One day while managing the Boston Braves in 1941, Casey Stengel was having a rough first inning against the Giants—he watched his starter, Al Javery, give up three base hits on the first three pitches of the game. As Stengel walked out to the mound, he called over catcher Phil Masi to join in the conversation. Stengel asked Masi, "What kind of pitches has he been throwing?" "I dunno," replied Masi, "I haven't caught one yet."

AND THE RICK-ET'S RED GLARE

Former Cubs first baseman Mark Grace often recounts this story about pitcher Rick Sutcliffe: "One day Rick gave up back-to-back

home runs in Cincinnati. And in Cincinnati, they shoot off fire-works after a Red hits a home run. And Sutcliffe was pretty intense on the day he pitched. So Eric Davis takes him deep and Paul O'Neill takes him deep right after that. So Sutcliffe is all mad, and Billy Connors comes out to the mound and Sutcliffe yells at him, 'I know I gave up f***ing back-to-back home runs and get your f***ing a** back in the dugout and tell Zimmer to f***ing settle down there, too!' Billy looks at him and says, 'I know you have everything under control, Rick. I just wanted to give that guy running the fireworks a little time to reload.'"

PUTTING ON A SHOW

Umpire Tim McClelland recounted this story on MLB.com: "A long time ago at a game in Triple-A, Jack McKeon was the man-ager in Omaha. He came out and said, 'I know you got that call right, but I have a big, full house here and my team isn't playing very well. Can we just stand out here and argue a little bit? I am just going to stand here and bob my head and raise my hands a little bit, but I am not mad at you. I just want to put on a little bit of a show. When I'm done you run me and I'll go to the dugout.'

"I said, 'That's fine, whatever you need to do, go ahead and do it.' So I told him I had a good dinner last night at a restaurant and asked if he's ever been there. He said no, and started kicking the dirt and raising his hands and said, 'Maybe I should try it out sometime!' Then he said, 'Well, I think this was enough, why don't you run me now?' So I did and he walked away."

A NOTE FOR YOU

Umpire Doug Harvey knew very well that Dodgers pitcher Don Sutton liked to doctor up baseballs with sandpaper (Sutton's nick-name: "Black and Decker"), and one afternoon Harvey thought he'd caught him in the act. He walked out to the mound and asked to inspect Sutton's glove. The pitcher gave the ump an innocent look and said, "Sure, go ahead." Sure enough, Harvey found a small piece of paper concealed in Sutton's mitt. He pulled it out and unfolded it. It wasn't sandpaper—it was note that read: "You're getting warm, but it's not here."

Sweeeet! A line drive or grounder hit up the middle close to 2nd base is called a *honey.*

WHO'D THEY GET FOR...

Building a team is like gambling. Actually, it is gambling. Some trades go your way; others make you want to bury your head in the sand.

BRIAN GUINN?
Following the 1986 season, the Oakland Athletics traded three young prospects to the Chicago Cubs: David Wilder, Brian Guinn, and Mark Leonette. In return, the A's got pitcher Dennis Eckersley, a 12-year veteran and former ace who'd just pitched a dismal 6–11 season. In his first year in Oakland, Eckersley continued his mediocre streak, going 6–8. Then manager Tony La Russa switched him to relief pitching, where he became massively successful. From 1988 to '90, Eckersley saved 128 games and Oakland went to the World Series all three years. In 1992 he won the Cy Young Award and was eventually elected to the Hall of Fame. Wilder, Guinn, and Leonette never made it out of the minor leagues.

...MILT PAPPAS?
In 1966 the Baltimore Orioles sent two-time All-Star pitcher Milt Pappas (who had a record of 110–74 at that point) to the Cincinnati Reds. In return, the Orioles got Frank Robinson, an established star—he was the 1956 Rookie of the Year and the 1961 MVP—who, Reds execs said, was fading. But when he got to Baltimore, he did even better than he'd done in Cincinnati, leading the American League in hits, home runs, RBIs, and batting average. Robinson was the 1966 MVP and led the Orioles to a World Series championship. Pappas lasted only two years in Cincinnati, going 30–29 before being traded to Atlanta.

...DINNER?
On the day of the trade deadline in 1994, Minnesota traded superstar Dave Winfield to Cleveland for "a player for be named later." The 1994 players' strike began two weeks later. Winfield didn't play for the Indians because the strike ended the season, and then he became a free agent. To settle the trade, Cleveland and Minnesota executives went out to dinner, and the Indians picked up the tab. Winfield is the only player in history to be traded for a dinner.

Only player to get caught stealing to end the World Series: Babe Ruth, in 1926.

...LARRY ANDERSEN?

Houston traded veteran pitcher Larry Andersen to Boston in 1990 for minor leaguer Jeff Bagwell, a player Boston picked in the 1989 amateur draft. Bagwell got called up to the Astros in 1991, where he had 15 home runs, a .294 average and was named the National League's Rookie of the Year. In 1994 he hit .368 with 39 home runs and was the league's MVP. Andersen, who'd spent two-thirds of his previous 15 seasons in the minor leagues, retired in 1994 with a lifetime 40–39 record.

...FRED MANRIQUE?

In the middle of the 1989 season, the Texas Rangers traded 21-year-old Sammy Sosa (he'd only played 25 games) to the Chicago White Sox, along with shortstop Scott Fletcher and rookie pitcher Wilson Alvarez, for Fred Manrique and veteran home-run hitter Harold Baines. Sosa went on to become a superstar—in 1998 he hit 66 home runs and was the National League MVP. He currently has 609 home runs, the fifth-highest total ever. The owner of the Rangers at the time, George W. Bush, later called the trade "the biggest mistake of my adulthood."

...DOYLE ALEXANDER?

In 1988 the Atlanta Braves traded Alexander, a solid pitcher who'd won 194 games and struck out over 1,500 hitters, to Detroit in exchange for 21-year-old minor league pitcher named John Smoltz. Alexander was nearing the end of his career (1988 was his 18th season), but Smoltz went on to become part of the Braves' dominant 1990s pitching rotation. Pitching in a roster that included Tom Glavine and Greg Maddux, Smoltz led Atlanta to 14 straight postseason appearances.

...JIM FREGOSI?

After the 1971 season, the California Angels sent Fregosi to the New York Mets. Once a solid hitter who'd averaged 170 hits each season for a decade, Fregosi slumped to just 81 in 1971, prompting his trade. The Angels got four players in return: Don Rose, Leroy Stanton, Frank Estrada...and Nolan Ryan, a pitcher with a lifetime record of 29–38 at the time. But Ryan blossomed when he got to California, winning 19, 21, and 22 games in his first three seasons, and setting off his Hall of Fame career.

UNIFORMS THROUGH THE AGES, PART I

The world's first organized baseball club, the Knickerbockers, was founded in New York 1845, but four more years would pass before they adopted an official team uniform. Here's a timeline to show how baseball uniforms have changed continuously ever since.

1849

On April 24, 1849, the Knickerbocker Base Ball Club adopted the first uniform in the history of organized baseball: blue wool "pantaloons" (pants), white flannel collared shirts, and straw hats. Hot, scratchy woolen uniforms wouldn't make much sense today...and they didn't then, either. But that was beside the point. The Knickerbocker club was first and foremost an exclusive social club, one that happened to be organized around baseball. Merchants, stockbrokers, insurance salesmen, and several idly rich "gentlemen" were counted among its members, and these dignified fellows prided themselves on not playing the game too roughly. Even if they had, more durable fabrics like cotton, denim, and canvas were unacceptable—they were too "working-class." For many years, the "best" baseball clubs avoided the color red for the same reason: Because red dye was cheap and widely available, it was common among small-town and working-class athletic clubs.

1850–60s

• In the late 1850s, some teams began modeling their baseball togs after the uniforms worn by volunteer firemen. Many uniforms included "shield-front" jerseys, which featured a shield-shaped piece of fabric sewn and/or buttoned to the front of the shirt, often featuring the team's town name or initials.

• Another common feature of baseball uniforms of the 1850s and 1860s: ties. Bow ties were worn with shield-front jerseys; regular neckties were worn with (and tucked into) jerseys that had laced or button-down shirt fronts.

• In 1860 the Brooklyn Excelsiors began wearing belts with the word "EXCELSIOR" displayed in large letters across the front.

Final year the White Sox actually *wore* solid white socks: 1948.

This makes them the first team to display their team nickname anywhere on their uniforms.

• As baseball grew increasingly competitive and aggressive, full-length pantaloons became a problem—players tripped over the flapping pant legs as they ran. Some teams experimented with pants so tight that they needed buttons from calf to ankle just to get the pants on and off. Others secured their pants with straps, the way bicyclists use straps to keep their pant legs out of bicycle chains.

• In 1868 the newly founded Cincinnati Red Stockings borrowed an idea from cricket teams and started wearing knee-length knickers. Over the next few years, so many teams copied the style that sporting goods manufacturers begin selling them as "baseball pants." These short pants were what made nicknames like Red Stockings or White Stockings possible: For the first time, fans could see the color of their favorite team's socks.

1870s

• After years of popularity, shield-front jerseys fell out of favor, and baseball teams switched to jerseys that laced up the front. This style of jersey would remain popular through the 1890s.

• In 1877 *Spalding's Base Ball Guide*, the nation's premier baseball catalog, introduced its "Base Ball Hat," a slightly flattened derby or bowler hat (it never caught on). By the late 1880s, the catalog offered ten different styles of hat, including four pillbox-shaped hats with bills and five others that looked kind of like modern caps—some with smaller bills, some with larger ones; some with rigid crowns, others with floppy cloth crowns. The one closest in appearance to modern caps was probably the "Jockey Shape Cap," a larger version of the cap worn by jockeys in horse races.

1880s

• As the game got even rougher, baseball equipment manufacturers started offering baseball pants with built-in quilted padding.

• Major league baseball's biggest-ever uniform experiment took place in 1882, when league officials decreed that henceforth, each *position* on a team would have its own unique uniform. All first basemen in the league would wear silk jerseys with vertical red and white stripes and a matching baseball cap, center fielders would wear red and black stripes, and so on. All players on all

---

First team to fly to a baseball game: the Marysville Merchants (California), in August 1921.

teams would wear white pants, white belts, and white ties. The only indicator of *which* team a player plays for: the color of his stockings—Chicago would wear white stockings, Cleveland would wear navy blue, and so on. League officials had high hopes for the new color scheme, but no one else did—the players hated the "clown costumes" from the start, and so did the fans, who found them confusing. Were they even necessary? A first baseman is pretty easy to identify—*he's the guy standing on first base*. Clown costumes lasted only half a season before they were laughed and booed out of ballparks forever.

• Three major teams experimented with pinstriped uniforms in 1888: the Washington Senators, the Detroit Wolverines, and the Brooklyn Bridegrooms. The Senators and the Wolverines had bad seasons, which may be why they dropped the pinstripes in 1889. Brooklyn had a good year, and the following season they added *horizontal* pinstripes, creating a uniform covered entirely with squares. The team, later called the Superbas and then the Dodgers, would revive the checkered look in 1907 and again in 1916 before finally dumping it for good in 1917.

1890s
• As the 1800s drew to a close, laced-front baseball jerseys went out of style. By 1901 only two teams, the Boston Americans and the Boston Nationals, were still wearing them (every other team had switched to buttoned jerseys), but both teams abandoned the lace-up look after the 1910 season.

*For more baseball uniform origins, turn to
Part II of our timeline on page 171.*

*   *   *

BIG NAME MATCHUP
On May 29, 1996, Giants pitcher William Van Landingham took the mound against the Mets' Jason Isringhausen. At 25 letters, that sets the record for the longest combined last names of two opposing pitchers in the history of major league baseball.

First major leaguer to wear his birthday on his back: Carlos May (#17), born on May 17, 1948.

PITCHER'S MENTALITY

How does a big-leaguer deal with the pressure of pitching? Here are some insights.

"I hate all hitters. I start a game mad and I stay that way until it's over."
—Don Drysdale

"Hitting is timing. Pitching is upsetting timing."
—Warren Spahn

"Just take the ball and throw it where you want to. Throw strikes. Home plate don't move."
—Satchel Paige

"It's no fun throwing fastballs to guys who can't hit them. The real challenge is getting them out on stuff they can hit."
—Sam McDowell

"When I'm pitching well, it's like I'm in a nice little ballet. Everything is going slow all around me. It's very peaceful."
—Barry Zito

"Pitching is the art of instilling fear."
—Sandy Koufax

"When you can throw 97 miles an hour and put the ball over the plate anytime you want, it's fun."
—Randy Johnson

"I exploit the greed of all hitters."
—Lew Burdette

"Everybody kind of perceives me as being angry. It's not anger, it's motivation."
—Roger Clemens

"I was in the outfield and he was walking out of the bullpen. He was grumping, 'I don't have a thing today. Nothing!' I asked, 'Then why are you going in?' He said, 'The hitters don't know that.'"
—Dave Schneck, on Tug McGraw

"It helps if the hitter thinks you're a little crazy."
—Nolan Ryan

"Control is what kept me in the big leagues for 22 years."
—Cy Young

"I focus on making that one pitch. That's what I tell myself, 'One pitch.' You can't worry about the next one. Even with a good hitter, he'll get out seven times out of ten. I want to make sure that this is one of those seven."
—Tom "Flash" Gordon

"Good pitching will always stop good hitting and vice-versa." —Casey Stengel

HITTER'S MENTALITY

How does a big-leaguer deal with the pressure of batting? Here are some insights.

"The pitcher has got only a ball. I've got a bat. So the percentage of weapons is in my favor and I let the fellow with the ball do the fretting."
—Hank Aaron

"Every great batter works on the theory that the pitcher is more afraid of him than he is of the pitcher."
—Ty Cobb

"Think. Don't just swing. Think about the pitcher, what he threw you last time up, his best pitch, who's up next. Think."
—Ted Williams

"You can't think and hit the ball at the same time."
—Yogi Berra

"Hitting is better than sex."
—Reggie Jackson

"I think of myself as 'catching' the ball with my bat and letting the pitcher supply the power."
—Barry Bonds

"A full mind is an empty bat."
—Branch Rickey

"When a pitcher's throwing a spitball, don't worry and don't complain. Just hit the dry side like I do."
—Stan Musial

"Never let the fear of striking out get in your way."
—Babe Ruth

"I study pitchers. I visualize pitches. That gives me a better chance every time I step into the box. That doesn't mean I'm going to get a hit every game, but that's one of the reasons I've come a long way as a hitter."
—Mark McGwire

"How hard is hitting? You ever walk into a pitch-black room full of furniture that you've never been in before and try to walk though it without bumping into anything? Well, it's harder than that."
—Ted Kluszewski

"Hit 'em where they ain't."
—Wee Willie Keeler

"Hitting the ball was easy. Running around the bases was the tough part."
—Mickey Mantle

"Good hitting will always stop good pitching and vice-versa." —Casey Stengel

TAMPATIENCE

The Tampa Bay, Florida, area has long been affiliated with baseball, hosting spring training facilities since the 1920s. But before Tampa Bay finally got a major league franchise, the Devil Rays, in 1995, they almost got the...

Tampa Bay Twins: In 1984 a group of investors led by Florida real estate developer Bill Mack attempted to buy the cash-strapped Minnesota Twins and move them to Tampa Bay. American League president Dr. Bobby Brown prevented the sale because he didn't think Tampa Bay was a large enough city to support a major league baseball team.

Tampa Bay Rangers: Four years later, Mack and his investors tried to buy the Texas Rangers with the stated intention of moving the team to Tampa Bay. Again, the league blocked the sale because of concerns that the local market was too small.

Tampa Bay White Sox: In 1989 Chicago White Sox owner Jerry Reinsdorf told the league and the city of Chicago that he'd move the team to Tampa Bay if he didn't get a new stadium. By a single vote, the Illinois legislature approved a new ballpark, and the White Sox stayed in Chicago.

Tampa Bay Mariners: After 13 seasons of losing games and losing money in Seattle, in 1990 the Mariners considered a move to Tampa Bay, impressed with the brand-new (and empty) Florida Suncoast Dome. The move never panned out.

Tampa Bay Nothings: After four teams almost moved there, Tampa was thought to be a shoo-in when the National League expanded in 1991. The new teams went to Denver and Miami instead.

Tampa Bay Giants: In 1992 San Francisco Giants owner Bob Lurie agreed to sell the team to a group of Tampa investors led by Vince Naimoli. Under pressure from San Francisco city officials, the league blocked the sale, and the Giants were purchased by a group of hometown investors.

Tampa Bay Devil Rays: In 1995 Major League Baseball expanded again. An American League franchise was awarded to...Tampa Bay.

April 26, 2006: The Yankees drew 14 walks in a game against Tampa Bay. None scored.

ATTACK OF THE KISSING BANDIT!

Were you ever at a game when Morganna Roberts, the "Kissing Bandit," bounded out onto the field? In her day, she was one of the most famous baseball fans in the entire country.

ON A BET
One summer afternoon in 1971, a 17-year-old woman named Morganna Roberts went to Riverfront Stadium to see a Cincinnati Reds game with a friend. The game was pretty uneventful until Roberts's friend "dirty double-dared" her to run out onto the field and give Pete Rose a kiss. Why not? Roberts climbed over the railing, ran across the field, and gave the startled but welcoming Rose a big smooch as fans roared their approval.

Roberts must have enjoyed the experience, because a few games later she ran out onto the field to kiss another player…and then another…and another. Blonde, with a top-heavy Dolly Parton build (she claimed measurements of 60-24-39), Roberts got a lot of attention. Her profile rose with each pucker and she soon found her way into the newspapers, where a Cincinnati sportswriter dubbed her "The Kissing Bandit."

SOMETHING TO SEE

If you ever got a chance to see the Kissing Bandit at work, you probably never forgot it. Fans aren't allowed on the field for security reasons, no matter how famous they are, so Morganna typically had to sneak into the baseball park incognito, her ample attributes concealed beneath a bulky jacket or some other loose-fitting garment. Then, at the opportune moment, she'd throw off her disguise and jump down to the playing field wearing a tight T-shirt and short shorts and bound across the field to the object of that day's affection.

Roberts parlayed her fame into a career as an exotic dancer, and, thanks to bookings in nightclubs and strip joints all over the country, she was able to visit nearly every ballpark in major league baseball. Over the years she kissed everyone from Johnny Bench

---

The Cubs have won more games than any other pro team in any sport.

and Don Mattingly to Nolan Ryan and Cal Ripken Jr. Why stop at baseball? Morganna also snuck into pro basketball games to kiss Kareem Abdul-Jabbar, Charles Barkley, and other greats.

Stadium officials weren't crazy about her breaking the rules, but the players liked her, and many grew to see her as a good luck charm. After she kissed George Brett of the Kansas City Royals in the mid-1980s, his team went on to win the next 22 of 23 games. In 1988 she tried to kiss Ryne Sandberg of the Chicago Cubs but failed when she was blocked by an umpire. Sandberg hit the next pitch out of the park. (Maybe the umpire shouldn't have gotten involved—the Cubs still lost the game.)

BUST-ED

Roberts's antics got her arrested more than once over the years. In 1985 she was charged with criminal trespassing after she ran onto the field during the Houston Astros season opener to kiss pitcher Nolan Ryan. Her attorney claimed that she was a victim of physics—when she leaned over the railing "the laws of gravity took over," he explained. "She ran out onto the field and saw police chasing her, so where would she run but to the safety of the pitcher?" Roberts managed to beat that rap, but when she was arrested in 1988 during the Baltimore Orioles "Fantastic Fan Night," she spent a night in jail before the prosecutor set aside the charges as long as she stayed off the field at Memorial Stadium.

GAME OVER

Roberts was a part of baseball for nearly 30 years, from her late teens into her late forties. But in 1999, she decided to hang it up. She never formally announced her retirement, she just dropped out of sight and stopped giving interviews. When the Seattle *Post-Intelligencer* ran a profile on her in 2001, she again refused to participate, but after the story ran she called the newspaper at 4 a.m. and left a message explaining that she had retired to a "dream life" with her husband and three dogs, in a house alongside a creek and a running trail in the suburbs of Columbus, Ohio. "I just got sick of talking about myself and always being the center of attention," she said in her message. "I had a great time. All the fans were wonderful. All the players were wonderful. But I just had enough."

BRANCHING OUT

What's a washed-up ballplayer to do? In Branch Rickey's case, he moves into the front office…and changes the game of baseball.

MIDDLE MANAGEMENT
Branch Rickey wasn't much of a baseball player. A devoutly religious man who once promised his mother he'd never play baseball on Sunday, he had a brief and unspectacular career as a big-league catcher. In the course of three seasons with the St. Louis Browns and New York Highlanders between 1905 and 1907, he hit .239. And in one game, a record 13 runners stole bases while he was behind the plate. Realizing he didn't have the skills to be a successful player, Rickey quit in 1907 and went back to school. He studied (and played baseball) at Ohio Wesleyan University and earned a law degree (and served as baseball coach) at the University of Michigan.

In 1913 Rickey returned to the big leagues as an executive with the St. Louis Browns. He quickly established himself as a scout, signing future Hall of Famer George Sisler, and was "promoted" to on-field manager of the Browns, where he stayed through the next two seasons, compiling a mediocre 139–180 record. In 1916 Philip Ball bought the Browns and fired Rickey, who enlisted in the Army. With World War I under way, Rickey was assigned to lead a chemical weapons training unit (in his unit: Ty Cobb and Christy Mathewson).

After the war ended, Rickey returned to St. Louis in 1919, this time as manager—and general manager—of the National League's Cardinals. It was in that capacity that Rickey would make his first big contribution to big-league baseball: He invented the modern farm system.

HOME GROWN
Before radio and television broadcast major league games, fans who didn't live in the same town as one of the 16 major league teams got their baseball fix from their local minor league team. These teams served as a de facto farm system, with big-league clubs buying the contracts of promising young players from the

---

Abbott & Costello's "Who's on First" skit has been translated into 30 languages.

independent minor league clubs that owned them. Rickey cut out the middlemen by leading the Cardinals to buy their own minor league teams (at one point, the Cardinals owned at least a part of 32 farm teams). That way, they could sign their own undeveloped talent, assign the young players to one of their affiliated teams at whatever level of play was appropriate, and bring them along on their own terms.

The farm system meant that Rickey and the Cardinals no longer had to engage in costly bidding wars with other teams over hot prospects. Rickey believed that if he signed enough players and gave them a chance to develop, the system would always produce enough genuine big-leaguers to fill out the Cardinals' roster. Time proved him right. With the best player development system in baseball, St. Louis became a National League powerhouse. Cardinal squads won nine pennants and six World Series between 1926 and 1946, led by farm-system graduates like Dizzy Dean, Rogers Hornsby, Stan Musial, Ducky Medwick, and Enos Slaughter. Today, every major league team has at least one farm team at four different minor league levels.

CROSSING THE LINE

In 1943 the Brooklyn Dodgers hired Rickey away from St. Louis, and he continued his pioneering work developing new talent for them. Brooklyn had a lot more money to spend the Cardinals did, and under his direction, the Dodgers built the first permanent spring training facility on a defunct naval air base in Vero Beach, Florida. Today, following Rickey's lead, all teams have permanent spring training camps, in either Florida or Arizona.

His greatest contribution to the game, however, would come in 1945—when he stood up to the racism of the baseball establishment by crossing the color line and signing Jackie Robinson from the Negro National League. Back in 1903, while Rickey was player-manager at Ohio Wesleyan University, his team had been turned away from a hotel during a road trip because one of the players was black. The incident fostered an antiracist idealism in Rickey. The other, possibly even more motivating reason Rickey wanted to integrate baseball: his perpetual drive to discover and sign new talent. He realized that the Negro Leagues represented an untapped source of top-quality players, and whichever major league team got there first would be able to pick whoever they wanted.

After considering Satchel Paige and Josh Gibson, Rickey signed second baseman Jackie Robinson in 1945 and sent him to play for the Dodgers' Montreal farm team for a year. In 1947 Robinson became the first African-American player in the major leagues—and was the National League Rookie of the Year (for more on the integration of baseball, see page 273). Other former Negro Leaguers like Don Newcombe and Roy Campanella helped to create a baseball dynasty in Brooklyn in the late 1940s and 1950s. Between 1947 and the Dodgers' move to Los Angeles in 1958, the team won five pennants.

SHEA'S REBELLION
Rickey left the Dodgers in 1950, driven out by constant disagreements with owner Walter O'Malley, and became the general manager of the Pittsburgh Pirates. His five years there were largely uneventful, with one exception: In 1955 Rickey signed Roberto Clemente, one of the first Latino players in the big leagues.

In 1959, at age 78, Rickey settled into a well-earned retirement, though he briefly found himself embroiled in another power play with Major League Baseball. After the Dodgers and Giants both left New York for California in 1958, New York lawyer William Shea lobbied the National League for an expansion team. Baseball owners didn't want to share television revenues with any new teams, but Shea defiantly announced in 1959 that he was forming a third major league, the Continental League—with Branch Rickey as president. The idea was shelved after the National and American Leagues agreed to allow two expansion teams each, including the New York Mets. (For more on the Continental League, see page 138.)

That brush with major league baseball would prove to be Branch Rickey's last. He died in 1965, and was inducted into the Hall of Fame two years later.

*　　*　　*

"Man may penetrate the outer reaches of the universe, but for me, the ultimate human experience is to witness the flawless execution of a hit-and-run."

—Branch Rickey

THE POTATO MAN

He peeled...he threw...he became a legend.

HAVING A BALL

In August 1987, the Williamsport Bills (the Indians' Class A club) were playing the Reading Phillies. In the ninth inning, with the score tied, two outs, and two men on, Bills catcher Dave Bresnahan tried to pick off the runner at third but threw the "ball" into the outfield grass. When the Phillies runner tried to score, Bresnahan pulled the *real* ball out of his glove and tagged the him out at home. So what did Bresnahan throw into the outfield? A potato. Before the game, he had peeled the tuber and sculpted it into the shape of a baseball. Naturally, the Phillies protested the play. The umps agreed; they charged Bresnahan with an error, ejected him from the game, and called the runner safe. Result: Williamsport lost. The next day, Bresnahan was fined $50 and released from the team, ending his baseball career (he was a backup and only hitting .149). But that's not the end of the story.

FAVORITE SON

Bresnahan became a local folk hero. His creative stunt added some excitement to an otherwise lackluster season and made headlines across the country. A week later, Williamsport celebrated with "Potato Night"—fans who brought a potato got a reduced admission ($1.00 instead of $2.75), and Bresnahan himself autographed their potatoes. The following year, Bresnahan's number was retired. At the ceremony he said, "Lou Gehrig had to play in 2,130 consecutive games and hit .340 for his number to be retired, and all I had to do was bat .140 and throw a potato."

These days Bresnahan is a stockbroker and a married father of two, but his legend lives on. On August 18, 2007, the Williamsport Crosscutters (the new name of the Bills) honored the potato game's 20th anniversary by giving the first 1,000 fans Dave Bresnahan bobblehead dolls, each of which holds a little potato. When asked why he did it, Bresnahan explained, "A minor league season gets to be a long grind...I just wanted to have some fun and break up the monotony a little."

Nyah! Nyah! An umpire can have you removed from a stadium for heckling.

RANDOM BASEBALL FACTS

Ah, baseball: the crack of the bat, the roar of the crowd,
the hot dogs, cold beer...and an unlimited supply
of random facts, statistics, and trivia.

• Only player to win a batting title in three decades: George Brett (1976, 1980, 1990).

• When the Houston Astros entered the National League in 1962, they were called the Houston Colt .45s. The team changed its name to the Astros in 1965 in honor of NASA Mission Control, located in Houston (thanks to the influence of President Lyndon Johnson, a native Texan). Another reason for the name change: The Colt Firearms Company wanted a piece of "Colt .45s" merchandise sales.

• First Canadian in the major leagues: Bill Phillips, a first baseman from New Brunswick. He played for Cleveland in 1879.

• Who is Masanori Murakami? The first Japanese player in the major leagues. He pitched for the San Francisco Giants in 1964 and 1965.

• Most home runs by brothers: 768 by the Aarons— Hank Aaron hit 755 while his brother Tommie, who briefly played with the Braves in the 1960s, hit 13. Runners-up: the DiMaggios—Joe had 361, Vince had 125, and Dom had 87.

• During the Red Scare in the 1950s—the anti-Communist panic led by Senator Joseph McCarthy—the Cincinnati Reds changed their name to the Cincinnati Redlegs. (They changed it back to "Reds" in 1960.)

• In 1982 Joel Youngblood of the New York Mets drove in the game-winning run in an afternoon game against the Cubs. Later that day he was traded to the Montreal Expos, and that night he got a single in a game played in Philadelphia. This makes Youngblood the only player in history to get a hit for two different teams on the same day.

• So far, only 13 Rookie of the Year award winners (given out since 1947) have made it into the Hall of Fame. They are: Jackie Robinson, Willie Mays, Frank Robinson, Luis Aparicio, Orlando Cepeda, Willie McCovey, Rod Carew, Billy Williams, Tom Seaver, Johnny Bench, Carlton Fisk, Eddie Murray, and Cal Ripken Jr.

• Vice President Henry Wallace threw out the first pitch at the 1942 Washington Senators home opener. He threw it from his box seat over the players' heads and past second base, a distance of 200 feet. It was the longest first pitch in history.

• Hoyt Wilhelm was the first relief pitcher elected to the Hall of Fame. He is also one of two Hall of Famers to get a home run in their first at-bat. The other is center fielder Earl Averill (Cleveland Indians).

• In 1982 Dave Kingman led the National League in home runs with 37. He also had a .204 batting average, the lowest ever for a regularly playing first baseman. It's also the lowest batting average ever for a home-run leader. It's also a record in that he had a lower batting average than that year's Cy Young Award-winning pitcher, Steve Carlton, who hit .218.

*   *   *

HE GETS AROUND

In a game in 1965, Kansas City A's shortstop Bert Campaneris played a different position every inning. The idea came from A's owner Charlie Finley, who was looking for a way to showcase the young Cuban's all-around skills. Campaneris did a great job (although he did commit an error while playing right field). As a pitcher in the 8th inning, he gave up two walks, a hit, and a run, but kept his team in the game. Stranger still, during that inning, Campaneris was a *switch* pitcher, throwing righty to righties and lefty to lefties. As a catcher, he was bowled over at the plate by a runner trying to steal home, but he held on for the out. The grand experiment was a success, as the A's won the game in extra innings. Since then, three other players have played all nine positions in one game: César Tovar, Twins (1968), Scott Sheldon, Rangers (2000), and Shane Halter, Tigers (2000).

Rogers Hornsby didn't read or watch movies in an effort to preserve his batting eye.

THE BIRTH OF BASEBALL, PART I

Compared to other professional sports, baseball has changed very little since the modern era began in 1893. Before that, though, it went through a lot of rough drafts. So where'd it come from in the first place?

R EWRITING HISTORY
One spring day in 1839 in Cooperstown, New York, a young man named Abner Doubleday drew up a diagram of a ball field in the dirt with a stick. He wrote down the rules on a piece of paper, declared the new game "Base Ball," and—voilà!—our national pastime was born. Fact? Unfortunately, no. That story is pure fiction.

Doubleday was a real person, a general who fought in the Civil War, but the account of his "invention" was fabricated at the turn of the 20th century by a former pitcher-turned-sporting-goods-magnate named Albert Spalding. His goal: to increase interest in baseball in order to increase sales of sporting equipment. So Spalding attributed the origin to the heroic Doubleday in an attempt to paint baseball as a truly American game—not a knockoff of the English game of cricket. The Doubleday myth became baseball "fact" for much of the 20th century, and Cooperstown became the official "Birthplace of Baseball."

A REALLY BIG, CONFUSING PUZZLE

So why did Spalding make up the Doubleday story? Because tracking the actual history of the game was difficult. It turns out that baseball wasn't so much "invented" as it was gradually modified from many other similar sports over many decades. Most changes came one or two at a time, like pieces of a puzzle, each bringing baseball a little bit closer to today's game. Baseball historians obsess and argue over basic questions: When was the game first played in the United States? When was it first called "base ball"? Which men were responsible for which rules?

What makes the history so difficult to piece together is that early players didn't think the game important enough to docu-

---

Pop quiz: What was Sam Malone's (*Cheers*) jersey number? A: 16.

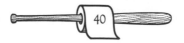
ment its every incarnation. Later in their lives, these same men (now seeing how important baseball had become) began taking credit for things they didn't do—or, in Spalding's case, giving credit to a man who may never have even *played* the game. "In short," says prominent baseball historian John Thorn, "recent scholarship has revealed the history of baseball's origin to be merely a lie agreed upon." Thorn and his contemporaries have been attempting to separate myth from reality, and, thanks to them, the fuzzy origin of baseball is becoming clearer.

THE OLD BALL GAME

Ancient Egyptian hieroglyphics reveal that people have been playing stick-and-ball games since at least 1500 B.C. Similar games turn up over the next two and a half millennia in many parts of Europe and Asia. The games that directly led to baseball, however, trace their origins to Great Britain, starting in the Middle Ages.

• **Stoolball.** The common ancestor of both cricket and baseball, stoolball is believed to have been first mentioned in 1086 in the *Domesday Book*, an English land ownership survey (kind of like a census). Gaining popularity in the 16th century, stoolball was played by milkmaids: One attempted to throw a ball at a milking stool while another tried to bat it away with her hand. A version of stoolball is still played (though not exclusively by milkmaids) in Sussex, England, where it is said to have originated.

• **Cricket.** A "wicket" replaced the milkmaid's stool, and a bat was used instead of bare hands. Originating sometime around the the 1200s, cricket became England's national sport in the 1700s—and the only one considered acceptable for the well-to-do to play. It's a much different game than baseball—for starters, the bat isn't round—it's flat. One similarity: The batsman is called "out" if a hit ball is caught before it hits the ground.

• **Base ball.** In 1744 British author John Newberry wrote a poem about this sport in *A Little Pretty Pocket-Book*: "The ball once struck / Away flies the boy / From each abandoned post / To the next with joy." This is not the same baseball that we know, but the "abandoned post" is a precursor to the base. One other important word shows up: "boy." Base ball was a game for kids.

- **Rounders.** Much closer to baseball than to cricket, rounders originated in Ireland and became a favorite children's game. Like base ball, it featured four abandoned posts that a batter had to run to (whether he hit the ball or not), laid out in a pentagon-shaped field, perhaps the forerunner of the baseball diamond.
- **Town ball.** Based on rounders, town ball was popular in New England in the 1800s. Not only did its rules vary from town to town, it was known by different names, sometimes going by "cat" when there weren't enough players available for town ball. Some versions included baseball-like features such as, most notably, the first instance of "three strikes, you're out." But the bases were still unmanned pegs sticking up out of the grass; the "striker" hit a piece of wood, not a ball; a runner was retired by "plugging," or throwing the piece of wood at him; and as many as 50 players could play on each team.

THE JOY OF RUNNING AROUND
The first stick-and-ball contests crossed the Atlantic with the Pilgrims in 1620. According to Governor William Bradford's journal, the boys were "pitching ye ball, some at stoole ball and shuch-like sport." These games traveled well because they were easy to teach and required few pieces of equipment—just a good stick and something to hit. With the exception of cricket, though, none were taken seriously. The only reason that "base ball" was even mentioned in a 1791 ordinance from Pittsfield, Massachusetts: Playing it was banned within 80 yards of the town's meeting hall.

By the early 1800s, working people were able to enjoy something we take for granted today: leisure time. Up until the 19th century, unless you were rich or a member of the royalty, every day required long hours of work. But at the onset of the Industrial Revolution, urbanization and factories created America's first middle class, which led to shorter workdays and, even better, weekends.

CHIRP CHIRP
In the early 1800s, cricket was the only field sport in America with organized teams, making it the only "respectable" sport. But as strict Puritan values eased and the taboo against grown men running around playing games began to diminish, a new bias

against cricket crept in. In addition to originating in England—from which the United States had only recently gained independence—cricket had another drawback, described by an early baseball player from New York City named William Rufus Wheaton:

> Myself and intimates, young merchants, lawyers, and physicians, found cricket too slow and lazy a game. We couldn't get enough exercise out of it. Only the bowler and the batter had anything to do, and the rest of the players might stand around all the afternoon without getting a chance to stretch their legs.... We had to have a good outdoor game, and as the games then in vogue didn't suit us we decided to remodel three-cornered cat and make a new game. We first organized what we called the Gotham Base Ball Club. This was the first ball organization in the United States, and it was completed in 1837.

Was Wheaton telling the truth? He shared this story in an interview he gave in his later years. And when it comes to taking credit for the invention of baseball, Wheaton is far from alone.

PROUD PAPAS

"Every good idea has a multitude of fathers and a bad idea none," writes John Thorn. "Baseball has been unusually blessed with claimants to paternity." In 2001 a newspaper account from 1823 was discovered in New York City that mentioned the sport by name (without describing it in detail), making *that* the birthplace of baseball...until the 1791 Pittsfield ordinance was discovered a few years later. As other local historical societies dig through their archives, who knows what new evidence will be revealed?

Historians do agree on one thing: The "modern" version of the game truly took form when the men who played it took the time to write down the rules. That happened in New York when Wheaton's Gothams and their crosstown rivals, the Knickerbockers, first played each other in the 1840s with teams of nine players each. After that, tracking the evolution of the game gets a little easier.

For Part II of the Birth of Baseball, turn to page 159.

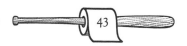
CALLING HISTORY

As a little kid playing ball, Uncle John would provide his own imaginary announcer to call his game-winning home run. Do big-leaguers do the same thing? They don't have to—they have real announcers to do it.

HOLY COW!

Situation: On October 1, 1961, the last day of the Yankees' season, Roger Maris was one swing away from breaking Babe Ruth's single-season home run record. At home against the Red Sox, Maris stepped up to the plate in the fourth inning.

Sportscaster: Phil Rizzuto, Yankees radio

The Call: "Here comes Roger Maris. They're standing up, waiting to see if Roger is going to hit number 61. Here's the windup, the pitch to Roger, way outside, ball one. The fans are starting to boo. Low—ball two. That one was in the dirt and the boos get louder. Two balls, no strikes on Roger Maris. Here's the windup, fastball, hit deep to right, this could be it...way back there...holy cow! He did it! Sixty-one home runs! They're fighting for the ball out there. Holy cow!"

"LOOKY THERE!"

Situation: On September 8, 1998, in his attempt to tie Roger Maris's 37-year-old home run record, Cardinals first baseman Mark McGwire went for his 61st home run of the season. In the fourth inning, with two outs, McGwire entered the batter's box.

Sportscaster: Joe Buck, Cardinals Radio

The Call: "Mike Morgan is the pitcher. Here's the pitch to McGwire...swing! Looky there! Looky there! McGwire Flight #61 to Planet Maris! Pardon me for a moment while I stand and applaud!"

"IT'S GONE!"

Situation: In the Atlanta Braves' 1974 home opener, Hank Aaron entered the game tied with Babe Ruth for the all-time home run record. More than 53,000 Braves fans were on hand as Aaron came up in the fourth to face the Dodgers' starter, Al Downing.

"The key to winning baseball games is pitching, fundamentals, and 3-run homers." —Earl Weaver

Sportscaster: Milo Hamilton, Braves radio
The Call: "Now here is Henry Aaron. This crowd is up all around. The pitch to him, bounced it up there, ball one. Henry Aaron in the second inning walked and scored. He's sitting on 714. Here's the pitch by Downing, swinging, there's a drive into left centerfield, that ball is gonna be outta here! It's gone! It's 715! There's a new home run champion of all time and it's Henry Aaron! The fireworks are going. Henry Aaron is coming around third, his teammates are at home plate. Listen to this crowd!"

"AN EXTRAORDINARY SHOT!"
Situation: On August 7, 2007, the Giants' Barry Bonds was still stuck at home run #755, trying to break Hank Aaron's all-time record. In the bottom of the fifth, Bonds came to the plate.
Sportscaster: Jon Miller, Giants radio
The Call: "Bonds is one home run away from history. He swings, and there's a long one, deep into right-center field, way back there…it's gone! A home run into the center field bleachers, to the left of the 421-foot marker! An extraordinary shot to the deepest part of the yard! And Barry Bonds, with 756 home runs, he has hit more home runs than anyone who has ever played the game!"

"TOUCH 'EM ALL, JOE!"
Situation: In Game 6 of the 1993 World Series, the Blue Jays were up three games to two against the Phillies, but down a run in the bottom of the ninth. With two men on, Joe Carter came up to bat against Mitch Williams, against whom Carter had never had a hit.
Sportscaster: Tom Cheek, Blue Jays radio
The Call: "Here's the pitch…a swing and a belt! Left field…way back…Blue Jays win it! The Blue Jays are World Series champions as Joe Carter hits a three-run home run in the ninth inning and the Blue Jays have repeated as World Series champions! Touch 'em all, Joe! You will never hit a bigger home run in your life!"

And the readers are stunned by these amazing calls!
Now they're racing over to page 197 to read some more!

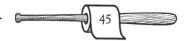

THE STATS ON BATS

A short swing through the history of the baseball player's best friend.

BAT-GROUND
Baseball's original 1845 rules contain only one mention of the word "bat," but with no description or specifications. The first official guidelines for big-league bats appeared in 1857 in the National Association of Base Ball Players' rules: "The bat must be round, and must not exceed two and a half inches in diameter in the thickest part. It must be made of wood, and may be of any length to suit the striker."

The rules have changed numerous times over the years, but the current Official Baseball Rules define a bat as "a smooth, round stick not more than 2¾ inches in diameter at the thickest part and not more than 42 inches in length. The bat shall be one piece of solid wood."

BAT-STORY
In the 1880s, 17-year-old Bud Hillerich invited a player from his local team, the Louisville (Kentucky) Eclipse, to his father's woodshop. The player was slumping, so Hillerich offered to make him a new bat. The next day, the player got three hits with the custom-made bat. In 1894 Hillerich took over his father's business and decided to focus on just making baseball bats. The company's name: Louisville Slugger. Here's how they make their famous bats:

Most bats are made from the wood of the northern white ash tree, which grows primarily in Pennsylvania and New York. An ash tree has to grow for at least 50 years and develop a trunk diameter of 14 to 16 inches before it's big enough to be turned into bats. (One ash tree provides enough lumber for 50 to 60 bats.)

The trees are cut down, taken to a mill, and cut into forty-by-five inch "splits." They are then placed on an automatic lathe and the corners are removed. These cylindrical "billets" are then seasoned: they are stacked and stored until the sap and gum have dried out, a process that takes anywhere from six months to two years.

Once dried, they are auto-lathed to the basic baseball bat shape, sanded, weighed, and stacked and stored again. A "turner"

Most ejections in a managerial career: Bobby Cox of Atlanta, with 132.

then picks a billet of the right weight for a given order, and puts it on a hand lathe. A finished bat of the model desired (a "Hank Aaron" model, for example) is used to compare measurements along the new bat's length as it is lathed and sanded until the shape and weight are perfect.

A slight, bowl-shaped dip is then cut into the "know" end (the handle side) to erase the lathe mark. If desired by the player ordering the bat, a substantial "cup" is cut into the barrel end, which some players like because they say it helps them stay balanced when hitting. The company trademark is then applied to the barrel, and the bat is painted or stained according to the order or model. And the final step: the bats are varnished.

BAT-FACTS

• There's no rule limiting bat weight, but the MLB average is 33 ounces.

• Other big-league rules: no laminated, colored, or "experimental" bats are allowed.

• More than 60 percent of all major leaguers, past and present, use Louisville Sluggers. To date, more than 100 million have been sold.

• Heavy hickory bats were popular in baseball's early days, but as pitching improved in the late 19th century, they were too heavy to be effective anymore. Most players switched to ash bats.

• Bats don't have to be made out of traditional wood. Some companies make bats out of compressed strips of bamboo.

• Many ballplayers are superstitious about their bats. For example, during the off-season, Hall of Famer Frankie Frisch hung his bats in a barn to "cure" them.

• In the strike-shortened 1994 season, the Padres' Tony Gwynn batted .394...with a single bat. Gwynn retired the lucky stick at the end of the season, but used it again when he was slumping in spring training the next season. He broke it in practice.

• Batting with the stars: Hank Aaron used a 35-inch, 33 ounce bat; Mickey Mantle's was a 35-inch, 32 ounce bat. Babe Ruth used 50-ounce hickory bats.

• According to Louisville Slugger, 1920s and '30s Athletics star Al Simmons used the longest bat in history: 38 inches.

HOT DIGGETY DOG!

It's practically a Pavlovian reaction: Get to the stadium, get a hot dog.
But not all hot dogs are created equal—they vary from region to
region, and stadium to stadium. Which is the best? It's hard
to say...but there sure are a lot to choose from.

WHERE DO LITTLE DOGS COME FROM? In 1852 a butcher in Frankfurt, Germany, created smoked, mild-tasting pork sausages and called them "frankfurters." (He made the sausages slightly curved to resemble his dachshund.) They came to America with German immigrants, who sold frankfurters on pushcarts in New York City in the 1860s. In 1880 a German street vendor named Antoine Fechutwanger devised a long, split bun to hold the sausage so his patrons wouldn't burn their hands, and called the sandwich a "red hot." In April 1902, Harry Stevens, the concessions director for N.Y. Giants games at the Polo Grounds, was having a hard time selling ice cream on cold days. So he offered red hots, marking the first time they were ever sold at a baseball game. When a newspaper cartoonist heard a vendor offer "red hot dachshund sausages," he drew a cartoon of a frankfurter with the legs, head, and tail of a dachshund, which he couldn't spell, so he labeled it a "hot dog."

Today the most popular game-day wiener is the Dodger Dog. Introduced at Dodger Stadium in 1962, it's a grilled, skinny, 13" hot dog that flops over both ends of the 10" bun. There's also a Super Dodger dog that's bun-length, but more than twice the diameter of the standard Dodger Dog.

KNOW YOUR DOGS

How many names can there be for a long skinny tube of meat on a bun? Apparently a lot, as this stadium-by-stadium list shows:

AT&T PARK (San Francisco Giants)
Top Dogs: They offer 20 varieties of hot dogs and sausages, but the most popular is the grilled Giant Dog, followed by the Home Run Dog, and the Sheboygan Sausage with grilled onions and sauerkraut.

CHASE FIELD (Arizona Diamondbacks)
Top Dogs: There's the foot-long Mexi Dog, the Arizona Dog (with nacho cheese sauce, chorizo sausage, and tortilla strips), the Cincinnati Dog (with diced onions, cheese, chili, and jalapeño peppers), and the Texas Dog (with cheese, bacon, barbecue sauce, and crisp onion rings).

JACOBS FIELD (Cleveland Indians)
Top Dog: Foot-long hot dogs, always served with Ohio's own spicy brown Bertman Ball Park Mustard.

COORS FIELD (Colorado Rockies)
Top Dog: The Rockie Dog, a foot-long hot dog with grilled peppers, sauerkraut, and onions.

GREAT AMERICAN BALL PARK (Cincinnati Reds)
Top Dog: The Coney Island Dog (even though Cincinnati is 600 miles from New York), topped with a cinnamon chili topping, cheddar cheese, diced onions, and mustard.

KAUFFMAN STADIUM (Kansas City Royals)
Top Dog: The most popular dog is topped with sauerkraut and melted Swiss cheese, served on a sesame-seed bun.

ANGEL STADIUM (Los Angeles Angels)
Top Dogs: The Super Dog, the Grand Slam Dog, the Half Pound Dog, and the Corned Dog.

McAFEE COLISEUM (Oakland A's)
Top Dogs: Coliseum Dog, Big Dog, Stadium Dog, Veggie Dog, Corn Dog, Pretzel Dog, Chili Cheese Dog, and Big Chili Cheese Dog, Hot Link Sausage, and Big Atomic Hot Sausage.

MILLER PARK (Milwaukee Brewers)
Top Dog: Brewers fans prefer grilled brats dipped in "Secret Stadium Sauce," served with sauerkraut and spicy brown mustard on a crusty roll.

FENWAY PARK (Boston Red Sox)
Top Dog: The Fenway Frank, which is boiled, then grilled, then served on a New England-style bun, which looks like the top

halves of two slices of white bread joined across the bottom by a little white-bread bridge.

MINUTE MAID PARK (Houston Astros)
Top Dog: The Texas Dog, topped with chili, cheese, and jalapeños.

METRODOME (Minnesota Twins)
Top Dog: The quarter-pound Dome Dog is served with a pile of chips on top.

PETCO PARK (San Diego Padres)
Top Dog: The Friar Frank, a plain grilled hot dog with the standard fixings. Other dogs: the spicy Diego Dog, topped with cabbage, salsa, and mustard; and the half-pound RJ Slugger Dog named after pitcher Randy Jones.

SAFECO FIELD (Seattle Mariners)
Top Dog: They do have regular hot dogs, but the signature dog is the IvarDog, a batter-coated white fish fillet over a bed of coleslaw on a fresh-baked roll.

YANKEE STADIUM (New York Yankees)
Top Dog: The official Yankee hot dogs are Hebrew National (kosher) and Nathan's skinless all-beef franks (not kosher).

WRIGLEY FIELD (Chicago Cubs)
Top Dog: Chicagoans like their dogs with yellow mustard, dark-green relish, chopped raw onions, tomato slices, a dash of celery salt, and a dill pickle spear, on a poppy-seed bun.

HOT DOG FACTS

• The National Hot Dog and Sausage Council estimates that, laid end to end, the hot dogs Americans ate at major league ballparks in 2007 would "stretch from RFK Stadium in Washington, D.C. to AT&T Park in San Francisco."

• The top 10 hot-dog-eating stadiums in 2005 were (from #1 to #10): Dodger Stadium, Coors Field, Wrigley Field, Yankee Stadium, Minute Maid Park, Angel Stadium, Metrodome, Citizens Bank Park, Shea Stadium, and U.S. Cellular Field.

• Babe Ruth once ate 24 hot dogs between games of a doubleheader.

BASEBALL BY THE NUMBERS

Little-known facts from around the diamond.

6 Players Who Had Candy Bars Named After Them

1. Cap Anson
2. Babe Ruth (until the makers of Baby Ruth sued for trademark infringement and won)
3. Ken Griffey Jr.
4. Kirby Puckett
5. Albert Belle
6. Reggie Jackson

3 Games Called or Suspended on Account of Gnat Swarms

1. Cubs vs. Dodgers, 9/15/46
2. White Sox vs. Orioles, 6/2/59
3. Blue Jays vs. Brewers, 8/27/90

2 Players who Changed Their Names to Fit Inside Box Scores

1. Al Simmons (Szymanski)
2. Cass Michaels (Kwietniewski)

2 Big-Leaguers with Felony Records

1. Gates Brown, Detroit Tigers (breaking and entering, while in high school)
2. Ron LeFlore (armed robbery), recruited by the Tigers in 1973 while still in prison. Bonus fact: He's the only player ever to lead both leagues in *steals.*

7 Players Who Played Musical Instruments

1. Phil Linz (harmonica)
2. John Smoltz (accordion)
3. Eddie Basinski (violin)
4. Maury Wills (banjo)
5. Stan Musial (harmonica)
6. Denny McLain (organ)
7. Scott Radinsky (drums)

4 People Banned from Baseball

1. George Steinbrenner (illegal contributions to Richard Nixon's reelection campaign), 1974
2. Ray Fisher, Cincinnati Reds, 1921 (breach of contract)
3. Lee Magee, Chicago Cubs, 1921 (fixing games)
4. Benny Kauff, New York Giants, 1920 (auto theft)

1 Baseball Owner Who Received a Presidential Pardon for the Crime That Got Him Banned from Baseball

1. George Steinbrenner, pardoned by Ronald Reagan. (Steinbrenner was banned *again* in 1990, for paying a private investigator $40,000 to dig up dirt on one of his own players. He was re-instated in 1993.)

The 1869 Cincinnati Red Stockings went 65–0...and turned a profit of $1.39.

BONEHEAD PLAYS

There's something oddly satisfying about seeing major leaguers goof up to the point that they look like Little Leaguers. (Our apologies to all you skilled Little Leaguers out there.)

FOUR! Only once has a big-league player committed four errors on a single play: In 1895 New York Giants third baseman Mike Grady tried to field a routine ground ball, but bobbled it (1). He threw the ball to first, but it sailed over the head of the first baseman (2), who retrieved it and threw it back to Grady as the runner rounded second base. Grady missed the catch (3) and the ball went rolling toward the dugout. He ran over and scooped it up, then tried to throw it to home, but it sailed over the catcher (4), allowing the runner to score on what should have been an easy out at first.

NIGHT OF THE LIVING EDS. In the early 1950s, Phillies right fielder Bill Nicholson hit a high pop-up that was destined to come down somewhere near the mound. Pittsburgh pitcher Bill Werle called for one of his fielders to step in. "Eddie's got it! Eddie's got it!" he shouted. Then everyone in the Pirates' infield stood and watched as the ball landed on the grass…including catcher Eddie Fitzgerald, first baseman Eddie Stevens, and third baseman Eddie Bockman.

FREE PASS. In 1976 Phillies catcher Tim McCarver came up to bat with the bases loaded. Not known for his power, McCarver hit a deep fly ball. He watched it as he ran toward first base…and was elated when it sailed over the wall! McCarver put his head down and kept on running. One problem: Gary Maddox, the runner at first, held up to make sure the ball wasn't caught. McCarver ran right by him. By the time he realized his goof, it was too late—he was called out for passing a runner, thus negating his grand slam. Asked how he did it, McCarver replied, "Sheer speed."

THE BALL WAS JOOST. During a game between the Red Sox and the Philadelphia A's in 1948, Boston's Billy Goodman came up to bat with Ted Williams on at third. Goodman hit a sharp

grounder to A's shortstop Eddie Joost. The ball took a strange hop at the edge of the infield grass—it bounced over Joost's glove, rolled up his arm, and came to rest somewhere inside his jersey. He quickly untucked his shirt and started dancing (it looked like he was being stung by bees) until the ball finally fell out. By the time Joost picked it up, it was too late to even try to throw out Goodman at first. Luckily, the error didn't cost the A's a run—Williams was laughing so hard at Joost's dance that he forgot to run home.

HEAD GAMES. In 1993 Rangers center fielder Jose Canseco ran down a deep fly ball all the way to the warning track, but lost it in the lights. The ball bounced off of Canseco's head...and over the wall for a home run. The error has since become legendary. The television show *This Week In Baseball* awarded it the best blooper in its first 21 years of broadcasting. Also impressed by Canseco's heading skills was a professional indoor soccer team called the Harrisburg Heat, who offered Canseco a contract (which he turned down).

PICK ME UP. In the bottom of the ninth inning, in a tie game with first place on the line in August 2005, Angels closer Francisco Rodriguez threw ball one to Eric Chavez of the A's. Jason Kendall, representing the winning run, was standing on third. The catcher tossed the ball back to the mound. Rodriguez put his glove up...but the ball bounced out and fell softly onto the grass. Rodriguez just looked at it; the rest of his teammates later said they thought the ball wasn't even in play. But Kendall was paying attention. "You're never supposed to take your eye off the pitcher," he said after scoring the winning run just as Rodriguez went to pick up the ball. "That is the first time I've ever seen that happen," said Rodriguez. "Unfortunately, it happened to me."

WHAT RECORD? A reporter asked Red Sox catcher Doug Mirabelli, "Had the streak reached the point where no one on the team wanted to break it?" Mirabelli replied, "Streak?" Apparently, Boston had entered that July 2006 game with the all-time major league team record of 17 games without committing an error. "We set a record?" asked Mirabelli. Yes, they did...until Mirabelli made a high throw to second on a stolen-base attempt. "And I ended it?" he asked. "Sweet. Got to be remembered for something."

The Human Magnet: In 1971 the Expos' Ron Hunt was hit by pitches 50 times.

NINE INNINGS, NO HITS

Amid a sea of statistics, no-hitters and perfect games stand out as baseball's extra-special events. And they happen so seldom that every one of them is a story worth telling.

A BRIEF HISTORY OF PITCHING

Professional baseball was nearly 30 years old before the term "no-hitter" was even coined. That's because in the game's early days, the pitcher's main objective was to put the ball in play; the batter called for a high or low throw and the pitcher tossed it in underhand. But as the game became more competitive with the rise of the National League in the 1870s, pitchers started trying to throw the ball *past* the hitter. When overhand pitches were made legal in 1884, pitchers gained such an advantage that in 1893 the "pitching spot" was moved back 10 feet to its present distance of 60 feet, 6 inches from home plate (beginning the "modern" era). This gave the advantage back to the hitters, and batting averages went up throughout the N.L. Pitchers responded by requesting that their groundskeepers build them a mound that would allow more of a downward motion on their overhand delivery, giving *them* the advantage. As the mound height fluctuated over the years (its height is now 10 inches), pitchers and hitters constantly sought ways to gain the advantage, from spitballs to corked bats to stealing signs. By the turn of the 20th century, the two forces were so evenly matched that *not* allowing a single hit in a game was something to be celebrated.

DEFINING THE NO-NO

The exact definition of a no-hitter has also fluctuated over the years. If a pitcher doesn't allow a hit in nine innings but gives one up in extra innings, is it still a no-hitter? What about not allowing a hit in a game that was shortened by rain? Baseball writers argued back and forth until 1991, when MLB's Committee for Statistical Accuracy enacted rigid requirements: A no-hitter occurs only "when a pitcher (or pitchers) allows no hits during the entire course of a game, which consists of at least nine innings." That negated any no-hitters that lasted less than nine innings, as well

---

Why is the mound 60'6" away from home plate, and not just 60'? A measuring error in 1893.

as any in which a hit was allowed in extra innings. To define and distinguish perfect games, the committee ruled that under no circumstances could a batter reach first base. So even if a batter reaches first by way of an error and then makes an out while stealing (or being doubled up), it's considered a no-hitter and not a perfect game, even though only 27 men came to the plate. Given those specifications, tracing no-hitters and perfect games throughout history has become simpler.

THE FIRST "OFFICIAL" NO-HITTERS
• In 1876, during the inaugural season of the National League, George Bradley pitched all 64 games for the St. Louis Browns, winning 45 of them. Along the way, he set a still-standing major league record of 16 shutouts in a season. Bradley also threw the first recognized no-hitter, a 2–0 victory against the Hartford Dark Blues on July 15.

• The first modern no-hitter occurred in 1893, not long after the pitching distance was moved back. It was thrown by the Baltimore Orioles' Bill Hawke against the Washington Senators.

THE PERFECT GAME
On June 12, 1880, 23-year-old John Lee Richmond of the N.L. Worcester Ruby Legs retired every member of the Cleveland Blues in order—27 up, 27 down. Just as in each of the 16 perfect games that have been thrown since, Richmond was helped along by some stellar defense, most notably when right fielder Lon Knight threw out a runner going to first on what normally would have been a single to the outfield.

But the term "perfect game" wouldn't be invented for another 28 years. In one of the most nail-biting games in history, Cleveland's Addie Joss faced off against the Chicago White Sox on October 2, 1908. With both teams in a pennant race, Joss pitched one of the best games...ever. He needed just 74 pitches to retire all 27 White Sox batters in order, giving Cleveland the 1–0 victory. At the time, the accomplishment was only classified as a no-hitter, but many noted that not allowing a single batter to reach first base should have its own category. But what to call it? The term came from *Chicago Tribune* sportswriter I. E. Sanborn, who described Joss's pitching performance as "an absolutely perfect

---

The first perfect game in A.L. history was thrown by Cy Young on May 5, 1904.

game, without run, without hit, and without letting an opponent reach first base by hook or crook, on hit, walk, or error, in nine innings." Joss would go on to no-hit the White Sox again two years later, becoming the only pitcher to throw a perfect game and a no-hitter against the same team.

PLAYING CATCH

As any pitcher will admit, a great catcher is essential to throwing a no-hitter. A few catchers seem tailor made for the job. Ray Schalk of the White Sox caught *four* no-hitters between 1914 and 1922. Fifteen other catchers have caught three (including Yogi Berra). The only catcher behind the plate for two perfect games was Ron Hassey—the first for the Indians' Len Barker in 1981 and the second a decade later for the Expos' Dennis Martinez. In all, 58 catchers have been involved in more than one no-hitter.

ENCORE!

In 1938, his first full year in the majors, the Reds' Johnny Vander Meer had a reputation as a wild lefty who threw more walks than strikeouts, making him one of the least likely candidates to pitch a no-hitter. But that happened on June 11 in Cincinnati: Vander Meer gave up three walks and struck out four against the Boston Bees, winning 3–0. In his next start, just four days later, he had even less control, giving up eight walks against the Dodgers in Brooklyn (in the first night game at Ebbets Field). He almost lost the game after walking the bases loaded in the ninth inning. With two outs, Dodger shortstop Leo Durocher came up to bat; he got a good swing at the ball but popped out, giving Vander Meer the 6–0 win—and, to everyone's surprise, his second no-hitter in a row, a record that can only be broken by a pitcher who tosses *three* no-hitters in as many starts. That hasn't happened…yet.

Want to read some more no-hit stories?
Try bunting your way onto page 165.

*   *   *

"Every strike brings me closer to the next home run."
—**Babe Ruth**

Only member of Rock and Roll *and* Little League Halls of Fame: Bruce Springsteen.

LUCKY LOHRKE

After 20 years of making Bathroom Readers, we can't believe that we never heard this story before. It's one of the most amazing, tragic, and surreal tales in baseball—and American—history.

BACKGROUND

Perhaps no one's ever deserved the nickname "Lucky" more than Jack Lohrke. As a ballplayer, he was a decent hitter and utility infielder for the Giants and Phillies from 1947 to '53. But Lohrke's most incredible achievement may have been just living long enough to play in the majors at all. Born in Los Angeles in 1924, he started playing minor league ball in 1942, when he was 18 years old. But then his life—along with those of thousands of other young men—was put on hold when he was called up to serve in World War II. And that's where this story begins.

BRUSH WITH DEATH #1: The Train

Riding on a troop train through California to ship off to war, Lohrke's railcar came off the tracks. Three men were killed in the horrific wreck while many of the survivors were severely burned by scalding water that rushed through the car. Lohrke walked away uninjured.

BRUSH WITH DEATH #2: The War

A year later, Lohrke survived the Battle of Normandy. Then he fought in the Battle of the Bulge, the deadliest campaign of World War II for American GIs, in which 19,000 U.S. servicemen were killed. On four separate occasions, the soldiers on either side of Lohrke were killed. Each time, he walked away uninjured.

BRUSH WITH DEATH #3: The Colonel's Seat

In 1945 Lohrke was sent home. Arriving in New Jersey, he boarded a plane for his flight back to California. Just as the plane was preparing to take off, a colonel marched onto the plane and took Lohrke's seat, forcing him to wait at the airport for the next transport. Less than an hour later, the plane crashed in Ohio. There were no survivors.

"This kid has the best arm I've ever seen in my life. Could be...

BRUSH WITH DEATH #4: The Phone Call

A year later, Lohrke was playing for the Double-A Spokane Indians in the Western International League. On a rainy day in June, the team's bus was negotiating Washington's Snoqualmie Pass through the Cascade Mountains on their way to a weekend series near Seattle. The Indians stopped for lunch at a diner in Ellensburg, and as they were preparing to get back on the bus, Lohrke was told he had a phone call. He thought that was odd, considering that he was in a small town in the mountains. But the team's owner had somehow tracked him down at the diner. And he had good news: Lohrke, who was on a hitting tear, had been promoted to the Triple-A San Diego Padres (then in the Pacific Coast League).

At first, Lohrke was ecstatic. But then he had to make a choice: Did he want to continue with the team to the Seattle area and take a train back to Spokane from there? Or could he make his way back home on his own? Lohrke thought about it…and chose to hitchhike directly back to Spokane. He bid his teammates farewell and watched them board the bus. About 30 minutes later, the bus skidded on the wet highway and crashed through a guardrail before tumbling 350 feet down into a ravine, where the gas tank exploded. Nine players were killed, eight of whom were recent war veterans. To this day, it remains one of the worst disasters in the history of American sports.

"I've often wondered how the Spokane owner knew we'd stop at that particular diner," Lohrke later said. "That was pure fate."

THE MIRACLE MAN

Although he was devastated by the loss of his teammates, Lohrke stuck with baseball and performed well enough in San Diego to make it the majors. As luck would have it, Lohrke was the third baseman on the 1951 New York Giants, the team that famously came back from a seemingly insurmountable deficit to win the National League pennant. Unfortunately, Lucky's off-the-field luck didn't show up in that year's World Series—he went hitless in a losing effort against the Yankees.

Lucky Lohrke retired from baseball in 1953 and, as of 2008, he's 84 years old and still very much alive.

SCANDAL!

Steroids and Pete Rose may have tarnished the game, but they're not the only scandals that have torn apart the world of baseball.

ALL-STAR VOTING

Beginning in 1947, the starting lineups for each league's All-Star team were determined by fan voting. But in 1957, seven of the eight starting positions (pitchers were chosen by managers) went, almost inexplicably, to Cincinnati Reds players. The only non-Red: St. Louis Cardinals first baseman Stan Musial. A prompt investigation by the National League revealed that Reds fans had stuffed the ballot boxes: Half of all votes cast came from the Cincinnati area, many of them pre-marked ballots that had been printed in the *Cincinnati Enquirer*. There were even rumors that some Cincinnati bars refused to serve any patron who didn't first fill out an All-Star ballot. Commissioner Ford Frick decided to let five Reds players start the game, but substituted Willie Mays of the Giants and Hank Aaron of the Braves for Gus Bell and Wally Post of the Reds. The larger impact: Frick temporarily halted All-Star voting by fans, letting players, managers, and coaches elect the teams. Fan voting was reinstated in 1969.

DANNY ALMONTE

In 2001 the Rolando Paulino All-Stars, a team from the Bronx, New York, made it into the semifinals of the Little League World Series. They got there largely on the strength of pitcher Danny Almonte. But Almonte was so good (and so tall) that rumors started to spread that he was a ringer—older than Little League's age limit of 12. Officials from the league and in Moca, Dominican Republic (where Almonte was born), supported Almonte's assertion that he was born in April 1989. Ultimately, Almonte's team finished third in the Little League World Series, but Almonte had thrown a perfect game (with 16 strikeouts) in the series opener, which made him the breakout star of the tournament, and the Rolando Paulino All-Stars were awarded a key to the city of New York. But the rumors persisted. So a few weeks after the Series, two reporters from *Sports Illustrated* went to the civil records building in Moca and easily found a birth ledger that listed Almonte's birthday as April 7, 1987, making him 14, not 12…and way too old for Little League. Almonte's team had to forfeit all of their wins (and their third-place trophy). Team manager Paulino was banned from Little League for life for knowingly using a ringer. Almonte himself was cleared of wrongdoing—he spoke no English and was unaware of the conspiracy and the age limit.

THE PINE TAR INCIDENT

In July 1983, George Brett of the Kansas City Royals hit a home run in the top of the ninth inning off pitcher Rich Gossage of the rival New York Yankees. But as Brett crossed home plate, Yankees manager Billy Martin asked umpires to examine the bat because, he said, it had too much pine tar on it. Pine tar itself is legal—it merely helps hitters grip the bat better. The problem was that Brett used *too much*. Martin cited an obscure rule that pine tar can be present on no more than 18 inches of a bat, while Brett's bat had it on 24 inches. The umpires immediately changed the home run to an out, infuriating Brett, who stormed onto the field and screamed at Martin and the umpires while pacing around and flailing his arms in rage and disbelief. League officials later ruled that the bat had to be removed from the game, but the homer counted. A month later, the game was resumed from the point of Brett's home run…and the Yankees lost.

HANK GREENBERG

Greenberg was a star first baseman for the Detroit Tigers in the 1930s and a two-time MVP with a .313 lifetime average. He was also one of the first Jewish players in the league, and was often subjected to verbal abuse from spectators and even from other players. In the 1934 World Series, for example, players on the St. Louis Cardinals yelled to their pitchers "throw him a pork chop, he can't hit that," mocking the kosher ban on eating pork. And heading into the final weeks of the 1938 season, Greenberg had 58 home runs and appeared to have a lock on breaking Babe Ruth's single-season record of 60. As the end of the season neared, Greenberg began drawing a lot of intentional walks, sparking rumors that opposing pitchers didn't want a Jewish player to break Ruth's record. Whether or not there was actually a conspiracy, Greenberg ended the season with only 58 home runs.

George Steinbrenner hired and fired managers 23 times in 13 years (1977–90).

THE DESIGNATED HITTER

The DH is arguably the most divisive element in modern baseball. Supporters say it makes the game more action-packed. Opponents say it damages the tradition, symmetry, and strategy of the game. Whichever side you come down on, here's how it came about and the effect it's had on baseball.

B ACKGROUND
Because they focus on pitching techniques and try to rest their arms, pitchers are almost always lousy hitters. So the American League uses a "designated hitter," who does no fielding; he bats for the pitcher.

• The DH has only been used for about 30 years, but the idea was first conceived more than 100 years ago. In 1906 Philadelphia Athletics manager Connie Mack suggested a "designated pinch hitter" to bat in place of pitchers, who were poor batters even then. Mack couldn't talk any other teams into trying it out, so the idea died and faded away.

• But at the 1928 Winter Owner Meetings, National League president John Heydler discussed his concern that poor-hitting pitchers were slowing down games to the point that paying fans were starting to get bored. His solution: use Mack's idea for the designated pinch hitter. The plan gained some traction (New York Giants manager John McGraw helped drum up support) and the N.L. approved the DPH. But the American League didn't. Unable to reach a compromise, the new rule was abandoned again.

MODERN TIMES
By the early 1970s, the A.L. was dominated by pitchers.

• Major aces at the time included future Hall of Famers Gaylord Perry, Jim Perry, Catfish Hunter, Jim Palmer, and Nolan Ryan.

• American League hitters were struggling. In 1972 A.L. teams scored an average of 3.47 runs per game, while the National League average was almost 4.

• Heydler's prediction was coming true: The lack of offensive excitement in the A.L. turned off fans. Between 1969 and 1972, the A.L. drew 36% fewer fans than the N.L.

According to researchers, a corked bat actually has less hitting power.

Attendance equals money...and that led A.L. owners to act. At the winter meetings following the 1972 season, Oakland Athletics owner Charlie Finley reintroduced the idea of a permanent hitter to bat in place of the pitcher to increase scoring, and, hopefully, attendance. "The average fan comes to the park to see action—home runs," Finley said. "I can't think of anything more boring than to see a pitcher come up, when the average pitcher can't hit my grandmother."

Supported by two other owners who were frustrated by dwindling attendance (Bud Selig of the Milwaukee Brewers and Bob Short of the Texas Rangers), Finley took the DH proposal to a vote on January 11, 1973. A.L. owners unanimously approved it as a three-year experiment; N.L. owners unanimously rejected it. This time, a simple compromise was reached: The American League would have a designated hitter and the National League wouldn't. And so, on April 6, 1973, Ron Blomberg of the New York Yankees became the first designated hitter in major league history. (Having an extra hitter didn't help the Yankees—in his first at-bat, Blomberg walked and the Yankees lost the game to the Red Sox 15–5.)

RUNS BATTED IN

But did the DH ultimately increase offense and attendance? Here are the American League stats from 1972 to 1973:

- Game scores increased an average of 23%.
- Teams scored 29% more runs overall.
- Home run production increased by 32%.
- The league batting average rose from .239 to .259.
- Attendance jumped from 11.4 million to 13.4 million.

Since 1973, A.L. teams average more runs per game than N.L. teams. In every year but one, A.L. teams have had higher batting averages and hit more total home runs. Attendance between the two leagues equaled out in 1980, but in 1990 the A.L. surpassed the N.L. In terms of offense and attendance—the reasons for using the DH—the "experiment" has been wildly successful.

PERMANENT WAVE

After the 1975 season, A.L. owners voted to make the DH a permanent part of the game. The idea has spread throughout base-

---

Hall of Fame inductees include 227 players, 17 managers, 8 umpires, and 28 "others."

ball: One of Japan's two major leagues use a DH, as do most high-school teams, college teams, and minor and semi-pro leagues.

The DH rule also gives players nearing retirement or suffering from minor injuries to contribute: They bat, but don't have to physically endure fielding. (For this concept alone, the DH rule is supported by the Major League Baseball Players Association.) Some players who moved to DH late in their careers include Carl Yastrzemski, Dave Winfield, Frank Thomas, Al Kaline, Harmon Killebrew, Paul Molitor, and George Brett.

THE OTHER SIDE

Still, many fans and pros hate the DH rule. Some critics say the DH eliminates some late-game strategy, such as how to pitch to a pitcher (walk him, pitch to him, or use a pinch hitter). The DH may even increase the number of hit batsmen. In the A.L., if a pitcher beans a batter, the pitcher never faces repercussions from the other team because he never comes to bat. In the N.L., he does, which probably makes pitchers a little more cautious about throwing beanballs. Result: Over the last five years, A.L. teams averaged 60 batters per season who get hit by pitches, and N.L. teams averaged 55.

*   *   *

KNOW YOUR 19th CENTURY BASEBALL TERMS

Aces: Runs
The Behind: The Catcher
The Club Nine: The Team
Cranks: Fans
Dew Drop: Slow Pitch
Foul Tick: Foul Ball
The Hurler: The Pitcher
A Match: A Game
A Muff: An Error
The Striker: The Batter
The Tally: The Score

Who were the Blondes and the Brunettes? The first paid all-female baseball teams (1875).

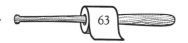

RAY CHAPMAN, R.I.P.

Sitting at home watching a game on TV, it may be hard to comprehend how dangerous it is for a batter to face a pitcher who's throwing 90 mph fastballs at him. What happens if the pitcher misses the strike zone?

THE WINDUP

Shortstop Ray Chapman joined the Cleveland Indians in 1912 and although he wasn't a superstar, he was one of the team's most consistent players. "Chappie" batted over .300 three times, led the team in stolen bases four times, and in 1918 led the American League in runs and walks.

On August 16, 1920, the Indians played the New York Yankees at the Polo Grounds in Manhattan. The 29-year-old Chapman entered the game hitting .303 for the season.

THE PITCH

At the time, it was common for pitchers to do whatever they could do to a baseball to make it difficult to see and even more difficult to hit. They'd smear it with dirt or tobacco juice; they'd scuff it, sandpaper it, or cut it. Yankees pitcher Carl Mays was no different—and he favored the spitball, which made his pitches curve wildly and unpredictably.

In the fifth inning, Chapman came up to bat. Chapman crouched over the plate. Mays delivered a low, sidearm spitball. It was a fastball meant to cross the plate low in the strike zone. But the ball was covered in dirt, as well as spit, and the bright late-afternoon sun was shining directly into Chapman's eyes. The pitch headed straight for the batter's head—way off course—and Chapman made no effort to get out of the way. He simply couldn't see the ball.

THE HIT

The pitch slammed into the left side of Chapman's skull. (Batting helmets weren't used at the time.) Mays couldn't see where the pitch had landed, so when it hit Chapman with enough force (along with a loud cracking sound) that it bounced back to the pitcher's mound, Mays fielded what he thought was a lightly hit grounder and threw it to first base. Only after the play was over

---

Phil Rizzuto was so afraid of lightning that he'd leave the broadcast booth at the first clap of thunder.

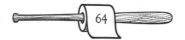

did he look around to see stunned teammates, a silent crowd, and the umpire at home plate calling into the stands for a doctor. Chapman was an unmoving crumpled mass on the ground.

The umpires called off the rest of the game. (The Indians were ahead, 4–3.) Chapman's teammates carried him from the field to the clubhouse to await an ambulance. He reportedly regained consciousness for a few minutes and said, "Tell Mays not to worry."

THE TRAGEDY

Chapman slipped into a coma and was taken to New York's St. Lawrence Hospital. Following eight hours of tests and observation, chief of surgery Dr. T. M. Merrigan determined that he had to operate on Chapman. The impact of the ball had left a 3½"-long depression in the left side of Chapman's head. Merrigan removed a one-inch piece of Chapman's skull next to the depression and found that the pitch had hit him so hard that blood clots and lacerations had formed at the point of impact—causing, essentially, an internal hemorrhage. And while the ball hit the left side of Chapman's head, it struck with such force that the right side of the brain was damaged, too—the force of the blow moved the brain, jamming it against the skull. The injuries were so severe that there was nothing Merrigan could do. At 4:40 a.m., after four hours of surgery, Ray Chapman died.

THE AFTERMATH

Wracked with guilt, Mays turned himself in to police and went before the New York district attorney, but he was completely exonerated of any wrongdoing. For the rest of the season, the Indians wore black armbands in Chapman's honor. Harry Lunte replaced Chapman at shortstop, and the Indians went on to win the American League pennant and the 1920 World Series. A plaque honoring Chapman still hangs in a team history exhibit at Jacobs Field, the Indians' current ballpark.

The Chapman tragedy led directly to two permanent changes in Major League Baseball: First, the spitball was banned almost immediately. Second, despite resistance from the players, batting helmets were gradually introduced to help prevent such a catastrophe from occurring again. Chapman remains the only major league player ever killed by a pitch.

CASEY AT THE MIC

After managing the Yankees to seven World Series championships from 1949 to 1960, followed by a bunch of losing seasons managing the Mets, Casey Stengel developed a unique perspective on the game and what makes the players tick.

"I broke in with four hits and the writers promptly decided they had seen the new Ty Cobb. It took me only a few days to correct that impression."

"Being with a woman all night never hurt no professional baseball player. It's staying up all night looking for a woman that does him in."

"You have to have a catcher because if you don't you're likely to have a lot of passed balls."

"If everyone on this team commenced breaking the furniture every time we did bad, there'd be no place to sit."

"The only thing worse than a Mets game is a Mets double-header."

"I've been in this game a hundred years, but I see new ways to lose I never knew existed before."

"The team has come along slow, but fast."

"If you're playing baseball and thinking about managing, you're crazy. You'd be better off thinking about being an owner."

"Old-Timer Games, weekends, and airplane landings are all alike. If you can walk away from them, they're successful."

"There are three things you can do in a baseball game. You can win, you can lose, or it can rain."

"Managing is getting paid for home runs someone else hits."

"Son, we'd like to keep you around this season, but we're going to try and win a pennant instead."

"The secret of successful managing is to keep the five guys who hate you away from the four guys who haven't made up their minds."

"There comes a time in every man's life, and I've had plenty of them."

"Accordion" to historians, the first song written about baseball was "The Baseball Polka" (1858).

THE WORST

It's hard to determine who was "the worst player of all time." Truly bad players don't make it to the big leagues. Still, there are some players who made it...and left behind some unfortunate statistics.

• Bill Bergen was a catcher who played from 1901 to 1911, mostly with Brooklyn. He had a lifetime batting average of .170, the all-time worst for a regular player (a player with more than 2,500 life-time at-bats). His worst season was 1909, when he hit .139, a record low, including a streak of 46 straight hitless at-bats (a record for a non-pitcher). In fact, during his eight years with Brooklyn, the pitchers outhit Bergen .169 to .162. So how did he stay in the big leagues for so long? Bergen was an excellent defensive catcher. In 1909 he had a .989 fielding percentage, at the time a record for catchers. He once threw out six base runners in one game, another major league record.

• Pitchers are notoriously bad hitters, but who was the worst? From 1961 to 1963, Bob Buhl, a pitcher for the Braves and the Cubs, went hitless in 88 straight at-bats. He didn't have a single hit in the entire 1962 season.

• The worst fielder of all time: Herman Long, a shortstop who played with many teams from 1889 to 1904. He played in 1,881 games and committed 1,096 errors, still a record. That means Long averaged almost two errors *per game*. (Fortunately for Long, he was a pretty good hitter, with over 2,100 hits and a .277 career batting average.)

• Frank Emmer played shortstop for the Cincinnati Reds in 1916. He had a dismal season, with 13 hits (a .146 average), and played in only 42 games. He got sent down to the minor leagues and eventually worked his way back to the Reds...an agonizing 10 years later. And once he got back to the majors, he hadn't improved much: he batted .196, with 44 hits in 224 tries.

• John Gochnauer was so forgettably bad that *Total Baseball*, the official encyclopedia of baseball, misspelled his name as "Gochenaur." After a few games with Brooklyn in 1901, he was

---

traded to Cleveland, where he went .185 in 459 at-bats in 1902. In 1903 he again hit .185. He was as bad a fielder as he was a hitter, committing 146 errors over those two seasons.

• The Mendoza Line is a term baseball players use to refer to the barrier between "adequate" and "terrible." That line is a .200 batting average—over .200 is adequate, under .200 is terrible. The term, named after shortstop Mario Mendoza, is commonly attributed to George Brett, who, during a slump in the middle of the 1979 season, commented to reporters that he knew he was doing badly because he was "below the Mendoza Line." (Mendoza was hitting .198 at the time.)

• Joe Travers pitched one spectacularly awful game for Detroit in May 1912. He worked eight innings, giving up 24 runs on 26 hits and seven walks. That's an ERA of 15.75. It's the worst single-game pitching performance in history.

• Jack Nabors was a starting pitcher for the Philadelphia Athletics from 1915 to 1917. In his first season, he went 0–5. Then, in his second season, he started 40 games. His record: 1–20. Strangely, his 3.47 ERA wasn't that bad. So how did he lose so many games? The rest of the Athletics were terrible—in 1916 the team went 36–117.

*   *   *

TWO STADIUM MUSIC FIRSTS

• In 1977 Nancy Faust, the organist at White Sox home games, became the first to serenade outgoing visiting pitchers with the song "Na-Na-Hey-Hey (Kiss Him Goodbye)." (At the White Sox crosstown rivals' home park, the Cubs' Wrigley Field, it's *never* played.)

• As a joke during a Mariners home game in June 2000, Gregg Greene, Seattle's director of promotions, played the song "Who Let the Dogs Out" when backup catcher Joe Oliver came to the plate. It probably would have been a one-shot deal, but two days later, star shortstop Alex Rodriguez requested the song when *he* came up to bat. After that, "Who Let the Dogs Out" became the Mariners' unofficial anthem...and remains a staple at big-league ball parks to this day. (Thanks a lot, Alex.)

Who (still) holds the A.L. record for most homers in a season? Roger Maris, with 61.

ON THE BALL, PART I

*"The human hand is made complete
by the addition of a baseball." —Paul Dickson*

SELF-HELP

If you and some friends wanted to play a game of baseball but you didn't have an actual baseball handy, what would you do? Today you have plenty of options—is there a town in America that doesn't have at least one store that sells baseballs? You could also wing it with a tennis ball, a softball, or a racquet ball. But things were different 150 years ago, when the sport was in its infancy. If you wanted to play baseball, there was only one option: You had to make the ball yourself.

ANATOMY

For all the things about baseballs that have changed over the years, the basic construction method has remained surprisingly unchanged. If you've ever taken a baseball apart to see what's inside, you already have a sense of how they were made back when players made their own.

1) You start with a small, firm object to serve as the "pill," the core of the ball. Round objects are preferable, but anything that's handy will work: In the 1800s, people used walnuts, rocks, or corks from liquor bottles; soldiers even used bullets. If you had an old rubber shoe, that was ideal: You could cut off strips of rubber and tie them into a small bundle or, better yet, melt them into a rubber ball.

2) Next, take some yarn or string and wind it as tightly as possible around the pill, taking care to create a spherical shape as you go. If you had been at a baseball game 150 years ago and noticed that a player was wearing only one sock (or no socks), it would have been a safe bet that he was the guy who "donated" the yarn to make the ball.

3) The dimensions of finished baseballs varied widely back then; they might be as small as a golf ball or as big as a grapefruit, depending on local custom. Whatever the case, when you'd wound enough yarn around the ball to get it to the desired size,

you sewed a cover made from scraps of old leather, horsehide or sheepskin—or even from tongues of old shoes—over the yarn to keep it in place. Baseballs weren't white in those days; they were whatever color the leather was.

• Today's baseball covers are called "figure-eights" because they are made from two identical pieces of leather, each shaped like the number 8. Early baseballs were different—they were often made with a single piece of leather called a "rose petal" or a "lemon peel." Picture a lemon being peeled into four equal sections, except that the sections remain connected at the base of the fruit. That's what lemon-peel baseball covers looked like when they were laid out flat. You pulled the four sections up over the ball and sewed them together, creating an X-shaped seam at the top of the ball.

SOFT BALL

These early baseballs left a lot to be desired. Because the yarn was not wound nearly as tightly as it is today, the balls were very light and players could only throw them about 200 feet. They were so soft that until 1845 it was legal to get a player "out" by firing the ball right at them—if the ball hit the runner, he was out.

The X-shaped seam on a lemon-peel ball had another problem: Having the stitches intersect at a single point threw off the aerodynamics of the ball, and because they concentrated all the tension on one side, the shape of the ball was easily distorted. The stitching was also prone to unravelling at the X, especially when this vulnerable area was hit square on by the bat. All of these factors combined to make lemon-peel balls travel unpredictably when pitched, hit, or thrown.

EIGHT BALL

The solution to the problem, the classic two-piece figure-eight cover that's still used on baseballs today, took more than 20 years to catch on. It has been credited to a Stoughton, Massachusetts, schoolboy named Ellis Drake, who came up with it in the 1840s while doodling in class. (Drake never patented his design and never made a dime off of it.) His father, a shoemaker, made the very first figure-eight balls, but it wasn't until the late 1850s that a company began producing them in large quantities. Figure-eights

competed alongside lemon peels until the early 1870s, when professional teams began using them exclusively.

Baseballs continued to be made by hand into the 1880s. They were like snowflakes: No two balls were identical, and their characteristics varied widely from one maker to another. Some firms specialized in "dead" balls: small rubber pills and loosely wound yarn kept these balls from traveling very far, even when smashed by a power hitter. Other makers sold "lively" balls: These had large pills and yarn that was repeatedly pounded and rewound to make it especially tight. Big companies like Spalding had entire lines of live, dead, and medium balls to choose from.

CHOICES, CHOICES

Deciding which kind of ball to use in a game was an important part of baseball strategy in the late 1800s. The home team usually supplied the baseball, so if they had a lot of strong hitters they used a lively ball. But if their strength was in fielding, they provided a dead ball. If a team was well-rounded, they used a medium ball.

The condition of the ball was also a big consideration: In those days, budgets were tight and teams used the same ball until it was literally falling apart. Was the cover scuffed or torn? Had the yarn soaked up enough water to make the ball a soggy, misshapen mess? It didn't matter—the ball stayed in the game. Even foul balls and home run balls were recovered from the stands and used again, whether the fans liked it or not. As late as 1922, an 11-year-old boy at a Philadelphia Phillies game spent a night in jail after he refused to give back a foul ball. Teams adjusted their strategy to accommodate deteriorating balls by aiming for home runs in the early innings of the game, while the baseball was still hard enough and round enough to be hit great distances.

THE MACHINE AGE

By 1883 most of the steps of manufacturing a baseball—cutting the covers, winding the yarn around the pill, etc.—had been automated by machines. (*Most*, but not *all*: No one has ever been able to perfect a machine than can sew the leather covers onto baseballs.) You could still buy dead, live, and medium balls, but for the first time in history every ball within each category was virtually identical to the next.

PUT A CORK IN IT

The next big improvement came in 1909, when the Reach base-ball company hit on the idea of replacing the ball's rubber pill with one made of cork. Until that time, baseball manufacturers had assumed that a ball with an elastic pill would travel farther than a ball with a rigid, unyielding pill. The theory was that when a batter hit the ball, the shape of the rubber pill was momentarily distorted by the force of the blow. As the rubber pill sprang back to its original shape, it would push off of the bat, and this extra push would cause the ball to travel farther than it would have if the pill had been made of something rigid...or so people thought.

It turns out that the *opposite* was true: They didn't realize that the rubber pill didn't spring back to its original shape until after the ball was no longer in contact with the bat, so there was no extra push. In fact, by distorting its shape in response to the blow, the pill was actually acting as a shock absorber and causing the ball to travel a *shorter* distance than it would have had the pill been made of a more rigid material like cork.

NEW AND IMPROVED

The new cork-centered balls were snuck into the 1910 World Series and when they performed satisfactorily they were adopted for the 1911 season. The results were immediate—in 1910 only 27 major league hitters batted .300 or higher; in 1911 the number jumped to 57. Batting averages remained high for the next three seasons, until 1914, by which time pitchers had developed enough mastery over the new balls—and over tricky pitches like spitballs, emery balls, and knuckleballs—to drive batting averages back down to where they had been before the introduction of cork.

For Part II of the history of the ball,
turn to page 155.

*   *   *

"The guy in the stands with the biggest stomach will be the first to take off his shirt."

—Glenn Dickey

...by slamming it in the door of his Porsche on the way to the bank.

THE DISABLED (AND EMBARRASSED) LIST

Uncle John was supposed to have this article done a month ago, but he broke three of the fingers on his typing hand when he jammed them in the toilet paper dispenser. It turns out he's not the only guy to hurt himself in a way that he'd rather not talk about.

Vince Coleman (St. Louis Cardinals, 1985): Bruised his leg and chipped a bone in his knee when a mechanical tarp at Busch Stadium rolled over him while he was stretching before a playoff game. (He wasn't paying attention.) Coleman ended up missing the rest of the postseason, including the World Series, which the Cardinals lost to the Kansas City Royals in seven games. "That tarp was a real maneater," said Coleman.

• **Bill Lee (Montreal Expos, 1979):** While jogging in Montreal, Lee jumped into the street to avoid a cat and was hit by a taxi.

• **Pea Ridge Day (St. Louis Cardinals, 1920s):** Famous for his hog calls and his ability to snap leather belts by expanding his chest, Day broke three ribs while demonstrating the latter.

• **Dwight Gooden (New York Mets, 1990):** Suffered a broken toe when teammate Mackey Sasser placed a metal folding chair on his left foot and sat on it without looking. The incident caused Gooden to miss a game; three years later he missed another game when Vince Coleman smashed Gooden's shoulder with a nine-iron while practicing his golf swing in the locker room.

• **Marty Cordova (Baltimore Orioles, 2002):** Fell asleep in a tanning bed and suffered burns to his face and other body parts.

• **Joe Oliver (Cincinnati Reds, 1993):** Tripped while unloading the dishwasher and gashed his forearm with a knife. It took 12 stitches to close the wound.

• **Adam Eaton (San Diego Padres, 2001):** Stabbed himself in the stomach with a paring knife while attempting to remove the shrink-wrap from a DVD.

• **Al Kaline (Detroit Tigers, 1967):** Broke a finger jamming his bat

into the bat rack after he was struck out during a close American League pennant-race game. He missed the next 28 games, and the Tigers ended up in second place, one game behind the Red Sox.

• **Jerry May (Pittsburgh Pirates, 1969):** Crashed into the dugout while trying to make a catch. While being rushed to the hospital for that injury, he injured his shoulder when the ambulance he was riding in got into an accident. *That* injury cost May his job with the Pirates; his career never recovered.

• **Eric Show (Oakland A's, 1991):** Stabbed himself in the finger with a toothpick; the resulting infection kept him out for 15 days.

• **Clarence Blethen (Boston Red Sox, 1923):** Blethen, who'd lost all his teeth by the age of 30, liked to intimidate batters by removing his dentures and grimacing when he pitched. During a game in September, he forgot to put them back in after batting; they were still in his back pocket when he slid into second base. He is the only player in major league history (as far as we know, anyway) to bite himself in the butt during a game.

• **Greg Minton (San Francisco Giants, 1985):** Drove a nail into his pitching hand while trying to shoe a horse.

• **Wade Boggs (Boston Red Sox, mid-1980s):** Sprained his back after he lost his balance while trying to remove his cowboy boots.

• **Steve Sparks (Milwaukee Brewers, 1994):** Pitcher Sparks dislocated his shoulder while trying to tear a phone book in half, a stunt demonstrated to him earlier in the week by motivational speakers hired by the team.

• **Sammy Sosa (Chicago Cubs, 1998):** Missed that year's Home Run Derby and the All-Star Game because of a sore shoulder caused by sleeping in an awkward position.

• **Jose Cardenal (Chicago Cubs, 1972):** Missed a game due to exhaustion when crickets in his hotel room kept him up all night.

• **Randy Veres (Florida Marlins, 1995):** Another hotel-related injury: Veres injured the tendon in his right pinkie while punching his headboard several times when the people in the next room wouldn't quiet down.

• **Glenallen Hill (Toronto Blue Jays, 1990):** A sleepwalker who's also terrified of spiders, Hill suffered cuts and bruises on his hands,

feet, and elbow after he smashed his foot through a glass coffee table and fell down a flight of stairs while "fleeing" the spiders in one of his dreams. The incident landed him on the 15-day disabled list and earned him the nickname "Spiderman."

• **Bret Barberie (Florida Marlins, 1995):** Missed a game after he was "blinded" by his chili-pepper nachos—he failed to wash his hands thoroughly before putting in his contact lenses.

• **David Wells (San Diego Padres, 2004):** Kicked a 40-lb. iron bar stool, lost his balance, and fell on a beer glass, cutting his left hand and a tendon in his right wrist.

• **Bob Stanley (Boston Red Sox, 1988):** Cut the nerves and tendons in his pitching hand after he fell down the stairs while taking out the trash and landed on broken glass.

• **Ben McDonald (Baltimore Orioles, 1991):** The pitcher missed a start when he cut his fingernails so short that he could no longer properly grip the ball.

BONUS SECTION: Three Strange Baseball Player Deaths

• **Ed Delahanty (Washington Senators, 1903):** While returning home from a game in Detroit, Delahanty, who was drunk and threatening the other passengers in his sleeper car with a straight razor, was thrown off the team's train near the International Bridge in upstate New York. Delahanty began to walk across the drawbridge, but it had been opened for a boat; he either jumped or fell into the river and became the first and (so far) only major league baseball player to be swept over Niagara Falls.

• **Thomas J. O'Brien (Pittsburgh Pirates, 1901):** While on a trip to Cuba to play a series of exhibition games, O'Brien was told that he could prevent seasickness by drinking large quantities of seawater. He drank so much that he became violently ill and was too sick to play in any of the exhibition games. His health never recovered. He died two months later at the age of 27.

• **Jake Powell (Washington Senators, New York Yankees, and Philadelphia Phillies, 1930s and '40s):** Powell, who retired in 1945, choked to death in 1948 while demonstrating his claimed ability to consume an entire steak in one bite. (Last words: "Watch this!")

Most valuable baseball card: A Honus Wagner T-206 was, as of 2008, worth over $2 million.

THE OLD BALL GAME

Compared to sports like football and basketball, baseball isn't all that
physically punishing. Result: Many pro baseball players continue to
play the game into their late 30s, early 40s...or even longer.

OLD BALL GAMER: Nolan Ryan
STORY: Ryan was one of the greatest pitchers of all
time, winning 324 games with a record 5,714 strikeouts
and seven no-hitters. He started his career in 1966 playing for the
New York Mets and retired at the end of the 1993 season, at 46
years old, after playing a record 27 seasons. He was the last active
player from the 1960s.

OLD BALL GAMER: Carlton Fisk
STORY: The Hall of Famer played 24 seasons from 1969 to
1993 with the Boston Red Sox and Chicago White Sox. The 11-
time All-Star retired from the majors at the age of 45. That's not
as old as some of the others on this list, but Fisk is special
because he was a catcher: Catchers generally retire earlier than
other players because of the constant strain on their knees from
crouching behind home plate.

OLD BALL GAMER: Connie Mack
STORY: Mack was a catcher in the National League in the 1880s
before becoming a player-manager in 1894. When the American
League formed in 1901, he bought into the Philadelphia franchise
and became the Athletics' co-owner and manager. He managed
the team from 1901 until 1950, when he left the game at age 88—
the oldest member of a professional coaching staff in American
team sports history.

OLD BALL GAMER: Jim Palmer
STORY: Palmer pitched for the Baltimore Orioles for 19 years,
winning 268 games and striking out 2,212 batters, and was elected
to the Hall of Fame in 1990. In 1991—seven years after he retired—
the 45-year-old Palmer attempted a comeback. He pitched in a
spring training game for the Orioles and gave up five hits in two

innings. (It was rumored that the notoriously vain Palmer did it to show that he was just as good as Nolan Ryan, who was 44 and still playing at the time.)

OLD BALL GAMER: Rickey Henderson

STORY: The stolen-base king (1,406) played in 25 seasons, from 1979 to 2003. Henderson played in the minor leagues in 2004 and '05, then took a job as the Mets' hitting coach in 2006. Oakland A's general manager Billy Beane considered signing Henderson to play in one late-season, ceremonial appearance in 2007, but it ultimately never happened. Henderson played his last major league game at age 44. Had Beane signed him, he would have played at age 48.

OLD BALL GAMER: Julio Franco

STORY: First baseman Julio Franco entered the majors in 1982. As of 2008, he's still playing (and he's gathered 2,586 career hits). But how old is he? It's unclear. Murky biographical records from his home country, the Dominican Republic, suggest that Franco was born in either 1954, 1957, or 1958, making him 50 at the youngest and 54 at the oldest.

OLD BALL GAMER: Satchel Paige

STORY: Paige was a star pitcher in the Negro Leagues in the 1930s, but was past his prime when the major leagues integrated in 1947. Paige pitched for the Cleveland Indians and then the St. Louis Browns from 1948 to 1953, retiring at the age of 48, which by itself makes him one of the oldest players of all time. But in 1965, Paige came back for one more game. Kansas City A's owner Chuck Finley signed him to play in one game as publicity stunt. At 59, he was the oldest man to ever play in a major league game. As part of the stunt, Paige, as a relief pitcher, waited in the bullpen in a rocking chair, tended by an actress dressed as a nurse.

OLD BALL GAMER: The Senior League

STORY: In 1989 the Senior Professional Baseball Association began play as an eight-team winter league for players over the age of 35. Marquee players included Rollie Fingers (43 years old), Ferguson Jenkins (45), and Vida Blue (40). Most players were in their late 30s and had just retired from the major leagues. Pitcher Ed Rakow was the oldest player at age 54. (The league folded in 1990.)

Fined $25 for speeding, Satchel Paige gave the judge $50, saying, "Here, I'll be back tomorrow."

IT ONLY HAPPENED ONCE

As of this writing, anyway. But in baseball, who knows what's possible?

DOUBLE HAT TRICK
On September 25, 2001, Jeromy Burnitz of the Milwaukee Brewers hit three home runs against the Arizona Diamondbacks. That's remarkable in itself, but what was even more unusual was that his teammate, Richie Sexson, also hit three homers—the only time in major league history that two teammates both hit three home runs in the same game.

CY VS. CY

Game 1 of the 1968 World Series pitted two great pitchers against each other: the Tigers' Denny McLain and the Cardinals' Bob Gibson. It was the first time a season's two Cy Young winners had ever faced each other in the World Series (the two had combined for 53 wins that season). Who won the game? Gibson, striking out 17 batters…but the Tigers won the Series in seven games.

THE OHIO–KENTUCKY EXPRESS

On August 10, 2004, Adam Dunn, the Reds' left fielder, walloped a pitch off Dodgers pitcher José Lima. The ball flew out of Cincinnati's Great American Ballpark and finally came to rest on a piece of driftwood in the Ohio River, which is considered Kentucky territory. Estimated distance: 540 feet. It was the only time a player has ever hit a ball into *another state*. A new deck has since been added behind Great American's center field, meaning that this feat that will probably never happen again.

ALL-STAR INFIELD

In the 1963 All-Star Game, the National League's starting infield consisted of first baseman Bill White, second baseman Julian Javier, shortstop Dick Groat, and third baseman Ken Boyer. The four players knew each other well—they were also the starting infield for the St. Louis Cardinals. It's still the only time a single team has supplied an entire All-Star infield.

Only player to win the All-Star MVP and World Series MVP in the same season: Derek Jeter (2000).

FIVE TO ONE

October 12, 1982, was a big day for Paul Molitor of the Brewers—he got five hits in Game 1 of the World Series against the Cardinals. No one had ever had five hits in a World Series game before, and no one's done it since.

EIGHT IS (NOT) ENOUGH

Only once has a team scored at least eight runs in the top of an inning only to have the home team score a greater number of runs in the bottom half. The game: Detroit Tigers vs. Texas Rangers, on May 8, 2004. Detroit opened the fifth inning with eight runs and Texas answered with 10.

WORST TO FIRST

The 1991 World Series, which saw the Twins beat the Braves in seven nail-biting games, is regarded as one of the most exciting ever. But that Series has another distinction: It's the only time that opposing pennant-winning teams were both last-place finishers the previous season.

STORYBOOK ENDING

Every young baseball player's dream is to win the World Series with one swing of the bat in the bottom of the ninth with two outs, when his team is facing elimination in the deciding game. Keep dreaming—it's never even happened in real life. In fact, the only postseason series to even come close was the seventh game of the 1992 National League Championship Series. The hero was the Braves' Francisco Cabrera: His pennant-winning pinch-hit single was the only time that a postseason series has ended on a come-from-behind, walk-off hit with two outs in the bottom of the ninth facing elimination. (Got all that?)

*   *   *

DID HE WORK FOR PEANUTS?

A pitcher for the Cleveland Spiders in 1897 gave up 30 hits and 25 runs in only 24 innings before the team released him from his contract. He never played in the major leagues again. His name: Charlie Brown.

As of 2007, no team in history has come back from a 3–0 World Series deficit.

SPECTATOR SPORT

Where would baseball be without its loyal fan base? Let's take a moment to celebrate our almost obsessive devotion to the game and its players.

"A baseball fan has the digestive apparatus of a billy goat. He can, and does, devour any set of diamond statistics with insatiable appetite and then nuzzles hungrily for more."
—**Arthur Daley**

"Baseball fans love numbers. They love to swirl them around their mouths like Bordeaux wine."
—**Pat Conroy**

"I have discovered in 20 years of moving around a ballpark, that knowledge of the game is usually in inverse proportion to the price of the seats."
—**Bill Veeck**

"Why, certainly I'd like to have that fellow who hits a home run every time at bat, who strikes out every opposing batter when he's pitching, who throws strikes to any base when he's playing outfield. The only trouble is to get him to put down his cup of beer and come down out of the stands and do those things."
—**Danny Murtaugh**

"I don't love baseball. I don't love most of today's players. I don't love the owners. I do, however, love the baseball that is in the heads of baseball fans. I love the dreams of glory of 10-year-olds, the reminiscences of 70-year-olds. The greatest baseball arena is in our heads."
—**Stan Isaacs**

"Baseball is a slow game with frequent and trivial interruptions, offering the spectator many opportunities to reflect at leisure upon the situation on the field: That's what a fan loves most about the game."
—**Edward Abbey**

"Baseball fans are junkies, and their heroin is the statistic."
—**Robert S. Wieder**

"Baseball is not necessarily an obsessive-compulsive disorder, like washing your hands 100 times a day, but it's beginning to seem that way. We're reaching the point where you can be a truly dedicated, state-of-the-art fan, or you can have a life. Take your pick."
—**Thomas Boswell**

The ivy that covers the walls of Chicago's Wrigley Field is Japanese bittersweet ivy and Boston ivy.

FATHER OF THE FASTBALL

How many baseball players can legitimately claim to have reinvented the game? Here's one player who did...and you've probably never even heard of him.

ON THE MOUND: James Creighton Jr. (1841–1862), baseball's first modern pitcher, its first true superstar...and its first baseball-related fatality.

BACKGROUND: For the first 15 years of organized baseball, the pitcher's job was to *assist* the opposing team's batters by throwing pitches they could hit. The rules said that pitches had to be thrown underhand, with the elbow and wrist rigid and unbent. Then, in 1859, a team called the Brooklyn Niagaras began to lose badly to another Brooklyn team called the Stars. In the fifth inning, 18-year-old Creighton replaced the regular pitcher. Creighton had figured out a way to throw illegal "speedballs" by snapping his wrist in a way that was imperceptible (so he didn't get caught), and that put a spin on the ball that caused it to rise as high as the batter's chin. By alternating his ordinary "dewdrop" pitches with speedballs, instead of enabling batters to hit, Creighton struck them out one after another. The Niagaras still lost the game, but baseball would never be the same again.

A WHOLE NEW BALLGAME: In 1860 Creighton signed with another team—the Excelsior of Brooklyn—and spent two seasons touring the eastern seaboard demonstrating his new and exciting style of play. His team not only defeated virtually every opponent, they reinvented the game of baseball as pitchers everywhere adopted Creighton's adversarial approach. Several youth teams even named themselves the Creightons in his honor.

GAME OVER: Just 21 years of age in 1862, Creighton should have had a long career ahead of him. But in a game against the Unions of Morrisania that October, he swung so hard at a pitch that he felt what he thought was his belt snapping. It wasn't: After rounding the bases for a home run, Creighton collapsed in agony. He died four days later, felled by what was then thought to be a ruptured bladder, but what is now believed to be an inguinal hernia. (Rather than risk tarnishing the young game's image as a healthy pursuit, his teammates claimed he died playing *cricket*.)

Cuba has won three Olympic gold medals in baseball, the United States one.

BASEBALL 101

Think you know a lot about baseball? Here are a few basic questions to test whether you're really a baseball expert.

1. What is a "regulation" game?

a) A procedural "perfect game"—any game in which no rules or regulations are broken.

b) Any regular-season major league game that is officiated by league-approved umpires.

c) A game that has progressed beyond four and a half innings (if the home team is ahead) or five innings (if the visiting team is ahead or the game is tied).

2. What is the strike zone?

a) The area adjacent to the batter's box where the umpire must stand in order for his strike calls to be legal. If he stands outside the strike zone, the batter or team manager can appeal his calls.

b) An imaginary rectangle over home plate through which a pitch must pass to be counted as a strike if a batter does not swing.

c) The period of the regular season, beginning on the first day of spring training and ending 72 hours before the first playoff game, in which the players may lawfully call a labor strike.

3. What's a walk-off home run?

a) If a batter hits a ball over the outfield wall for a home run, there's nothing in the official rules that requires him to run around the bases. He can walk off the field and go to the dugout.

b) A home run at the bottom of the last inning of a game that ends the game by giving the home team the lead. So called because the home team walks off the field immediately afterward.

c) If a batter hits a home run, then develops a leg cramp while running the bases, the rules allow him 90 seconds to walk it off.

4. What is a sacrifice fly?

a) A fly ball that is hit intentionally, though it is likely to be caught, so that a player on third base can score a run.

Reggie Jackson's three homers in game 6 of the '77 WS were all hit on the first pitch.

b) A fly that the fielder closest to the play allows another teammate to catch, so that the teammate can improve his fielding average.

c) A fly ball that a fielder intentionally drops so that he can attempt a double play, instead of just the one out he would have gotten by catching the fly.

5. What is the infield fly rule?

a) If a fielder drops a fair fly ball that, in the umpire's judgment, could have been caught with ordinary effort, the fielder can, at the umpire's discretion, be charged with two errors.

b) If an infielder drops a fair fly ball that, in the umpire's judgment, could have been caught with ordinary effort, the batter is automatically out regardless of whether the fly is caught or not.

c) A throwback to the Victorian era: Any infielder caught with his fly open "where he can be easily seen by ladies viewing the game" is automatically ejected from the game.

6. What's a fielder's choice?

a) In the American League, fielders who wish to avoid the risk of injury have the right to choose not to play in exhibition games or late-season games that have no bearing on the pennant race.

b) When a fielder handles a fair ground ball and, rather than throw the runner out at first base, he throws to another base to get another runner out. It's his *choice* to try for a different out.

c) Taster's Choice Coffee provides an exclusive blend of coffee to every major league dugout, which they call "Fielder's Choice."

7. What's a squeeze play?

a) When a runner is caught between bases, the opposing fielders throw the ball to each other, moving closer and closer, squeezing the base path until it's so narrow that they can easily tag him out.

b) When a manager makes a last minute change to his lineup, he is said to be squeezing players into the game.

c) When the team at bat has a runner on third base and the batter bunts the ball in an attempt to bring the runner home.

Answers are on page 283.

Answers are on page 283.

On an episode of *Mr. Ed*, the horse hits an inside-the-park homer off Sandy Koufax.

FDR GIVES BASEBALL THE GREEN LIGHT

Which is more important: playing baseball or winning a war?

BACKGROUND

The beginning of the 1940s was an uncertain time in the United States. With Communism and Fascism on the rise, the nations of Europe and Asia were divided between the Axis and the Allies and were battling each other in the second "Great War." At home, the debate raged on as to whether America should enter the escalating conflict. That question was answered when the Japanese attacked Pearl Harbor on December 7, 1941, and Germany declared war on the United States four days later. The nation immediately went to work for the war effort: hundreds of thousands of men enlisted in the armed forces; factories halted production on novelty items and instead began manufacturing airplanes, supplies, and ammunition.

And with baseball in the middle of its off-season, a new question loomed: should the boys of summer suit up in the spring—at least those who were ineligible to fight in the war? Would a baseball season be seen as a waste of time and resources? Baseball Commissioner Kenesaw Mountain Landis agonized over it, to the point of writing to President Roosevelt to ask for his opinion. Here is FDR's response, referred to today as the "Green Light Letter."

> January 15, 1942
>
> My dear Judge:
>
> Thank you for yours of January fourteenth. As you will, of course, realize the final decision about the baseball season must rest with you and the Baseball club owners, so what I am going to say is solely a personal and not an official point of view.
>
> I honestly feel that it would be best for the country to keep baseball going. There will be fewer people unemployed and everybody will work longer hours and harder than ever before.

May 28, 1998: Barry Bonds was intentionally walked...with the bases loaded.

And that means that they ought to have a chance for recreation and for taking their minds off their work even more than before.

Baseball provides a recreation which does not last over two hours or two hours and a half, and which can be got for very little cost. And, incidentally, I hope that night games can be extended because it gives an opportunity to the day shift to see a game occasionally.

As to the players themselves, I know you agree with me that the individual players who are active military or naval age should go, without question, into the services. Even if the actual quality to the teams is lowered by the greater use of older players, this will not dampen the popularity of the sport. Of course, if an individual has some particular aptitude in a trade or profession, he ought to serve the Government. That, however, is a matter which I know you can handle with complete justice.

Here is another way of looking at it—if 300 teams use 5,000 or 6,000 players, these players are a definite recreational asset to at least 20,000,000 of their fellow citizens—and that in my judgment is thoroughly worthwhile.

With every best wish,

Very sincerely yours,

Franklin D. Roosevelt

PLAY BALL!

Landis was overjoyed. "I hope that our performance will be such as to justify the president's faith," he wrote in his response letter. So while the majority of baseball's best players suited up for war—including Yogi Berra, Bob Feller, Ted Williams, Joe DiMaggio, Hoyt Wilhelm, Stan Musial, and Warren Spahn—a ragtag crew of has-beens and women suited up on the diamond and kept the game going for the folks at home.

After the war, Spahn (who would eventually win 363 games, more than any other lefthanded pitcher), said that "the Green Light Letter proves that baseball is a part of the American way. The game, that tradition, and the love affair that the American public has for baseball survived, and it always will."

In 1888 a new rule allowed bats to have one flat side. (It was revoked the next year.)

A DAY AT THE (FOOD) RACES

Our favorite sport to watch is baseball. Our second favorite sport to watch is people dressed up like food chasing each other around a ballpark.

DO YOUR WURST

It's moments before the 7th inning at a game in Milwaukee in 2003. The crowd waits as the four contestants enter through the left field fence. "Sausages, take your marks," says the public address announcer. "Get set...go!" The wieners start running along the foul line toward the infield. Guido the Italian sausage, wearing a chef's hat, takes an early lead. Trailing close behind are Frankie Furter, a hot dog in a baseball uniform, Brett Wurst in lederhosen, and Stosh the Polish Sausage in a rugby shirt. They're running link and link...until Pirates first baseman Randall Simon steps out of his dugout and hits the top-heavy Guido in back of the head with his bat! The Italian sausage goes down and takes the hot dog with him! Frankie gets up and keeps running. Finally, with the aid of Brett Wurst, Guido gets back up and hobbles to the finish line...in last place.

After the melee, Simon apologized profusely, saying, "I wasn't trying to knock her out. I was just trying to get a tap at the costume." *Her* was the costume wearer: 19-year-old Mandy Block, a Brewers employee. Simon was arrested for assault and taken away in handcuffs, but the 5'3" Block (over 7' tall in her costume) didn't press charges. "It's such a silly little thing," she said. "I'm just a sausage, guys. It's not a big deal. I'm fine." Simon was fined $432 and suspended for three games. He autographed the bat and gave it to Block.

MEAT ME AT THE PARK

Milwaukee's Sausage Races have been a Brewers tradition since 1994. They began as animated characters on the videoboard, but in 2000 the real-life wieners started racing at every home game. (In 2006 they added Cinco, a Chorizo sausage who wears a sombrero.)

Roger Clemens built a horseshoe pit at George H. W. Bush's Texas home.

Not long after the Sausage Races became a sensation, other big-league parks decided to pit their "fast food" against each other:

- **The Great Pierogi Race:** The Pirates' Pierogies consist of Cheese Chester (yellow hat), Jalapeño Hannah (green hat), Sauerkraut Saul (in red), and Oliver Onion (in purple). A big hit at home games since 1999, the races begin as cartoons on the videoboard, with the pierogies dashing around Pittsburgh. Finally, they bound into the park from right field. (Twice a year, they take on the Brewers' Sausages in home/home relay races.)

- **Hot Dog Derby:** At every Friday home game in Kansas City, three costumed hot dogs chase each other down the right-field line, each wiener wearing a cap that corresponds to its preferred condiment: red for ketchup, yellow for mustard, and green for relish. (Mustard was the season champ in 2007.)

- **Racing Chili Peppers:** Accompanied by the Mexican Hat Dance and Speedy Gonzalez's shouts of "Arriba, arriba! Andele, andele!" red, yellow, and green chili peppers race each other down the right-field line at Toronto's Rogers Centre.

- **Hot Dog Bun, Ketchup Bottle, and Mustard Bottle** race each other around a virtual diamond on the videoboard at Baltimore's Camden Yards. There are actually more virtual races than real races at big-league ballparks, and not all are centered around food: Seattle has boats, New York has subways, Washington, D.C., has the four presidents from Mt. Rushmore (actually, these are real people in costumes), and, perhaps most exciting, Oakland's virtual race features four dots that chase each other around the screen.

*　　*　　*

HOW TO MAKE A BASEBALL FILM

"There is an unwritten rule in Hollywood that no baseball movie shall be made where the team actually has the fundamentals down at the start. Also, the first 15 minutes must include at least one scene where four fielders converge on a pop-up that falls between them."

—**Paul Katcher, ESPN**

RECORD ROUTS

It's a baseball inevitability: over the course of a long season, there will be those games where one team's offense can do no wrong and the other team's pitching can do no right…and home plate could use a turnstile.

THE ROUT OF THE (NEW) CENTURY

Heading into the top of the fourth inning on August 22, 2007, the Orioles had a 3–0 lead against the visiting last-place Rangers. Then the O's gave up 30 unanswered runs—the most scored by one team in a big-league game in 110 years and the largest-ever margin of victory for a visiting team. The Rangers needed only four innings to inflict the damage: 5 runs in the fourth, 9 in the sixth, 10 in the eighth, and 6 in the ninth (final score: 30–3). The O's became the only team in history to have four pitchers each allow six earned runs in a single game. So what was it like to play in that game? "Freaky," said Marlon Byrd, who hit a grand slam. "You won't see anything like this again for a long, long time." Travis Metcalf, who also hit a grand slam, added, "It was AMAZING in capital letters!" (That was just the first game of a doubleheader—the Rangers won the second game, too, 9–7.)

RANGERS VS. ORIOLES, THE PREQUEL

The highlight of an April 1996 Rangers/Orioles game was the bottom of the eighth inning. Taking nearly an hour to complete, Texas scored 16 runs in what turned out to be the highest-scoring eighth inning in MLB history (final score: 26–7). So many Rangers came up to bat that the Orioles ran out of relief pitchers. Solution: Back-up infielder Manny Alexander took a turn the mound. Result: He walked four batters, including three with the bases loaded, then gave up a grand slam to Kevin Elster. After the game, O's manager Davey Johnson accused his Rangers counterpart, Johnny Oates, of running up the score. "I've seen it all, but guys tagging up from second with an 18-run lead? It's ridiculous." In his response, Oates produced a newspaper clipping about an International League game that Johnson managed in 1983, in which Johnson had a man steal second with a nine-run lead. So Oates wasn't hearing any of Johnson's complaining. "Davey didn't have to use an infielder to pitch that inning," he said.

"I managed good, but boy, did they play bad." —Rocky Bridges

A PERFECT 10

"We tried looking for the record-breaking ball out beyond the fence in right, but there were too many of them out there," deadpanned Orioles pitcher Mike Flanagan after his team gave up 10 home runs against the Blue Jays on September 14, 1987. Here's how the Jays set the major league record for homers in a game by one team: Ernie Whitt hit three, Rance Mulliniks hit two, George Bell hit two, and Fred McGriff, Lloyd Moseby, and Rob Ducey hit one apiece. Final score: 18–3. After the game, O's general manager Hank Peters ordered the team's video department to create a montage of all 10 homers—it was sent down to their farm system to teach young pitchers how *not* to pitch in the big leagues.

FOUR TD'S, TWO FIELD GOALS, AND A SAFETY

On June 29, 1897, the Chicago Colts (a few years before they were the Cubs) racked up 36 runs against the Louisville Colonels. Even Chicago's starting pitcher, Nixey Callahan, contributed: He had five of his team's 32 hits. Louisville fielded two pitchers that day. The starter, Chick Fraser, lasted only 2 ⅔ innings; he was pulled after giving up 12 hits and 14 runs. Coming in to relieve Fraser was 20-year-old Jim Jones, in his second major league appearance. Over the remaining 6 ⅓ innings, Jones surrendered 19 hits and 22 runs. Neither pitcher struck out a batter, and to this day no major league team has allowed more runs in a single game.

DEM BUMS WHIP DA WHIP

On May 21, 1952, after the Dodgers' lead-off man, Billy Cox, grounded out to start the game against the Reds at Ebbets Field in Brooklyn, it looked like it was going to be a normal first inning. Pitching for Cincinnati was Ewell "The Whip" Blackwell, who'd had great success against Brooklyn. But after retiring Cox, Blackwell couldn't get another out. Two walks and three hits later, Reds skipper Luke Sewell pulled him. Legend has it that Blackwell had enough time to shower and go to his hotel room…and still see the remainder of the inning on television. "The Dodgers were going around those bases like a merry-go-round," he said. That first inning saw 19 batters reach base in consecutive order, a major league record. Brooklyn went through two more Cincinnati pitch-

ers as they batted around nearly two and a half times in an inning that lasted 59 minutes. Final score: 19–1.

SEVENTH-INNING STRETCHERS

At Boston's Fenway Park on June 18, 1953, the day after the Red Sox disposed of the Tigers 17–1, the Sox matched that run total in one inning (the 7th) en route to a 23–3 win. Rookie outfielder Gene Stephen set the A.L. record for most hits in the inning, with three. Even the pitcher, Ellis Kinder, who went hitless the previous year, contributed two singles and two RBIs. In all, Boston sent 23 men to the plate, 14 of whom had a hit, both major league records for an inning. One more record: It was also the only time that five men came up to bat three times in one inning.

OTHER NOTABLE SCORING FRENZIES

• The 1950 Red Sox and the 1955 White Sox both played games in which they scored 29 runs, giving the pair of Soxes a tie for the 20th-century record. Boston did it against the dismal St. Louis Browns, winning 29–4. The White Sox trounced the Kansas City Athletics 29–6.

• The 22 runs that the Milwaukee Brewers scored against the Toronto Blue Jays on August 28, 1992, didn't set any scoring records. Milwaukee's 31 hits, however, did set the high mark for the most hits by one team in a nine-inning game since the Chicago Colts got 32 in 1897.

• This one isn't a exactly a rout, but it is a record...and the poor guy changing the scoreboard must have gotten pretty tired. On August 25, 1922, the Cubs and the Phillies combined for a record 49 runs in a game that also featured 51 hits, 23 walks, and 10 errors. The Cubs prevailed, 26–23. How must the Phillies have felt after scoring 23 runs...and losing? (Nearly 50 years later, the Phils got revenge: They beat the Cubs 23–22 on a home run by Mike Schmidt in the 10th inning.)

*　　*　　*

Actual Movie Title: *The Fable of the Kid Who Shifted His Ideals to Golf and Finally Became a Baseball Fan and Took the Only Known Cure* (1916)

STADIUM TRIVIA

Facts about the places where baseball magic happens.

• The Houston Astrodome, built in 1965, was the first covered ballpark in the world. It was also the first to offer spacious luxury boxes to corporate sponsors, now known as "Sky Boxes." (The Astros no longer play there.)

• Rogers Centre (formerly the SkyDome) in Toronto is the first stadium in the world with a fully retractable roof. Its four panels cover 345,000 square feet. It's also the first stadium with an adjacent hotel: 70 rooms overlook the field.

• The most notable feature of Boston's Fenway Park is the Green Monster: a 37-foot-high wall in left field. The Green Monster is also more than 240 feet long, giving it a total area of over 9,000 square feet. At Fenway, the Green Monster prevents a lot of home runs, turning what would be a sure homer at most other parks into a ball that bounces off the wall and onto the field.

• Camden Yards in Baltimore has a double-decker bullpen behind left field—the only one in Major League Baseball. And before the park was built, a building stood on what is now center field: Ruth's Cafe, a restaurant once operated by Babe Ruth's father.

• Prior to 1923, the Yankees played in the Polo Grounds, the stadium played in and owned by the New York Giants. When Babe Ruth joined the Yankees, the team started winning pennants and outdrawing Giants games. The Giants hinted at an eviction, so Yankees owners Tillinghast Huston and Jacob Ruppert put up $2.5 million for the construction of a new 60,000-seat stadium in the Bronx. They thought Babe Ruth's popularity could justify building a stadium twice as big as the average major league ballpark. (It did.) Yankee Stadium opened in 1923, nicknamed "The House That Ruth Built."

• Yankee Stadium has the largest capacity of all major league ballparks, seating 57,545. The smallest stadium: Oakland's McAfee Coliseum, which seats 34,077.

- Cost to build Wrigley Field in Chicago in 1914: $250,000. Cost to build Nationals Park in Washington, D.C., in 2007: $611 million.

- Kauffman Stadium in Kansas City is the only ballpark with waterfalls and a fountain in the outfield (they're turned on before and after games and between innings). Since the ballpark is owned by the city, the fountain, at 322 feet tall, is the world's largest government-operated manmade fountain.

- Dodger Stadium, which opened in 1962, is the only existing stadium that's never changed its seating capacity. It holds, and has always held, exactly 56,000 fans—the result of a conditional use permit from the city of Los Angeles.

- Most major league ballparks used to be named after a team, a person, or a location. In 1965 the Anheuser-Busch brewing company bought Sportsman's Park in St. Louis and wanted to rename it Budweiser Stadium. The National League wouldn't approve the name change, so they called it Busch Stadium instead (and, shortly after, introduced a new product: Busch Beer). Today, most major league ballparks have sold the "naming rights" to big corporations, such as Petco Park in San Diego, Citizens Bank Park in Philadelphia, and U.S. Cellular Field in Chicago. Sometimes the rights are resold. For example, the Diamondbacks play in Chase Field, but it used to be called Bank One Ballpark ("the BOB"). The Astros played at Enron Field in 2001, but after Enron collapsed later that year, Coca-Cola bought the rights and renamed it Minute Maid Park, after its Houston-based juice division.

*   *   *

"ERR" JORDAN

"Michael Jordan is leaving baseball to return to basketball. It is unclear whether the media will now refer to him by his old basketball nickname, 'Air Jordan,' or his more recent baseball nickname, 'Señor Crappy.'"

—**Norm MacDonald,** *Saturday Night Live*

Michael Jordan batted .202 with the Birmingham Barons, and .252 with the Scottsdale Scorpions.

QUIP-DRAW McGRAW

Tug McGraw was a solid relief pitcher for the Mets and Phillies in the 1960s, '70s, and '80s. He helped both teams win World Series. But he's equally notable for his humorous quips.

"Ninety percent of my salary I'll spend on good times, women, and Irish whiskey. The other ten percent I'll probably waste."

"In something like 50 million years, our sun will burn out and then the Earth will freeze up and drift through space like a giant frozen snowball. Now, when that happens, who's going to remember if I struck out Willie Stargell?"

"Kids should practice autographing balls. This is a skill that's often overlooked in Little League."

"I don't know—I've never smoked AstroTurf."
—when asked if he preferred playing on grass or AstroTurf

"It was like riding through an art gallery on a motorcycle."
—on winning the NLCS after a tough 10-inning game

"Always root for the winner. That way you won't be disappointed."

"I met her in a New York bar. We had a lot in common. We were both from California and we were both drunk."
—on meeting his future wife

"Maybe it's appropriate. I've had a love affair with baseball. The game stole my heart, and I was never a jilted suitor."
—announcing his retirement on Valentine's Day 1985

"The Phillies offered me a contract to come back. The only contingency was that I had to lose 20. So I lost 20, reported to spring training, only to find there was a huge misunderstanding. They were talking years, not pounds."
—on a possible comeback

"The same way as to anybody else, except don't let the ball go."
—explaining how to pitch to Hank Aaron

"I'm a flake, not a screwball."
—on being called a "screwball" by sportswriters

Ouch! Tug McGraw got his nickname from his mom because of the "aggressive" way he breastfed.

THE MUD MAN

Major league teams use up dozens of brand-new new baseballs in the course of a single game. But if you were picturing them as spotless, shiny balls fresh out of the box, think again—it turns out that the rules not only allow, but require the balls to be adulterated in one particular fashion before they're put to use.

FOUL BALLS

One afternoon in 1938, an umpire complained to Russell Aubrey "Lena" Blackburne, the third-base coach for the Philadelphia Athletics, about the poor quality of the baseballs that were being used in the game. It wasn't that the balls were old or damaged, it was that they were too *new*: For much of the pro game's history, balls had been reused until they were literally falling apart. That had all changed in 1920, after Ray Chapman of the Cleveland Indians died after being struck in the head by a dark and dirty ball while up at bat (see page 63). Had the poor condition of the ball contributed to Chapman's death? The Rules Committee that governed major league baseball suspected as much. Afterward they ordered that only new and clean balls could be used in games. And as soon as one ball became dirty, it had to be replaced by a brand-new one.

NEW...BUT NOT IMPROVED

But that created another problem: The shiny gloss on new balls made them difficult for pitchers to grip and even gave them blisters. And because the sunlight reflecting off the glossy balls could be blinding, batters hated them, too. Umpires tried to remove the gloss by rubbing them with everything from shoe polish to spit and tobacco juice to mud from the playing field. As the umpire complained to Lena Blackburne, these techniques often damaged the stitching and made the balls stinky, as well as too soft and prone to tampering.

Blackburne thought back to his childhood days fishing in the tributaries of the Delaware River along the Pennsylvania-New Jersey border. The mud there was silky smooth and had an unusual consistency that made him wonder if it would work better than

---

regular mud as a rubbing compound. On his trips back home he experimented with mud collected from different spots until he finally found what he thought was the perfect rubbing mud some-where along Pennsauken Creek in New Jersey, in a location that remains secret to this day.

MUDOPOLY

Blackburne brought some of his mud to the next Athletics game and gave it to the umpires. They were very impressed: The stuff coated the baseballs evenly and removed the gloss on new balls without damaging the stitching or discoloring the leather. It didn't stink, either. The Athletics started using the mud, and soon so did every team in the American League. The National League would have been happy to use it, too, but Blackburne's loyalty to his own league was so great that two decades passed before he finally agreed to sell it to them. When he finally did give in, "Magic Mud," as it had come to be known, became the rubbing mud of every team in major league baseball.

Before Blackburne died in 1968, he passed on the secret of where to harvest Magic Mud to his friend John Haas. Because Haas was already in his 70s, he gave the secret to his son-in-law, Burns Bintliff, who took over the business and began "farming" the mud with the help of his nine-year-old son, James. When Burns died in 2002, James took over the muddy reins; he's been running the company ever since.

SHHHH!

Today, more than 70 years after Blackburne first emerged from his secret mud hole, nearly everything about Magic Mud remains a closely guarded secret. James Bintliff has been known to take an occasional reporter out to what he *says* is the actual mud hole (only he knows for sure), but he always swears them to secrecy first, and even then he insists on blindfolding them during the drive out to the site. Bintliff says he makes about half a dozen trips out to the mud hole each summer in his pickup truck. If he sees anyone around, he leaves and comes back when the coast is clear, then wades out to a spot where the water is about a foot deep at low tide and begins shoveling the topmost, syrupy layer of mud into buckets. He collects about 900 pounds per trip; if caught in

the act by passersby, he says he collects the mud for his rosebushes or makes up some other excuse.

THE MUD-U-FACTURING PROCESS

When he gets back home, he filters the raw mud through a screen two or three times to remove debris, then mixes in a secret ingredient—perhaps to give Magic Mud its creamy, chocolate-pudding consistency, or perhaps to give it more grit. Then he ages the mud in 35-gallon trash cans for six to eight weeks before packing it into plastic containers for shipping.

A little bit of goo goes a long way: A single teaspoon, properly applied, can rub the gloss off half a dozen baseballs, and though a typical major league team uses as many as 30,000 baseballs a season, they need only two 32-ounce tubs of mud to treat them all, at a total cost of just $103.50 plus shipping and handling. At that meager price Bintliff not only isn't getting rich, he can't even quit his full-time job as a printing press operator. He sells mud to 30 major league teams, dozens more minor league teams, high-school and college teams, and baseball leagues in Puerto Rico, Italy, Israel, England, and the Dominican Republic. Yet for all that, he says he earns less than $20,000 a year on the stuff. "We don't charge much for it," Bintliff says. "It's just mud."

SLINGING MUD AT MUD

Baseball players can be a superstitious lot, and it's not unheard of for them to blame the mud when things go right or wrong. When the number of home runs spiked during the 1987 season, a lot of people wondered if Magic Mud had something to do with it. The speculation was even more intense when the number of home runs surged again in 2000. Might global warming be to blame, too? That year a severe drought struck the area where Bintliff collects his mud, and more than one clubhouse official (the people who get stuck with the job of rubbing the baseballs) reported that it smelled bad and didn't have its usual consistency. That year Chris Van Zant, the Atlanta Braves' baseball rubber, had to throw out one particularly stinky tub of the stuff after it made him break out in a rash.

Was Magic Mud really to blame for the surge in home runs? Not likely. There are plenty of other theories that have nothing to

do with mud. Illegal steriod use, for one thing. Another theory has it that the switch from different baseballs for the American and National Leagues to a single style printed with a large blue Major League Baseball logo has made it easier for hitters to see the rotation of the ball and figure out what kind of pitch they're being thrown.

CRACKING THE MUD CODE

So what is it about Magic Mud that makes it uniquely qualified to rub the gloss off of baseballs? In 1982 the *New York Times* commissioned a Princeton University professor to analyze samples of mud taken from an area thought to be very close to the secret mud hole. His finding: The "mud" didn't contain much real mud at all: Instead of being made up of mostly dirt and clay like garden-variety mud, it was actually about 90% finely ground quartz, one of the hardest minerals in existence. Rubbing a baseball with Magic Mud, it turns out, is like rubbing it with liquid sandpaper.

In his eight-year professional baseball career, Lena Blackburne played in 550 games, went up to bat 1,807 times...and hit only four home runs, an average of only one every other year. Not exactly Hall of Fame material, but when the folks at Cooperstown called Bintliff and told him that they wanted to include a tub of Magic Mud in their "Evolution of Equipment" exhibit, they told him that they also wanted to honor Blackburne in the process. So Bintliff renamed the product "Lena Blackburne Rubbing Mud," and it has been sold under that name ever since.

* * *

AT LEAST HE DIDN'T PREDICT AN A-BOMB

The San Francisco Giants played their crosstown rival Oakland Athletics in the 1989 World Series. In the October 17, 1989, *San Jose Mercury News* sports columnist Kevin Cowherd wrote, "These are two teams from California and God only knows if they'll even get all the games in. An earthquake could rip through the Bay Area before they sing the anthem for Game 3." That night, a devastating earthquake ripped through the Bay Area...just before the singing of the national anthem at Game 3.

Only Hall of Famer in the U.S. Senate: Jim Bunning (R-Kentucky).

MULTI-TASKERS

Hard: making it to the pro level in one sport. Harder: making it to the pro level in two sports. Here's our all-star team of baseball players who did a little moonlighting.

Pitcher: Gene Conley

Conley was an average pitcher with a lifetime 91–96 record. But he was the winning pitcher in the 1955 All-Star Game and was on the World Series-winning 1957 Milwaukee Braves. Conley was also a backup center with the Boston Celtics. He won three NBA titles in Boston (1959–1961), making him the only person to ever win championships in two different professional team sports.

Catcher: Jim Castiglia

He was a running back with the Philadelphia Eagles in the 1941 season, then abruptly quit in 1942 to play for the Philadelphia Athletics. Over three years, he played in just 16 games, but he got 7 hits in 18 at-bats (a lifetime .388 average), mostly as a pinch hitter. In 1945 Castiglia returned to the NFL, where he played for the Eagles, the Colts, and the Redskins.

First Base: Chuck Connors

Now best known as an actor—he starred in the TV Western *The Rifleman*—Connors was on the first Boston Celtics squad when the team began play in 1946. (In the Celtics' very first game in November 1946, Connors shattered the backboard—the first person ever to do so.) In 1947 he left the Celtics to play baseball, joining the Brooklyn Dodgers farm system. He played one game for the Dodgers and then was traded to the Cubs, where he played 66 games as a backup first baseman.

Second Base: Danny Ainge

Ainge was a star guard with the three NBA teams in the 1980s and early '90s—the Utah Jazz, the Phoenix Suns, and the Portland Trailblazers. But his professional sports career began with baseball.

Before he joined the St. Louis Cardinals, pitcher Bob Gibson played for the Harlem Globetrotters.

While still in college, he was a backup second baseman with the Toronto Blue Jays from 1979–1981.

Shortstop: Dick Groat
From 1948 to 1952, Groat was a basketball star at Duke University, a two-time All-American who averaged over 25 points per game. He was drafted into the NBA in 1952 by the Fort Wayne Pistons, where he averaged 11 points in 26 games. But that same year, Groat also played for the Pittsburgh Pirates. He left both sports when the army drafted him, and upon his discharge in 1955, tried to return to the Pistons. They didn't want him back, so he returned to the Pirates. Good choice: In 1960 Groat hit .325, was named the National League MVP and helped the Pirates win the World Series.

Third Base: Josh Booty
The Florida Marlins drafted Booty right out of high school in 1994. He spent five years bouncing back and forth between the Marlins and their minor league teams, and played on the Marlins' 1997 World Series championship team. After the 1998 season, Booty decided to quit baseball and return to college, specifically to play football. After two years at Louisiana State, Booty entered the NFL, where he was a backup quarterback in Cleveland for three years.

Left Field: Bo Jackson
Maybe the most famous of all two-sport athletes, Jackson was a media sensation in the late 1980s and early '90s, in part because of his high-profile "Bo Knows" ad campaign for Nike. Jackson played baseball full-time for the Kansas City Royals and was a part-time running back for the NFL's Los Angeles Raiders. (He picked baseball because it was a childhood dream; despite winning the Heisman Trophy in college, Jackson considered football just "a hobby.") It was a hip injury while playing football in 1991 that prematurely ended both of Jackson's careers. Jackson is still the only man to make the All-Star team in two different sports.

Center Field: Deion Sanders
Like Jackson, Sanders was embraced by the media in the early

On October 11, 1992, Deion Sanders played in...

1990s. He was flashy and boastful, calling himself "Prime Time" and "Neon Deion." Unlike Jackson, Sanders wasn't equally talented in baseball and football. Because of his spectacular play with the Atlanta Falcons, Sanders is considered one of the best and fastest cornerbacks of all time. In baseball, he was only a .263 hitter...but he did reach the World Series with the Atlanta Braves three times.

Right Field: George Halas

George "Papa Bear" Halas was a legendary player and coach with the Chicago Bears and helped move pro football from a regional pastime into a national multimillion-dollar league sport. He had 324 wins as a coach, an NFL record that stood for three decades. He'd played football in college, but in the 1910s, "pro football player" wasn't a viable career option, so he played baseball instead. He played in the minors before getting called up to play with the Yankees in 1919. After playing in just 12 games, a hip injury ended his baseball career.

* * *

HE DID IT HIS WAY

On June 19, 1942, Paul "Big Poison" Warner was only one hit away from 3,000—hoping to become only the sixth player to achieve the plateau. Warner, playing with the Boston Braves, came up to bat against his former team, the Pirates, and hit a line drive that was knocked down by the shortstop, who was a bit late trying to throw Warner out at first. It took the official scorekeeper a few minutes to rule it a base hit, giving Warner 3,000 for his career. Not so fast. Warner approached the scorer and asked him to change the ruling to an error. "I want my 3,000th to be a clean hit," he said. The scorer obliged and made the change. Later in the game, Warner whacked a "clean hit" to the outfield. Warner finished his career with 3,152 hits...and is still the only player known to have ever refused a base hit.

...both an NFL game in Miami and the NLCS in Pittsburgh.

GOOD COBB...

Ty Cobb was one of the best baseball players ever...

• Cobb set 90 American League hitting records (although many were eventually broken). Among them: 4,191 hits, 2,245 runs, 3,033 games played, 11,429 at-bats, 892 stolen bases, 96 stolen bases in a season, and 54 career steals of home.

• Cobb won 12 batting titles, still a record. He won his first at age 20, the youngest person ever to do so.

• His batting average was over .320 for 22 straight seasons. Three times, he hit over .400.

• Cobb made it to 3,000 hits at the youngest age of any player (34) and with the fewest at-bats (8,093).

• Not once, but six times, he reached first base on a single, then stole second, then stole third, and then stole home.

• In 1911 he led the American League in batting average (.420), hits (248), runs (147), RBIs (127), stolen bases (83), doubles (47), triples (24), and slugging percentage (.621). The only major category he didn't lead was home runs, in which he finished second.

• In 1936 Cobb was the first inductee into the Hall of Fame with 98.2% of the vote, among the highest ever.

• On the *Sporting News*'s 1998 list of baseball's greatest players, Cobb was ranked third, behind only Babe Ruth and Willie Mays.

• Cobb was a philanthropist. He donated $100,000 (in his parents' names) to his hometown of Royston, Georgia, to build a modern hospital. He also established the Cobb Educational Foundation, which awards scholarships to low-income, college-bound students in Georgia.

• Off the field, Cobb was a savvy businessman. He was one of Coca-Cola's first celebrity endorsers and he invested in the company. Cobb eventually owned 20,000 shares of Coke and three bottling plants, moves that made him very wealthy after he retired.

"When I began playing, baseball was about as gentlemanly as a kick in the crotch." —Ty Cobb

...BAD COBB

...but one of the most awful people to ever strap on cleats.

• In 1910 the winner of the A.L. batting title was set to receive a new car. Going into the last week of the season, Cobb led Nap Lajoie by 4/10th of a point. To preserve his lead, Cobb sat out the last five games...and won the batting title (and the car).

• After trading insults with a heckler named Claude Lueker for six innings at a 1912 game, Cobb climbed into the stands and started punching the man. When onlookers cried for him to stop because the heckler had only one hand, Copp kept punching Lueker and replied, "I don't care if he has no feet!"

• Cobb, an unabashed racist, once slapped an African-American elevator operator because he was "uppity." Another hotel employee intervened, and Cobb pulled out a knife and stabbed the man, who was also African-American.

• Unhappy with the conditions of the playing field at spring training in 1907, Cobb beat up an African-American grounds-keeper. When the man's wife came to her husband's assistance, Cobb attacked her too...and attempted to strangle her.

• In a 1921 game, Cobb contested a strike call, telling umpire Billy Evans, "I'll whip you right at home plate." Evans suggested they fight after the game; Cobb tried to strangle Evans. The two engaged in a bloody fistfight until players from both teams broke it up.

• He allegedly once tried to rape a cocktail waitress, but he was was unable to complete the act. He then paid the woman $1,000 to brag about his prowess.

• Ty Cobb Jr. didn't live up to his father's expectation that he would be a baseball player. The closest he got was playing varsity tennis at Princeton. When the younger Cobb nearly flunked out, his father went to the boy's dormitory and beat him with a whip.

• Cobb was forced to retire in 1926 when he and a Cleveland Indians pitcher were accused of conspiring to fix a game they'd bet on. (He was later exonerated.)

Ty Cobb once cheated at an Old-Timers Game.

YOU DON'T OWN ME

*To a lot of longtime sports fans, baseball has turned into millionaire-
ball. But that's a relatively recent phenomenon. Before the 1970s,
team owners had a secret weapon to keep players' salaries
as low as they wanted: the reserve clause.*

THE CARDINAL RULE

Curt Flood, a three-time All-Star, played center field for the St. Louis Cardinals from 1958 to 1969, including the World Series championship teams of 1964 and '67. In October 1969, the Cardinals traded Flood and three other players to the Philadelphia Phillies for star first baseman Dick Allen and two others. But Flood, an African American, didn't particularly want to play for the Phillies. His reasons: They were a mediocre team (63–99 that season), their stadium was falling apart, and when he'd played games in Philadelphia, he claimed, fans had heckled him with racist taunts.

But it wasn't just going to Philadelphia that angered Flood—it was the whole idea that he could be freely bought and sold against his wishes. To Flood, it was too much like slavery. So he refused to be traded and would not report to the Phillies. Instead, he wrote a letter to Major League Baseball Commissioner Bowie Kuhn, demanding to be declared a free agent.

"I do not feel I am a piece of property to be bought and sold irrespective of my wishes. I believe that any system which pro-duces that result is inconsistent with the laws of the United States," Flood wrote. "I have received a contract offer from the Philadelphia club, but I believe I have the right to consider offers from other clubs before making any decision."

PLAYING HARDBALL

Kuhn denied Flood's request. The Cardinals, he said, had every right to trade him because of his contract's *reserve clause*. A stan-dard part of a professional baseball player's contract since the National League formed in the 1870s, the reserve clause gave a team permanent rights to any player they signed. Those permanent rights were waived only if the player was released outright due to

old age, injury, or a perceived lack of talent, or if they were traded, at which point the new team got the player's permanent rights.

The clause had been challenged in court several times, but in 1922 the U.S. Supreme Court had ruled that the reserve clause was valid. Since Major League Baseball was deemed an entertainment entity (and not an interstate business), it wasn't subject to federal business regulations known as *antitrust laws*, and was allowed to conduct business—and police itself—however it wanted.

Nevertheless, Flood (with the moral and financial support of his union, the Players Association) filed a $4.1 million lawsuit against Kuhn and Major League Baseball in January 1970, alleging that the league's actions against him violated antitrust laws, regardless of baseball's antitrust exemption. Flood wasn't just suing for his right to negotiate and play where he wanted to—he was questioning the entire way the team owners conducted business.

TOUGH LUCK, OLD SPORT

Flood v. Kuhn went all the way to the U.S. Supreme Court. The gist of Flood's argument, as presented by his attorney, former Supreme Court Justice Arthur Goldberg, was that the reserve clause unfairly limited wages; team owners with lifelong rights to players could pay whatever they felt like. Attorneys for Major League Baseball simply countered that Kuhn's refusal to let Flood freely negotiate with other teams "preserved the good of the game."

In June 1972, the Supreme Court ruled 5–3…in favor of Major League Baseball. Why? The court said the Cardinals and the National League had acted lawfully, but only because the antitrust exemption made the reserve clause legal.

What happened to Curt Flood? Since he wouldn't play in Philadelphia (and no other team could legally sign him because his rights belonged to the Phillies), Flood sat out the entire 1970 season. In November 1970, the Phillies traded him to the Washington Senators, where he played in only 13 games. At the end of the season, he retired.

THE UNION SHALL STAND

Even though Flood lost, the Players Association wasn't ready to give up. Flood's legal battle brought baseball labor issues to the forefront. More importantly, it persuaded the union to try to

---

Hank Aaron's record-breaking 715th home run was nearly caught…by Bill Buckner.

change the way contracts and negotiations were handled.

In 1973 the Players Association proposed that Major League Baseball adopt a system of *binding salary arbitration*. Instead of owners deciding salaries or players negotiating with owners, a neutral third party would serve as a go-between in the negotiation process. The arbitrator would consider the owner's offer and the player's request, and come up with a salary figure. And because it was binding, both sides had to accept the arbitrator's decision. The owners agreed to it, reasoning that 1) it would help avoid a players strike and 2) they'd still have some control over salary levels.

It turned out to be an incredibly costly goof for the owners. Pitchers Andy Messersmith of the L.A. Dodgers and Dave McNally of the Montreal Expos both played the 1975 season, even though their contracts had expired in 1974, and the Players Association homed in on this as a loophole in the reserve clause. With the support of the union, in December 1975 Messersmith and McNally submitted a declaration of free agency to arbitrator Peter Seitz. Their argument: Since they'd worked without a contract for an entire season, they were no longer the property of their teams and technically they were free to sign with any club they chose. Seitz ruled in their favor, a decision that was later upheld by the U.S. Court of Appeals. (McNally ultimately decided to retire; Messersmith signed with Atlanta.)

BORN FREE

The league's owners, furious, immediately fired Seitz and briefly locked players out of 1976 spring training. In the negotiations after the lockout, the owners and the union reached a compromise: The reserve clause would stand, but only for players with less than six years of major league experience. For anybody who'd played for more than six years, when their contract was up, they were entitled to be a free agent. That meant they could negotiate —and sign—with any team that was interested.

Triggered by the events that occurred after Curt Flood's challenge to the reserve clause, the business of professional baseball dramatically changed forever. Players can now negotiate with any team, and teams can negotiate with any player. The result, for better or worse, is the big-money era of baseball, where owners scramble to top each other's offers, and star players (and average players) earn salaries that reach into the multimillion-dollar stratosphere.

Largest American cities without a major league team: San Antonio, San Jose, and Jacksonville.

THE BIONIC ARM

Tommy John gave up an arm (and part of another one) to pitch again. Here's the story of the surgery that saved his career…and the careers of dozens after him.

IT'S A BLOWOUT!

In July 1974, Tommy John, a left-hander with the Los Angeles Dodgers, was pitching in his 12th season. In the third inning of a game against the Expos, he injured his left elbow. It felt like he'd strained it, but an X-ray revealed worse news: Years of pitching had permanently weakened the ulnar collateral ligament in the elbow of his pitching arm. The same injury had prematurely ended Sandy Koufax's career in 1966. It looked like John would never pitch again.

John wasn't ready to retire, so he explored his options. The Dodgers referred him to Dr. Frank Jobe, a Los Angeles orthopedic surgeon specializing in sports medicine. Jobe had developed an experimental new surgery he called *UCL reconstruction*—the complete replacement of the ulnar collateral ligament. Jobe would remove the worn-out ligament and replace it with a tendon taken from somewhere else in the body, such as a forearm or leg.

Jobe had only performed the surgery three times—and never on a professional athlete. Even though he could give John only a 1% chance that the surgery would be successful enough that he could pitch again, John agreed to go under the knife. The biggest risks were nerve damage and restricted arm movement. But if it went perfectly, John could pitch again, and the new, unstrained tissue might make his arm stronger than ever.

BLOOD AND GUTS

In September 1974, Jobe performed the surgery. First, he drilled a series of narrow tunnels into John's ulna and humerus, the bones that meet at the elbow. Then he removed a tendon from John's right forearm and wove it in a figure-eight pattern over the bones and through the drilled bone tunnels. The whole operation took about three hours.

RECOVERY

John sat out the entire 1975 season to recover from the UCL reconstruction. According to Jobe, it takes the body a full year to recover. The main reason: The body has to convert an arm tendon into an elbow ligament. Tendons and ligaments perform different functions: A tendon attaches muscle to bone, while a ligament connects bones, stabilizing the joint. After the surgery, the tendon is initially very weak and the body has to get it to carry blood and train it to start working as a ligament. Rehabilitation has to be very slow and gradual. There's no way to shorten it—a year is just how long the body takes.

Amazingly, John returned to the Dodgers starting rotation in 1976, where he went 10–10. That's a decent record for most pitchers, but astounding for someone who'd just had experimental reconstructive surgery involving the implantation of new tissue in his pitching arm. The surgery turned John from having to retire in his prime into a pitcher with one of the longest careers in baseball history: John pitched in the major leagues until 1989, at the age of 46.

LEGACY

Today, UCL reconstruction (or as it's now more commonly known, "Tommy John surgery") is one of the most frequently performed medical procedures for baseball players. Since John, 89 other players (almost all pitchers) have undergone UCL reconstruction, prolonging their careers by many years. Among the top pitchers who have gone under the knife are David Wells, Mariano Rivera, John Smoltz, Eric Gagne, and Kenny Rogers.

The Tommy John surgery shows the extreme measures pitchers will go to to save their arms and their careers. Pitching at the big-league level can cause devastating damage, and often only major surgery can help. The good news is that the reconstructed arm is sometimes so strong that a pitcher may be better after the surgery than before. For example, Kerry Wood says that before the surgery, he used to top out at 90 mph. But now he can throw at 108 mph—and with improved accuracy. Chances of recovery today are up to 90%, and the procedure (performed by only three surgeons in the United States, including Jobe) now takes only about an hour.

Holy ground rule double, Batman! The name of Gotham City's pro baseball team: the Goliaths.

COMPLIMENTS, INSULTS, & WE'RE NOT SURE WHAT

Most accolades are boring, and most putdowns are just plain mean,
but a precious few are quite clever…or just plain weird.

COMPLIMENTS

"He's the only guy I know who can go four-for-three."
—**Alan Bannister,**
on Rod Carew

"He threw the ball as far from the bat and as close to the plate as possible."
—**Casey Stengel,**
on Satchel Paige

"One time he hit a line drive right past my ear. I turned around and saw the ball hit his ass sliding into second."
—**Satchel Paige,**
on Cool Papa Bell

"I'm beginning to see Brooks Robinson in my sleep. If I dropped a paper plate, he'd pick it up on one hop and throw me out at first."
—**Sparky Anderson**

"Sandy's fastball was so fast, some batters would start to swing as he was on his way to the mound."
—**Jim Murray,**
on Sandy Koufax

"Trying to sneak a fastball past Hank Aaron is like trying to sneak the sunrise past a rooster."
—**Joe Adcock**

"I've had pretty good success with Stan Musial…by throwing him my best pitch and then backing up third."
—**Carl Erskine**

"Back then, my idol was Bugs Bunny, because I saw a cartoon of him playing ball—you know, the one where he plays every position himself with nobody else on the field but him? You have to love a ballplayer like that."
—**Nomar Garciaparra**

"I can't very well tell batters, 'Don't hit it to him.' Wherever they hit it, he's there anyway."
—**Gil Hodges, on Willie Mays**

INSULTS

"If he raced his pregnant wife he'd finish third."
—**Tommy Lasorda,**
on catcher Mide Scioscia

Outfielder Edd Roush once fell asleep during a game.

"He'd give you the shirt off his back. Of course, he'd call a press conference to announce it."

—**Catfish Hunter,**
on Reggie Jackson

"Rex Barney would be the league's best pitcher if the plate were high and outside."

—**Bob Cooke, sportswriter**

"He's really turned his life around. He used to be depressed and miserable. Now he's miserable and depressed."

—**Harry Kalas,**
on Gary Maddox

WE'RE NOT SURE WHAT

"They say Yogi Berra is funny. Well, he has a lovely wife and family, a beautiful home, money in the bank, and he plays golf with millionaires. What's funny about that?"

—**Casey Stengel**

"Pete Rose is the most likable arrogant person I've ever met."

—**Mike Schmidt**

"He didn't sound like a baseball player. He said things like 'nevertheless' and 'if, in fact.'"

—**Dan Quisenberry,**
on Ted Simmons

"The more self-centered and egotistical a guy is, the better ballplayer he's going to be. You take a team with twenty-five a**holes and I'll show you the New York Yankees."

—**Bill Lee**

"Stan Musial's batting stance looks like a small boy looking around a corner to see if the cops are coming."

—**Ted Lyons**

"Every hitter likes fastballs, just like everybody likes ice cream. But you don't like it when someone's stuffing it into you by the gallon. That's what it feels like when Nolan Ryan's throwing balls by you."

—**Reggie Jackson**

"The only people I ever felt intimidated by were Bob Gibson and my daddy."

—**Dusty Baker**

*   *   *

A DUBIOUS ACHIEVEMENT

The Yankees' Lou Piniella was once "thrown out" for the cycle—making an out at 1st, 2nd, 3rd, and home plate all in one game.

Rogers Hornsby was a member of the Ku Klux Klan.

THE IRON HORSE, PART I

*Even if Lou Gehrig had taken a day off during the 14 years of his consecutive
games streak, he'd still be known as one of the game's greats. But that
dependability, which earned him the nickname "The Iron Horse"—
combined with the courageous way he met his untimely
end—made Gehrig into a national hero.*

THE PLAYER'S PLAYER

Growing up in poverty in New York City, Henry Louis
Gehrig excelled in school, both as a student and an athlete, and baseball was just a means to get into a good college.
But after two years at Columbia University, Gehrig had broken
so many pitching and hitting records that the New York Yankees came calling and offered him a job. He dropped out of college to join the team, much to the dismay of his hardworking
mother, Christina, who had instilled in her son a strong work
ethic and wanted him to be an architect or engineer. But for the
poor family, the offer was too good to pass up. After a couple of
years in the minors, Gehrig joined the Yankees full-time in
1925.

By most accounts, Gehrig's teammates were "swashbuckling,
tobacco-chewing, cursing tough-guys." Gehrig, on the other hand,
was a quiet man who never questioned the tight set of rules that
the Yankees' bosses set down. At first, that didn't make him a lot
of friends in the clubhouse, but as player after player would later
attest, it was impossible not to like Lou Gehrig and his workmanlike attitude. So for the young Gehrig, it was no big deal when, on
June 2, 1925, he was asked to fill in at first base for the struggling
Wally Pipp. After that, the Iron Horse didn't miss a game for the
next 14 seasons—playing through broken bones, bruises, and a
slew of other aches and pains.

THE NATURAL

The Yankees were a powerhouse during Gehrig's tenure, appearing
in seven Word Series and winning six of them. Batting in the
cleanup spot behind Babe Ruth in the famous "Murderer's Row,"
Gehrig amassed some amazing statistics:

Rookie Luke Stuart hit a home run his very first at-bat...then left the majors two games later.

- A lifetime .340 batting average, a .447 on-base percentage, and a .632 slugging percentage.
- A total of 1,995 RBIs, still #5 on the all-time list. He led the American League in RBIs in five different years, with his highest total coming in 1931 when he batted in 184 runs. Three of the top six RBI season records in history belong to Gehrig.
- MVP awards in 1927 and 1936, and the Triple Crown (highest batting average, most home runs, and most RBIs) in 1934.
- Gehrig's 23 career grand slams is still a Major League record. In all, he hit 493 home runs.

And who knows how many more records he would have collected had he kept playing at full strength. But in 1938 something started happening to him.

PLEASE TAKE ME OUT OF THE GAME

Gehrig was 35 years old and approaching 2,000 consecutive games played. But for him, 1938 was a "mediocre" year: After a strong start, he slowed down and ended the season with a .295 average with 114 RBIs and 29 homers. "I tired midseason," he said. "I don't know why, but I just couldn't get going again."

At first, Gehrig figured it was the same thing that all big leaguers go through when they reach that age. But that winter, he was so weak that his wife, Eleanor, insisted he see a doctor, who diagnosed him (incorrectly) with gall bladder problems. The following spring training, Gehrig had trouble swinging the bat and fielding. He knew it was serious when he found it difficult to tie his shoelaces. "I just can't understand," he said. "I am not sick. The stomach complaint which was revealed last year in three separate examinations has been cleared up by observance of a strict diet. My eye is sharp, yet I'm not swinging as of old."

By the end of April, Gehrig had batted in only one run...and he decided he just couldn't do it any more. On May 2, while the Yankees were preparing for a game in Detroit, Gehrig told manager Joe McCarthy, "I'm not helping this team any. I know I look terrible out there. This string of mine doesn't mean a thing to me. It isn't fair to the boys for me to stay in there. Joe, I want you to take me out of the lineup today." McCarthy was reluctant, but when he saw that Gehrig's mind was made up, he relented.

Moments before game time, the pubic address announcer told the crowd, "Ladies and gentlemen, Lou Gehrig's consecutive streak of 2,130 games played has ended." Tiger fans gave the Iron Horse a standing ovation. McCarthy hoped Gehrig just needed some time to recover and told him that first base was his for the asking.

A SOMBER REPORT

On June 19, his 36th birthday, after a week of tests at the Mayo Clinic in Rochester, Minnesota, Gehrig was informed that he suffered from a rare disease called *amyotrophic lateral sclerosis*. According to the ALS Association, the disorder is a "progressive neurodegenerative disease that attacks nerve cells and pathways in the brain and spinal cord. When these cells die, voluntary muscle control and movement dies with them." At Eleanor's request, Dr. Charles Mayo gave Lou a better prognosis than he really had. "There is a 50-50 chance of keeping me as I am," Lou wrote in a letter to his wife. "I may need a cane in 10 or 15 years. Playing is out of the question." But the doctors had told Eleanor the truth: Her husband would steadily grow weaker until his body couldn't function any more—he'd be dead in less than three years.

Lou realized this as well—his condition kept growing worse. The Gehrigs kept the seriousness of the disease mostly to themselves. Meanwhile, the reports of Lou Gehrig's absence from baseball spread around the country.

One thing that would not be affected by ALS was Gehrig's mind. Throughout his illness, he retained his keen senses, basically becoming a prisoner inside his degenerating body. But he kept his frustration to himself, especially in public, where he always reminded people of the bright side of things.

A BAD BREAK, BUT...

Such was the case on July 4, 1939, when Yankee Stadium celebrated "Lou Gehrig Appreciation Day" between games of a doubleheader. It was an emotional afternoon, with Yankees past and present in attendance, and speaker after speaker paying tribute. New York City mayor Fiorello LaGuardia said that Gehrig was the "prototype of good sportsmanship and citizenship." Yankees manager Joe McCarthy called him the "finest example of a ballplayer, sportsman, and citizen that baseball has ever known." Finally, it was Gehrig's turn, his body obviously weak, but his voice echoing through Yankee Stadium.

Fans, for the past two weeks you have been reading about a bad break I got. Yet today, I consider myself the luckiest man on the face of the earth. I have been in ballparks for seventeen years and have never received anything but kindness and encouragement from you fans.

Look at these grand men. Which of you wouldn't consider it the highlight of his career just to associate with them for even one day? Sure I'm lucky. Who wouldn't consider it an honor to have known Jacob Ruppert? Also, the builder of baseball's greatest empire, Ed Barrow? To have spent six years with that wonderful little fellow, Miller Huggins? Then to have spent the next nine years with that outstanding leader, that smart student of psychology, the best manager in baseball today, Joe McCarthy? Sure, I'm lucky.

When the New York Giants, a team you would give your right arm to beat, and vice versa, sends you a gift—that's something. When everybody down to the groundskeepers and those boys in white coats remember you with trophies—that's something. When you have a wonderful mother-in-law who takes sides with you in squabbles with her own daughter—that's something. When you have a father and a mother who work all their lives so that you can have an education and build your body—it's a blessing. When you have a wife who has been a tower of strength and shown more courage than you dreamed existed—that's the finest I know.

So I close in saying that I might have been given a bad break, but I've got an awful lot to live for. Thank you.

Gehrig wiped away his tears as more than 60,000 fans (including his wife and his parents) applauded for two solid minutes. Babe Ruth walked over and gave Gehrig a hug. The next day, the *New York Times* called the ceremony "one of the most touching scenes ever witnessed on a ball field."

After staying with the Yankees for several more months as honorary captain, Gehrig found the stress of traveling too much to handle and he officially retired from baseball.

But he wasn't done yet.

For the story of Gehrig's final years, streak over to page 264.

Lou Gehrig's #4 was the first number to be retired.

ANIMALS IN THE OUTFIELD

And the infield, the dugout, the uniforms, the pressbox...

JACOB'S SWATTER

In the 2007 A.L. division series, the Yankees were playing in Cleveland, down by one game but clinging to a 1–0 lead in the eighth inning. Coming in to hold the lead was 22-year-old Yankee reliever Joba Chamberlain, who hadn't blown a save all year. Also entering the game: a giant swarm of tiny gnatlike insects called *midges* (they were attracted to the stadium lights). As they enveloped the mound, Chamberlain tried swatting them with his cap, but that didn't work, so catcher Jorge Posada ran out and sprayed the pitcher with insect repellent. That didn't work, either. So, with tiny midges crawling all over his face and neck, Chamberlain kept pitching. Result: He gave up two walks, threw two wild pitches, and hit a batter, allowing the tying run to score. The Indians, who were used to the bugs, won the game in the 12th inning. Afterward, Chamberlain blamed himself: "Bugs are bugs. It's not the first time I had a bug near me." But Yankee shortstop Derek Jeter disagreed: "I guess that's home-field advantage for them—just let the bugs out."

FANGS FOR THE MEMORIES

During the fourth inning of a 2007 spring training game between the Indians and the Mets in Winter Haven, Florida, play was briefly halted when several reporters started screaming and running out of the press box. The culprit: a three-foot-long black snake that had slithered over their notebooks and computers. While fans (Floridians, who are accustomed to snakes) laughed at the reporters, a member of the grounds crew caught the snake and let it go in some woods near the parking lot.

FLY TO YOUR TOMORROW, SEAGULL

To this day, Dave Winfield swears he didn't do it on purpose. Between innings of a game in Toronto on August 4, 1983, the Yankee outfielder caught one last warm-up toss and then threw it to a ball boy waiting along the foul line. Perched on the field between Winfield and the boy, however, was a small white gull. After taking a

---

Cal Ripken Jr. refuses to endorse beer or underwear.

short hop, the baseball hit the bird hard…and killed it. As the groundskeepers quickly came in and took it away, Winfield raised his cap. Stunned Toronto fans saw this as disrespectful and threw things at the Yankee slugger for the rest of the game. And after the game, a group of Mounties arrested Winfield (in the visitor clubhouse) for "willfully causing unnecessary cruelty to an animal." Winfield denied it was willful, but cooperated and paid the $500 bail. The charges were later dropped, but Winfield's reputation in Canada was severely damaged. (When the Blue Jays later brought in a falcon to try and curb the ballpark's gull population, they named it "Winfield.")

Redeemed: Ironically, Winfield (the player, not the falcon) was later traded to the Blue Jays and helped win the 1992 World Series with a spectacular game-wining double in Game 6… earning him the nickname "Mr. Jay."

THE CAT'S MEOW

In May 1990, A's manager Tony La Russa was sitting in the dugout during an Oakland home game when a stray cat ran out onto the field. The players tried to catch it, but the frightened cat made a beeline for the dugout, where La Russa—a self-described "cat person"—was able to corral it. The crowd cheered, and the cat spent the rest of the game clinging to La Russa. (He kept the cat and named her Evie.) Inspired, La Russa and his wife Elaine founded ARF, the Animal Rescue Foundation, which auctions off baseball memorabilia and uses the funds to find homes for stray animals (so far, tens of thousands of them). La Russa, who owns three dogs and nine cats, says his animals help him keep things in perspective. "I get home, feeling like hell after we get beat, and then see the faces of my pets telling me that, really, everything's okay."

A TIP O' THE CAP

It's always tough to return to the home park of your former team, but Casey Stengel came prepared when he and his fellow Pirates showed up at Ebbets Field to play the Dodgers (who'd recently traded him) in 1919. The Dodger fans booed mercilessly as Stengel walked up to the plate, when he suddenly paused and turned to face the hecklers. Then, to everyone's astonishment, he tipped his cap and out came…a sparrow. It fluttered a few circles around the plate and then flew off into the sky. The fans roared and—at least temporarily—were in love with Casey again.

UNBREAKABLE?

Some records are unbreakable...until they're broken.

Record: 749 complete games pitched
Holder: Cy Young (1890–1911)
Why It Will Stand: From the late 1800s through the mid-20th century, pitchers routinely stayed in for the entire game. (Last pitcher to throw 20 complete games in a season: Fernando Valenzuela, in 1986.) Today's pitching strategy is to strike out as many batters as possible, which leads to more pitches thrown and more stress on a pitcher's arm. So managers generally replace a pitcher after about 120–130 total pitches, usually no more than seven innings. The active leader in complete games is 24-year veteran Roger Clemens, with 118, a sixth as many as Young.

Record: 1,406 career stolen bases
Holder: Rickey Henderson (1979–2003)
Why It Will Stand: Henderson's total dwarfs the second-place total: Lou Brock, with 938. This record will probably stand for a long time because no current player even comes close. Kenny Lofton is the closest active player with 622 and Barry Bonds is next with 514, but both of them are over 40 and neither will play long enough to break the record.

Record: 7 no-hitters pitched
Holder: Nolan Ryan (1966–1993)
Why It Will Stand: Because pitchers seldom pitch complete games anymore, the chance for no-hitters, especially multiple no-hitters, has significantly decreased. The current pitcher with the most no-hitters is Randy Johnson, with two.

Record: 5,714 strikeouts by a pitcher
Holder: Nolan Ryan (1966–1993)
Why It Will Stand: Ryan struck out 5,714 batters in his 27 years in baseball. Active pitchers in second and third place on the list:

What are "Uncle Charlies," "hammers," "yakkers," and "benders"? Curve balls.

Roger Clemens (4,672) and Randy Johnson (4,616). To overtake Ryan, Clemens or Johnson would have to strike out more than 1,000 batters in the remaining years of their careers—unlikely, since both are in their mid-40s and nearing retirement.

Record: 4,256 career hits
Holder: Pete Rose (1963–1986)
Why It Will Stand: Ty Cobb's record of 4,191 was considered untouchable until Rose hit it...and kept going. Third place: Hank Aaron, with 3,771. Rose's record is safe for now because he's so far ahead. The closest active players are Barry Bonds (2,935) and Omar Vizquel (2,598).

Record: Most seasons spent with one team: 23
Holders: Brooks Robinson (Baltimore Orioles, 1955–1977) and Carl Yastrzemski (Boston Red Sox, 1961–1983)
Why It Will Stand: Until the 1960s, players usually spent their entire careers with one team. That's because contracts were so restrictive: Teams owned the rights to their players for as long as they played, not for just a few years. Now, there's free agency—when a player's contract is up, he can sign up with any team he wants...usually the one that's offering the most money. For this reason, there's little chance a current or future player would ever match Robinson and Yastrzemski's mark. Active leader: John Smoltz, who has spent 18 seasons with Atlanta.

Record: Hitting in 56 straight games
Holder: Joe DiMaggio (1941)
Why It Will Stand: In a game where hitting the ball 30% of the time is considered exceptional, getting a hit in 56 straight games is nothing short of miraculous. In fact, after going hitless in game #57, Dimaggio hit in his next 16 games, meaning he got a hit in an amazing 72 out of 73 games. In his book *Triumph and Tragedy in Mudville: A Lifelong Passion for Baseball*, scientist Stephen Jay Gould theorized that DiMaggio's streak is the only record in sports that, based on statistical analysis and probability, was theoretically *impossible*. In other words, it probably won't happen again.

Record: 2,632 consecutive games played
Holder: Cal Ripken Jr. (1981–2001)
Why It Will Stand: Lou Gehrig's record of 2,130 consecutive games was once considered unbreakable. (That's 14 seasons without missing a game.) Very few people in *any* line of work never miss a day in 14 years, let alone a professional athlete. Ripken, despite playing at the physically taxing position of shortstop, started his streak in 1982, broke Gehrig's record in 1995, and played in every game until 1998. Miguel Tejada had a streak of 1,152 going until it ended in 2007 with an injury. Closest active leader: Dodgers outfielder Juan Pierre, with 434 games.

Record: .435 batting average in a season
Holder: Tip O'Neill (1887)
Why It Will Stand: O'Neill's record has stood for over a century, but what's more amazing is that nobody has even hit over .400 since Ted Williams made .406 in 1941. A few have come relatively close to Williams, including George Brett (.390 in 1980) and Rod Carew (.388 in 1977), but none have come anywhere near O'Neill. Why? Not only is the game more competitive, but strategies have changed. More pitchers are used per game, which means hitters have to contend with pitchers playing at full strength. Also, batting average is now seen as a less important statistical indicator than on-base percentage, meaning hitters are encouraged to draw walks and swing for the fences. Some baseball writers think certain intangibles also play a part in lowering averages. Examples: increased travel, artificial turf, and night games.

Record: 511 pitching wins
Holder: Cy Young (1890–1911)
Why It Will Stand: Young routinely started more than 40 games per season in a time when teams employed a three-man pitching rotation. Today, teams use a five-man rotation so that pitchers can rest their arms for as long as possible between games. Result: No pitcher will ever again *start* as many games as Young, let alone win as many.

Originally, A.L. balls were stitched with red and blue thread; N.L. balls with red and black.

EDDIE AT THE BAT

Eddie Gaedel may only have played a teensy-weensy, itsy-bitsy part in baseball history…but he made a huge impression.

PIG IN A POKE

In July 1951, Bill Veeck, (rhymes with "wreck") the new owner of the St. Louis Browns, decided he'd throw a 50th birthday party for the American League on August 19, in between the games of a doubleheader between the Browns and the Detroit Tigers. Veeck had to do *something* to get the fans into the ballpark for that game: The Tigers were the worst team in the league, and the Browns weren't far behind. Attendance at home games was already down, and few people were likely to turn out just to watch the game.

Veeck convinced the Browns' radio sponsor, the Falstaff Brewery, to pick up the tab by turning the "festival of surprises" he'd planned into a birthday party for the brewery, too. He promised to deliver a publicity stunt so spectacular that it would generate national exposure for Falstaff in the process. But there was a catch: To prevent word of the stunt from leaking out, Veeck refused to tell them what it was. He was asking them to foot the bill without even knowing what they were paying for.

JUST ONE SMALL PROBLEM

Veeck didn't know what they were paying for, either. With just two weeks to go until the game, he still hadn't come up with an idea for the publicity stunt. As he racked his brain for ideas, Veeck thought back to his childhood, when his father was the president of the Chicago Cubs and John McGraw, the manager of the New York Giants, would come to visit. Veeck remembered McGraw telling the story of Eddie Bennett, a hunchbacked dwarf who hung around the Giants ballpark and had become a sort of good-luck charm for the team. McGraw had sworn that one day he'd add Bennett to the batting lineup, but he never got around to doing it. The memory of that gave Veeck the idea he was looking for: He'd sign a "midget" to the baseball team and send him up to bat.

Veeck called a booking agent he knew in Chicago and asked him to find a young, athletic midget stage performer, but he didn't say what for. The agent found 26-year-old Eddie Gaedel and sent him to St. Louis. Veeck liked Gaedel at first sight. "Eddie," he asked, "how would you like to be a big-league ballplayer?"

NOW THAT'S A NO-HITTER

Gaedel was apprehensive at first, but Veeck sold him on the idea by telling him he'd make history. "You'll be famous, Eddie," Veeck told him. "You'll be immortal." Gaedel thought it over, swallowed his fears, and agreed to take the job.

Having inflated Gaedel's expectations, Veeck proceeded to let some of the air right back out again. He was hiring Gaedel for one game only, he explained, and for only one turn at bat. And he didn't want Gaedel to even lift the bat off of his shoulders, let alone try to swing at the pitches. Athletic or not, Gaedel wasn't a good enough ballplayer to score a hit off of a big-league pitcher. Instead, Veeck wanted him to draw a walk, something he thought would be easy. After all, Gaedel was only 3'7" tall; when he got into his batting stance, his strike zone—the distance between his armpits and the top of his knees—was about eight inches. With a little coaching from Veeck on how to "improve" his stance, he managed to shrink it to about an inch and a half. What pitcher could hit that?

Veeck told Gaedel that if he'd just stand there and let the pitches whiz past him, he'd get four balls in a row. After he got to first base he'd be replaced by a pinch runner and would be out of the game. To make sure Gaedel played along, Veeck upped the ante: "Eddie," he told Gaedel, "I'm going to be up on the roof with a high-powered rifle watching every move you make. If you so much as look as if you're going to swing, I'm going to shoot you dead."

PLAY BALL!

By the morning of game day, everything was ready. Gaedel suited up in a uniform borrowed from the seven-year-old son of a team official; his player number—"1/8"—was sewn on the back of his jersey. Both the Browns and the Falstaff Brewery had worked hard to promote the game, and more than 18,000 peo-

ple, the largest crowd in four years, had turned out. Every fan got cake and ice cream in honor of the American League's birthday, and each adult got a can of Falstaff Beer to in honor of the brewery's. Only one sportswriter noticed the entry "Gaedel 1/8" on the scorecard and asked about it, but team officials brushed him off.

MOMENT OF TRUTH

Veeck had scheduled a number of events for his Festival of Surprises: a parade of classic cars, men and women in period costumes, jugglers, a trampoline act, and a guy who could walk on his hands. Satchel Paige, who'd signed with the Browns that season, played drums with a quartet on home plate. None of it was very impressive, and the Falstaff executives started getting restless. Where was the big promotion they had paid for?

A short time later, a seven-foot-tall papier-mâché cake was wheeled out onto the field as the Browns' announcer said that the Browns' manager was getting a present of his own, "a brand-new Brownie." With that, Gaedel popped out of the cake and ran around in his uniform and pointy elf shoes, then disappeared into the dugout. *That* was the surprise? A midget jumping out of a cake? The Falstaff people couldn't believe it—they felt they'd been had. "This is the explosive thing you couldn't tell us about? This is going to get us national coverage?" one of the executives asked.

BUT WAIT...THERE'S MORE

Veeck put on an embarrassed face and apologized profusely to the Falstaff people. Their anger lasted until the second half of the first inning, when it was the Browns' turn to bat. Suddenly Gaedel emerged from the dugout, wearing baseball spikes instead of elf shoes and swinging three small bats. "Batting for the Browns," the announcer called out, "number one-eighth, Eddie Gaedel." The Falstaff executives quickly stopped grumbling and turned their attention back to the game. The umpire was in just as much disbelief as they were, but when the team manager presented him with Gaedel's signed contract and a copy of the team's active list with his name on it, he ran out of objections. He said, "Play ball!" and Gaedel went up to bat.

What is "template #R43" in the Louisville Slugger archives? The pattern for Babe Ruth's bat.

MISSION: IMPOSSIBLE

How do you even pitch to a guy who's less than four feet tall? Bob Swift, the Tigers' catcher, walked out to the mound for a quick conference with the pitcher, Bob Cain. "Keep it low," he suggested, then he went back to home plate and dropped to his knees.

The first pitch sailed right past Gaedel. He didn't even try to swing. Too high—ball one. He didn't swing at the second pitch, either. Too high—ball two. By now Cain had lost his composure and was laughing on the mound. Pitches three and four came in three feet over Gaedel's head. Ball three! Ball four! As the crowd roared and the press cameras clicked, the little man trotted out to first base, and then waited there until pinch-runner Jim Delsing replaced him.

The Browns' dugout was behind third base, so when Gaedel was relieved he walked slowly across the infield, stopping twice to wave his cap and bow as the cheering crowd gave him a standing ovation. "Man, I feel like Babe Root!" he said in his thick Chicago accent when he got to the dugout. (Jim Delsing never did make it home; he was stranded on third when the inning ended. The Browns lost the game 6–2).

MAN OF THE HOUR

In an age when you have your choice of 24-hour sports channels and can watch the World Series on your cell phone, sending a 3'7" player up to bat may not seem like a big deal, but in 1951 it was a *very* big deal. The Falstaff executives were more than satisfied when the story made the front page of just about every newspaper sports section in the country, plus additional coverage on radio and TV. Gaedel was paid only $100 for his appearance, but the publicity landed him paid appearances on several TV shows. In the end he earned nearly $20,000 for his single at-bat, more than most ballplayers made all season. More than 50 years after the fact, his turn at bat is still considered the most famous publicity stunt in the history of professional baseball.

One person who wasn't happy with the stunt was Will Harridge, the president of the American League. He thought it made a mockery of the game. The day after the game he voided Gaedel's contract, effectively barring him from major league baseball.

The 7th-inning stretch makes baseball the only sport where *spectators* do calisthenics.

THE LONG AND SHORT OF THINGS

Gaedel was shattered by the decision, and Veeck was disappointed, too. Though he certainly hadn't planned on using Gaedel in every game, he'd been looking into adding a 9'3" English giant he'd read about onto the team and alternating him in the lineup with Gaedel. Now that was out of the question. Veeck would hire Eddie Gaedel for more publicity stunts over the years—in 1959 Gaedel and three other little people dressed up as Martians and "invaded" a Browns-White Sox game by landing on the field in a helicopter. Two years later, he and several other little people dressed up as vendors and sold refreshments in the stands after someone complained that average-height vendors blocked the view of the game. But he never did get another chance to play in a major league game—in addition to being the shortest man ever to play in the big leagues, with only one at-bat (with an on-base percentage of 1.000), he also had one of the shortest careers in the history of professional baseball.

LIFE AFTER BASEBALL

Gaedel had a difficult time living in the shadow of his own fame once his big moment was over. He made a couple of appearances in minor league games, traveled with a rodeo and then a circus, and later played a bellhop in a Philip Morris cigarette TV commercial. But as he entered his 30s, a lifetime of being singled out and abused for being different caught up with him. He became increasingly bitter, developed a drinking problem, and got into one bar fight after another. By 1961 he was unemployed, living with his mother, and drinking more than ever. In June of that year, he was severely beaten by four or five other men in yet another bar fight and died from a "heart seizure" a few days later. He was 36.

With only one at-bat, Gaedel will never be elected into the Baseball Hall of Fame. But his jersey is on display there, and in August 2001 the Hall of Fame commemorated his moment in the limelight with a reenactment attended by more than 30 relatives and at least one teammate, his pinch runner, Jim Delsing. If you happened to be at the game in 1951 and got his autograph or saved the scorecard with his name on it, take care of it. His autographs are so rare that they're worth upwards of $15,000—more than Babe Ruth's.

"GOING, GOING...GONE!"

You've paid your dues at broadcasting school and have finally worked your way up to becoming a play-by-play announcer in the majors. Congratulations! Now all you need is your own signature home run call. (You can't use any of these—they're already taken.)

"Holy Cow!"
— **Phil Rizzuto, Yankees**

"It could be, it might be...it is, a home run!"
— **Harry Caray, Cubs**

"Whoa, boy! Next time around, bring me back my stomach!"
— **Jack Brickhouse, White Sox**

"Tell it 'Bye-Bye, baby!'"
— **Russ Hodges, Giants**

"Forget it!"
— **Vin Scully, Dodgers**

"Going back...at the track, at the wall...SSSEEEEE-YA!"
— **Michael Kay, Yankees**

"Get up, get outta here, gone for Yount!"
— **Bob Uecker, Brewers**

"Here's the swing and there it goes...light tower power!"
— **Jerry Trupiano, Red Sox**

"Get out the rye bread and mustard, grandma, cause it's grand salami time!"
— **Dave Niehaus, Mariners**

"It's deep, and I don't think it's playable."
— **Keith Olbermann, ESPN**

"Swung on and there it goes! That ball is high! It is far! It is...GONE!"
— **John Sterling, Yankees**

"Whaddaya think about that?"
— **Rob Faulds, Blue Jays**

"They usually show movies on a flight like that."
— **Ken Coleman, Indians, Red Sox, and Reds**

"It's going, going...gone!"
— **Harry Hartman, Reds (He coined it in 1929.)**

"A high fly ball hit to deep center. Took it to the track wall. See you later!"
— **Michael Reghi, Orioles**

Dodgers pitcher Ralph Branca, wearing #13, posed with black cats just before the 1951 playoffs.

"Kiss it goodbye!"
—Bob Prince, Pirates

"That ball is going and it ain't coming back!"
—Jeff Kingery, Rockies

"Long drive, way back, warning track, wall...you can touch em' all!"
—Greg Schulte, Diamondbacks

"You can put it on the board ...yes!"
—Ken "Hawk" Harrelson, White Sox

"To the wall and over the wall! Oh, Doctor!"
—Jerry Coleman, Yankees, Angels, Padres

"Goodbye, baseball!"
—Dick Risenhoover, Rangers

"Back, back, back, back... gone!"
—Chris Berman, ESPN

"Long gone!"
—Ernie Harwell, Tigers

"Open the window, Aunt Minnie, here it comes!"
—Rosey Roswell, Pirates

"That ball is...history!"
—Eric Nadel, Rangers

"Watch that baby...outta here!"
—Harry Kalas, Phillies

"A-B-C you later!"
—Frank Messer, Yankees

"*Bonsoir, elle est partie!*" (French for "So long, she's gone!")
—Rodger Brulotte, Expos

*   *   *

INTERNATIONAL APPEAL

In 1872 an American university professor named Horace Wilson traveled to Japan to teach English. He taught something else, too: baseball. The Japanese students took to it immediately, followed by the entire nation, mainly because the game of baseball incorporates a value that the Japanese hold in high regard: the spirit of *wa*—the willingness of one individual to sacrifice himself for the good of the group.

No B.S.: Harry Caray trained himself to say "Holy cow!" to avoid accidental profanity.

WHY *TWO* PAIRS OF SOCKS?

Wearing two socks—a colored "stirrup" sock over a white sock—is a baseball tradition that, on the surface, makes no sense. After all, other sports seem to get by just fine with only a single pair.

COLOR CODED

Identifying baseball teams by the color of their socks or stockings dates back to the earliest days of the sport—the Cincinnati Reds, professional baseball's oldest team, get their name from their socks—they were originally known as the Red Stockings when they were founded in 1868.

Believe it or not, something as simple and seemingly harmless as wearing colorful stockings came with serious health risks in the 1880s, when spiked shoes came into widespread use. "Spiking" another player by deliberately sliding into them with spikes exposed, or by baring your spikes as another player slid into you, became such a common occurrence that in 1895 there were calls for them to be banned. But they never were banned; if anything, the problem grew worse over time. Ty Cobb, who began his career in 1905, was infamous for sharpening his spikes so they would cut even deeper.

DYING FROM DYEING

If being gashed in the legs by mud- and manure-encrusted baseball spikes wasn't harmful enough, the potential danger was even greater if the victim wore colored socks. In those days, most dyes were not colorfast: The colors ran when the socks got wet...or bloody. The chemicals in the dye could seep into wounds, increasing the risk of infection. Infections were no laughing matter in the days before antibiotics—they could be deadly.

The issue came to a head in 1905, when Nap Lajoie, star second baseman for the Cleveland Naps, was spiked during a game and came down with a life-threatening case of blood poisoning

that was attributed to the dye in his socks. The infection kept him sidelined for two months.

DOUBLE PLAY

No macho ballplayer wanted his obituary to read, "Killed by his socks." So when sporting goods companies, capitalizing on the fear of blood poisoning, started offering undyed, "sanitary" white socks that could be worn underneath the team's colored socks, they found ready buyers.

Wearing two pairs of socks created a new problem—baseball shoes didn't fit as well, so players started cutting off the heels and toes of the dyed socks to create an improvised "stirrup" sock that reduced the bulk inside the shoe and let a little bit of the white sanitary sock show through. Soon sporting goods manufacturers began making their colored socks in that style. In those early days, the stirrups were small enough and low enough on the leg that very little of the white sock could be seen. But the stirrup socks stretched a little every time a player put them on, and fashions changed, too. As the years passed, more and more of the white sanitary sock peeked through, until the stirrup "look" became synonymous with baseball uniforms.

IT HAS ITS UPS AND DOWNS

By 1961 stirrups had gotten so long that baseball officials tried to intervene to prevent them from getting even longer, but they failed miserably. As the years passed, stirrups got longer...and longer...and longer, until so much of the stirrup had disappeared beneath the uniform pants that they didn't even look like stirrups anymore, they just looked like two strips of cloth running from the pants down into the shoe. This "whitewall tire" look remained dominant until the early 1990s, when uniform pants lengthened to the point that the stirrups are now almost completely concealed by the players' pant legs.

*　　*　　*

"It isn't hard to be good from time to time. What is tough is being good every day."

—Willie Mays

URBAN LEGENDS

Baseball has its share of myths. Here are a few.

Baseball Legend: Fidel Castro was one of Cuba's top amateur baseball players, and in 1949 the Washington Senators invited him to come to the United States for a tryout. Castro hit poorly, didn't make the team, and returned to Cuba, where he quickly rose through the ranks of the Cuban socialist movement, ultimately becoming dictator of the country in 1959.

Truth: Castro loves baseball and has fostered and encouraged the development of the game in Cuba, but he was never good enough to play at the professional level. He never tried out with the Senators, nor did he visit Washington in the 1940s. In fact, at the time of his supposed tryout, he was already involved with Cuba's socialist movement.

Baseball Legend: Gaylord Perry was a top pitcher but a very poor hitter. In 1963 Perry joked to a reporter, "They'll put a man on the moon before I hit a home run." Six years later, on July 20, 1969, the Apollo 11 ship landed on the moon and Neil Armstrong set foot on the lunar surface. Moments later, Perry hit the first home run of his career.

Truth: Amazingly, the story is true.

Baseball Legend: In 1997, when actor Kevin Costner was spending a lot of time at Baltimore Orioles games to research his role as a pitcher in the movie *For Love of the Game*, he stayed at Cal Ripken Jr.'s house. One August day, just before a game, Ripken found his wife, Kelly, in bed with Costner. Ripken was so emotionally devastated that he called the Orioles to tell them he wouldn't be playing that night. Not wanting to break his record 2,500-plus game streak, the Orioles cancelled that night's game, citing a "lighting problem."

Truth: The Orioles did, in fact, cancel a game in August 1997, but it was because a circuit breaker kept shorting out the stadium's lights. And while Costner was at a lot of Orioles games that summer, both Ripken and Costner deny that the alleged affair ever occurred.

In 12 games in his first season, Sandy Koufax had 12 at-bats and struck out 12 times.

WHAT'S IN A NAME?

Buy me some peanuts and…Crunch 'n Munch?

PINCH HITTER
In May 2004, the New York Yankees organization decided to replace Cracker Jack with a different caramel corn. The switch came about when Frito-Lay, which owns the Cracker Jack brand, decided to phase out Cracker Jack boxes and package their product in bags instead. Frito-Lay assured the Yankees that the bagged Cracker Jack would be fresher and that the bags would still include the prizes. But Yankee management refused to get on board. David Bernstein, the Yankees' director of hospitality, insisted, "Bags break open and don't sell as well." And a Yankee tasting panel preferred another product, ConAgra's Crunch 'n Munch, which comes in boxes, to the bagged Cracker Jack.

Lonn Trost, the Yanks' COO, told the *New York Times* that "Cracker Jack is just a brand name. We're selling a caramel crunch that is the same thing as Cracker Jack. It's the same difference as Frigidaire versus refrigerator, or aspirin and Bayer, or Jell-O and gelatin." Wrong. Fans raised such an outcry that the Yankees had to back down. On June 2, 2004, they brought back Cracker Jack. "The fans," Trost said, "have spoken."

CRACKER JACK FACTS
• Cracker Jack was first sold at the World's Columbian Exhibit of 1893, Chicago's first World's Fair, by Fritz and Louis Rueckheim.
• In 1908 Cracker Jack was famously referred to in "Take Me Out to the Ball Game," written by Jack Norworth and Albert Von Tilzer. But Von Tilzer never saw a baseball game until more than 20 years after the song came out, and Norworth saw his first one in 1940.
• The Rueckheim brothers started adding prizes to the boxes in 1912. More than 23 billion have been given out since then.
• What's in today's Cracker Jack? Sugar, corn syrup, popcorn, peanuts, molasses, salt, corn and/or soybean oil, and soy lecithin. Half a cup of Cracker Jack contains 120 calories, 2 grams of fat, and no cholesterol.
• July 5 is "National Cracker Jack Day."

A complete set (176) of 1915 Cracker Jack baseball cards sold for $800,000 in 2005.

CASEY AT THE BAT

Subtitled "A Ballad of the Republic Sung in the Year 1888," this classic poem was first published in the San Francisco Examiner in June 1888, but was popularized on the vaudeville circuit. It was written by 24-year-old sports-writer Ernest Thayer and is probably the most famous piece of literature ever written about baseball. Here's "Casey at the Bat" in its entirety.

The outlook wasn't brilliant for the Mudville Nine that day;
The score stood four to two, with but one inning more to play,
And then when Cooney died at first, and Barrows did the same,
A sickly silence fell upon the patrons of the game.

A straggling few got up to go in deep despair. The rest
Clung to that hope which springs eternal in the human breast;
They thought, if only Casey could get but a whack at that—
We'd put up even money, now, with Casey at the bat.

But Flynn preceded Casey, as did also Jimmy Blake,
And the former was a lulu and the latter was a cake;
So upon that stricken multitude grim melancholy sat,
For there seemed but little chance of Casey's getting to the bat.

But Flynn let drive a single, to the wonderment of all,
And Blake, the much despis-ed, tore the cover off the ball;
And when the dust had lifted, and they saw what had occurred,
There was Jimmy safe at second and Flynn a-hugging third.

Then from 5,000 throats and more there rose a lusty yell;
It rumbled through the valley, it rattled in the dell;
It knocked upon the mountain and recoiled upon the flat,
For Casey, mighty Casey, was advancing to the bat.

There was ease in Casey's manner as he stepped into his place;
There was pride in Casey's bearing and a smile on Casey's face.
And when, responding to the cheers, he lightly doffed his hat,
No stranger in the crowd could doubt 'twas Casey at the bat.

Ten thousand eyes were on him as he rubbed his hands with dirt;
Five thousand tongues applauded when he wiped them on his shirt.
Then while the writhing pitcher ground the ball into his hip,
Defiance gleamed in Casey's eye, a sneer curled Casey's lip.

And now the leather-covered sphere came hurtling through the air,
And Casey stood a-watching it in haughty grandeur there.
Close by the sturdy batsman the ball unheeded sped—
"That ain't my style," said Casey. "Strike one," the umpire said.

From the benches, black with people, there went up a muffled roar,
Like the beating of the storm-waves on a stern and distant shore.
"Kill him! Kill the umpire!" shouted someone on the stand;
And it's likely they'd a-killed him had not Casey raised his hand.

With a smile of Christian charity great Casey's visage shown;
He stilled the rising tumult; he bade the game go on;
He signaled to the pitcher, and once more the spheroid flew;
But Casey still ignored it, and the umpire said, "Strike two."

"Fraud!" cried the maddened thousands, and echo answered fraud;
But one scornful look from Casey and the audience was awed.
They saw his face grow stern and cold, they saw his muscles strain,
And they knew that Casey wouldn't let that ball go by again.

The sneer is gone from Casey's lip, his teeth are clenched in hate;
He pounds with cruel violence his bat upon the plate.
And now the pitcher holds the ball, and now he lets it go,
And now the air is shattered by the force of Casey's blow.

Oh, somewhere in this favored land the sun is shining bright;
The band is playing somewhere, and somewhere hearts are light,
And somewhere men are laughing, and somewhere children shout;
But there is no joy in Mudville—mighty Casey has struck out.

CASEY AT THE FACTS

• In 1907 sportswriter Grantland Rice wrote a sequel called
"Casey's Revenge," in which Casey faces a similar bottom-of-the-
ninth situation...and this time he hits a game-winning home run.

• "Casey at the Bat" was made into a movie (starring Wallace
Beery as Casey) in 1927, an opera by composer William Schuman
in 1953, and a *Mad* magazine parody in 1964 (it takes place in
Russia—when Casey strikes out, he's sent to the gulag).

• Two cities claim to be the inspiration for Mudville: a neighbor-
hood called Mudville in Holliston, Massachusetts, and Stockton,
California, which was actually called Mudville before it was incor-
porated as Stockton in 1850. Which one is the "real" Mudville?
Ernest Thayer claimed it was based on...nowhere in particular.

Only pitcher to strike out Maris, McGwire, Sosa, and Bonds: Nolan Ryan.

THE DOCK IS (FAR) OUT, PART I

No matter what a player does in his career, a single moment can overshadow everything else (just ask Bill Buckner). Take Dock Ellis, a pitcher who became a household name in the 1970s for his controversial comments and intense play (he once tried to bean every member of the Reds' lineup). But today Ellis is primarily known as "the guy who pitched a no-hitter on LSD."

CHIP ON HIS SHOULDER

As a teenager growing up in Los Angeles in the 1960s, Dock Ellis's angry streak was already in place. From his viewpoint, he was always being slighted because he was African American. In some cases Ellis was right, such as when he refused to play on his high-school baseball team because a teammate called him "spearchucker" and the coach didn't see anything wrong with that. But unlike his hero, Jackie Robinson, Ellis wasn't hesitant about retaliating. While playing in the minor leagues, he once ran into the stands, bat in hand, to confront a man who'd been yelling racial insults at him all afternoon.

The 23-year-old Ellis took that intensity into the majors when he started with the Pirates in 1968. Within a couple of years, the mainstream press had labeled the imposing 6' 4" pitcher as a "militant" (along with other outspoken black players, such as Curt Flood and Dick Allen). On the mound, though, Ellis was a great pitcher. He threw a no-hitter in 1970 (more on that later), and the following season he made the All-Star team on his way to a 19–9 record and a 3.06 ERA, culminating with a Pirates World Series victory. But by then, Ellis was known more for his inflammatory antics than for his pitching stats.

PUT ME IN, COACH

It was the 1971 All-Star Game that first put Ellis in the national spotlight as a troublemaker. After finding out he'd made the lineup for the National League squad, Ellis stated publicly that he deserved to be the starter. But because Baltimore's Earl Weaver had announced that pitcher Vida Blue, an African American,

---

would start for the A.L., Ellis told reporters he doubted that Sparky Anderson, the N.L. manager, would be brave enough to start an African-American pitcher as well. "They wouldn't pitch two brothers against each other," he told the press.

The comments made big news that summer: Sportswriters wrote about racism in baseball and argued over who Anderson should play. Ultimately, Anderson did choose to start Ellis (but claimed his decision was purely based on pitching ability), marking the first time that two black pitchers started an All-Star contest. The game was a classic, featuring 20 future Hall of Famers, including Reggie Jackson, who faced Ellis for the first time and hit a 520-foot home run off him. Ellis believed that Jackson "showboated" by taking too much time to run around the bases...and he would never forget that home run.

In the weeks that followed, Ellis received hundreds of hate letters, most race related, but also messages from baseball fans simply telling him to be quiet (Sparky Anderson was a fan favorite, and Ellis calling him out enraged a lot of people). But he did receive one letter of encouragement that reinforced his determination:

> I read your comments in our paper the last few days, and wanted you to know how much I appreciate your honesty. The news media, while knowing full well you are right and honest, will use every means to get back at you. Honors that should be yours will bypass you and the pressures will be great—try not to be left alone. There will be times when you ask yourself if it's worth it at all. I can only say, Dock, it is. Sincerely,
>
> Jackie Robinson

ACCESS DENIED

By 1972 Ellis was one of the best-known pro athletes in the United States. That's probably why he was so surprised when a security guard stopped him at the players' gate at Cincinnati's Riverfront Stadium before a game against the Reds. The guard, who was white, didn't believe Ellis's claim that he was a real player. Ellis tried using his World Series ring as identification, but the guard still wasn't convinced. An argument ensued in which Ellis "made threatening gestures with a clenched fist" while carrying a half of a bottle of wine...and the guard maced Ellis in the face.

The pitcher was arrested for disorderly conduct, but the charge

was later dropped. Amidst a flurry of bad press, the Reds' head office publicly apologized to Ellis and fired the guard. The incident added yet another layer to Ellis's mystique…and to his reputation for being a troublemaker. "There may be persons out there who hate my guts," he said, "but they don't know me."

EBONY AND IVORY

Ellis did have a lighter side, but even that got him into trouble. In 1973 the flamboyant athlete started showing up on game day wearing pink hair curlers in his afro. Inspired, *Ebony* magazine ran a pictorial featuring all of Ellis's hairstyles. Ellis loved the attention, so he started wearing curlers on the field during pregame warm-ups. That's when the Pirates executive office stepped in and ordered him to remove the curlers before entering the field of play. Ellis was upset. "I know the orders came from [baseball commissioner] Bowie Kuhn, and I don't like it. Look around. There are guys who wear white shoes in practice. Some wear jackets. Others don't wear hats. I wasn't going to say anything, but since they seem to be aiming in my direction, I'm going to say things." But the order stuck, and Ellis was further alienated. That year, a Pittsburgh newspaper headline called him "Probably the Most Unpopular Buc of All Time."

RAGE AGAINST THE MACHINE

Many people *really* stopped admiring Ellis after his next infamous incident. Unhappy with his team's lackluster performance at the beginning of the 1974 season, Ellis decided his Pirates needed a spark, and it would happen against their biggest rival: Cincinnati's "Big Red Machine," who'd come from behind to win the division title over Pittsburgh the previous year. On May 1, Ellis made a passionate speech to his teammates just before a game against the Reds: "Cincinnati will bullsh*t with us and kick our a** and laugh at us! They're the only team that can talk about us like a dog!" Full of fire, Ellis then announced, "We gonna get down. We gonna do the do. I'm going to hit these m*therf***ers!"

No one in the locker room really believed Ellis would do it…until he opened the game by hitting Pete Rose in the ribs, sending the Reds' best hitter to the dirt. Then Ellis beaned Joe Morgan and Dan Driessen to load the bases. After Tony Perez

dodged the Ellis attack to draw a walk (which brought in a run), Ellis threw the next two pitches at Johnny Bench's head (Bench dodged them both). Pittsburgh manager Danny Murtaugh yanked Ellis before he did any serious damage. But by then, the pitcher had made his point. Did his tactic work? Well, the Pirates won the division and, for the first time in three seasons, the Reds didn't.

HIT ME WITH YOUR BEST SHOT

Ellis's last good year as a pitcher came in 1976, when he was traded to the Yankees. Once again, though, his combative attitude over-shadowed his play. Ellis had been holding a grudge against Reggie Jackson ever since that home run in the 1971 All-Star Game, and now that he was in the American League, he finally had a chance for revenge. In a game against the Orioles, with whom Jackson was playing that year, Ellis threw a fastball that hit Jackson's cheek and knocked him unconscious. The future "Mr. October" missed the next 28 games.

Ellis was remorseless, simply saying, "I owed him one." Not only was he *not* punished by Major League Baseball, he said that a lot of players bought him drinks after he hit Jackson, who had a reputation for being conceited. But as Jackson's fame was rising to the level of superstar, Ellis's age was catching up with him—he bounced around the league for two more years, ending up where he began, in Pittsburgh.

A QUIET EXIT

Ellis retired after the 1979 season with decent—though not Hall of Fame—numbers: a 138–119 won-lost record, a 3.46 ERA, and twice as many strikeouts as walks. As the 1980s rolled in, the for-mer headline grabber faded into mainstream obscurity. He remained a hero in the black community, thanks to the 1976 biog-raphy *Dock Ellis in the Country of Baseball*. Written by poet Donald Hall, the book painted Ellis as a brave champion for civil rights—"Baseball's Muhammad Ali." But it was Ellis's shocking 1984 con-fession that, for many people, overshadowed everything else he ever did.

For the "trippy" part of Ellis's story,
float your way over to page 237.

BANNED!

The most famous permanent banishment in baseball history involved the eight Chicago White Sox players convicted of fixing the 1919 World Series. But they weren't the first—or last—players to get kicked out of baseball.

PHIL DOUGLAS. In 1922 Major League Baseball officials received a tip from Les Mann of the St. Louis Cardinals that pitcher Phil Douglas of the New York Giants had offered to leave New York and not play in the Giants' pennant-stretch games —if the Cardinals would bribe him. Reason: Giants manager John McGraw had fined Douglas $100, and skipping the games was how he planned to get even. Commissioner Kenesaw Mountain Landis banned Douglas from baseball for life.

JIMMY O'CONNELL. In September 1924, the Giants were in a close pennant race. The Giants' O'Connell offered shortstop Heinie Sand of the Philadelphia Phillies $500 to make fielding errors to ensure a Giants win (the Phillies were out of pennant contention). Sand told league officials. O'Connell was banned for life.

FERGUSON JENKINS. A star pitcher with the Cubs and Rangers, Jenkins was detained during a routine customs check in Toronto in 1980. Officials found a small amount of cocaine on his person. Commissioner Bowie Kuhn banned him for life, but the ban was reviewed by an independent arbitrator, who reinstated him. Jenkins was elected to the Hall of Fame in 1991.

BENNY KAUFF. Commissioner Kenesaw Mountain Landis banned Kauff, a player for the New York Giants, from baseball in 1921 after he was arrested on charges of selling stolen cars. Landis called him "no longer a fit companion for other ball players." Even though the charges were later dropped, Kauff was never reinstated.

MICKEY MANTLE AND WILLIE MAYS. Mantle and Mays, two of the best and most popular players of all time, retired in 1969 and 1973, respectively. But this was the era before massive salaries, and both needed work after their playing days. In 1983 the Claridge Resort and Casino in Atlantic City hired Mantle as a "community respresentative," and Bally's Resorts hired Mays as a

---

35 major league players have ended their careers with a home run in their final at-bat.

public relations executive. Commissioner Bowie Kuhn, who fervently opposed gambling, thought that their association with casinos tarnished baseball's image. Although Mantle and Mays were no longer involved with major league baseball in any way, Kuhn banned them from any association for life. The next commissioner, Peter Ueberroth, reinstated them both in 1985.

STEVE HOWE. Howe was the 1980 National League Rookie of the Year, but his potential was never realized due to ongoing problems with cocaine and alcohol. Howe was suspended for drug use three times in 1983, leading to a ban for the entire 1984 season. His drug abuse led to fines, being released by major and minor league teams, more suspensions, and an arrest before Commissioner Fay Vincent banned Howe from baseball completely in 1992. After Howe sued the league, an independent arbitrator reinstated him. Howe was never suspended by the league for drugs again, but in 1996 he was arrested for trying to carry a loaded gun onto an airplane. Howe retired from baseball in 1997 and died in a car accident nine years later while under the influence of methamphetamine.

HORACE FOGEL. In 1912 Fogel, the owner of the Philadelphia Phillies, told reporters that he was convinced umpires were conspiring to make the Phillies lose. Specifically, he thought umpires were making unfair calls against the Phillies when they played the New York Giants, allowing the Giants to win every time they played that season. For making what turned out to be unsubstantiated claims and bringing bad press to baseball, the league banned Fogel for life and forced him to sell the Phillies.

JOSEPH CREAMER. In 1908 Creamer, the team doctor for the New York Giants, was banned after he tried to bribe an umpire $2,500 to throw a playoff game against the Chicago Cubs.

PETE ROSE. Despite the fact that Rose is the all-time leader in hits, played on three World Series-winning teams, and was one of the most popular players of the 1970s, he's not in the Hall of Fame. Reason: In 1989, while the manager of the Cincinnati Reds, he was found to have bet on baseball games (including Reds games), which led Commissioner A. Bartlett Giamatti to banish Rose for life. (Rose was also charged with income-tax evasion, for which he served a five-month jail sentence in 1990.)

No rule in the book prohibits a batter from carrying his bat after he hits the ball.

LOST LEAGUES

Today we have the American League and the National League, but over the past hundred years, others have tried—and failed—to establish brand-new major leagues. Here are the stories of a few.

BIG IDEA: The Players' National League of Professional Base Ball Clubs

STORY: John M. Ward was the New York Giants' star shortstop in the 1880s. He was also president of baseball's first players union, the Brotherhood of Professional Base-Ball Players. At the time, players had to buy their own uniforms, and they were paid on a system that took into account personal conduct and on-field performance—basically, owners could arbitrarily pay players less if they felt like it. The Brotherhood felt this was unfair and prepared to strike on July 4, 1890, potentially cancelling the lucrative July 4th doubleheaders and costing the owners a lot of money. When preseason negotiations broke down, Ward staged a massive walkout to form his own league, draining the National League of nearly all its talent. Called the "Players League" for short, the Players' National League of Professional Base Ball Clubs put up teams in Boston, Brooklyn, New York, Chicago, Philadelphia, Pittsburgh, Cleveland, and Buffalo. Games were well attended because the teams were stacked with the National League's best players, but the league made very little money because it was being managed by baseball players with little (or no) business acumen. After the 1890 season—its only season—Ward dissolved the Players League. The Boston and Philadelphia teams joined the American Association (a major league on par with the N.L. at the time) while the Brooklyn, New York, Chicago, and Pittsburgh teams merged with the National League teams in those cities. Ward, his quarrels with the owners still unresolved, played with and managed the Brooklyn Grooms for two seasons, and then was sold back to the New York Giants in 1893 for $6,000.

BIG IDEA: The Federal League

STORY: It began as the minor Columbia League in 1912, but changed its name to to the Federal League in 1913. And since it had no affiliation with any major league teams, and all its teams

---

Wrigley Field is the only remaining Federal League ballpark.

were in large cities, league president James Gilmore declared it a major league at the beginning of the 1914 season. There were eight teams—Baltimore, Brooklyn, Chicago, Kansas City, Pittsburgh, St. Louis, Buffalo, and Indianapolis (they moved to Newark in 1915). After one financially unsuccessful season in which team owners realized they couldn't compete with the American and National Leagues, they sued the big leagues for antitrust violations, hoping to get bought out. No decision was made, so the Federal League played another season, the cost of which left most of the teams nearly bankrupt. The Pittsburgh, Newark, Buffalo, and Brooklyn teams were purchased by A.L. and N.L. owners and absorbed by existing franchises, while two Federal League owners, Phil Ball of St. Louis and Charlie Weeghman of Chicago, bought the financially struggling St. Louis Browns and Chicago Cubs, respectively. The Kansas City team went bankrupt, and the Baltimore owner rejected a buyout offer, choosing instead to once again sue Major League Baseball for antitrust violations in an attempt to get a higher buyout price. It backfired: In 1922 the Supreme Court ruled that Major League Baseball is an entertainment entity, not interstate commerce, and thus is exempt from antitrust laws, a finding that remains intact to this day.

BIG IDEA: The Continental League

STORY: After the Brooklyn Dodgers and New York Giants moved to California in 1958, New York lawyer William Shea wanted to bring a National League franchise to New York. Unable to get an existing team to move there, Shea decided to start a new league to pressure the N.L. into giving him what he wanted. He found several millionaires around the country willing to participate in the venture, hoping to get Major League Baseball to expand into their cities. In 1959 Shea announced the formation of the Continental League with teams in Denver, Houston, Minneapolis, Toronto, Atlanta, Dallas, Buffalo, and New York City. (Shea even hired former Brooklyn Dodgers owner Branch Rickey to be league president—essentially a publicity stunt.) Owners included Wheelock Whitney in Minneapolis (he also owned the NFL's Minnesota Vikings) and Jack Kent Cooke in Toronto (he would later own the Washington Redskins). The idea paid off: MLB owners panicked at the threat of competition and in late

1959 agreed to a major league expansion. Houston, Minneapolis, and New York would all get new teams. And Shea got what he wanted—a New York team, the Mets. Having no more need for the Continental League, and having never fielded a single "C.L." team, Shea and the other owners voted to disband in August 1960.

BIG IDEA: The Baseball League
STORY: In 1989 Richard Moss and David LeFevre, two New York attorneys who'd primarily worked with baseball players and teams, quietly announced that they were forming a new major baseball league called, simply enough, the Baseball League. The season would last for 154 games, and teams were slated for eight large cities, six of which didn't have major league teams at the time: Washington, D.C.; Miami; New Orleans; Denver; Vancouver, B.C.; Portland, Oregon; New York; and Los Angeles. The league had plenty of money: Donald Trump, who'd owned a team in the failed United States Football League, wanted to own the New York franchise. One possible reason for the new league was TV money. In 1990 ABC's multimillion-dollar contract to air Major League Baseball games was about to expire, and the network entered into talks with the Baseball League. But the real reason behind the new league: It was an elaborate tactic staged by the two lawyers (and a bevy of sports agents) on behalf of the Major League Baseball Players Association—the players union—to extract more money from MLB owners on the pretense of competition. The entire gambit fell apart amid rumors that Trump was trying to take over the league with the intention of playing one season and then merging with Major League Baseball, the way owners in the American Basketball Association made a bundle when the NBA absorbed it in 1976. No games were ever played.

*　　*　　*

"The difference between the old ballplayer and the new ballplayer is the jersey. The old ballplayer cared about the name on the front. The new ballplayer cares about the name on the back."
—Steve Garvey

WHY MUST THEY BOO?

Booooooooooooo!

"I don't understand why the fans were booing at me. They showed me today they just care about themselves. That's no fair. Because when you're struggling, you want to feel the support of the fans."

—**Carlos Zambrano, Cubs**

"They have the right to boo people because they've been waiting for 99 years (for a World Series) and sometimes we don't do a good job and they get frustrated, too."

—**Carlos Zambrano, one day after the previous quote**

"There's not a lot of teams that I've seen in a fight for the division, in control of a ballgame the whole time, never lose the lead, and still get booed. It's certainly a boost for us to play in front of a full ballpark. If they decided to root for us, that would be even better."

—**Scott Linebrink, Brewers**

"Philadelphia fans would boo funerals, an Easter egg hunt, a parade of armless war vets, and the Liberty Bell."

—**Bo Belinsky**

"I think the only sport where they don't boo is golf."

—**Lou Piniella**

"It's like going to a Broadway show, you pay for your tickets and expect to be entertained. When you're not, you have a right to complain."

—**Sparky Anderson**

"You're trying your damnedest, you strike out and they boo you. I act like it doesn't bother me, like I don't hear anything the fans say, but the truth is I hear every word of it and it kills me."

—**Mike Schmidt**

"Those boos really motivate me to go out and make something happen."

—**Barry Bonds**

"I kind of appreciated the fact that I was booed by the Yankees' fans. I was kind of like, 'Okay, I'm a major league player now.' I'll try not to get booed at Tropicana Field."

—**Akinori Iwamura, Devil Rays, after hitting a home run in New York**

"I actually welcome boos as part of the game. I love to see that from my opponents' fans. Last night I think those fans didn't boo hard enough."

—Ichiro Suzuki, Mariners

"There are always about 20,000 Red Sox fans here when we play them. Maybe it was only Sox fans who were booing."

—Mariano Rivera, Yankees, after blowing a save against the Sox

"I've been treated there just like everywhere else: everyone boos me. I take that as a compliment."

—Albert Belle, on playing in Baltimore

"The Expos fans discovered 'boo' is pronounced the same in French as it is in English."

—Harry Caray

"The fans here are too stupid. You have to play perfect every game. You can't make an error. You can't go 0-for-4. Are we like machines?"

—Rey Ordóñez, Mets, after getting booed for going 0-for-4 and making an error

"F*** those f***ing fans who come out here and say they're Cub fans that are supposed to be behind you, ripping every f***ing thing you do. I'll tell you one f***ing thing, I hope we get f***ing hotter than s***, just to stuff it up them 3,000 f***ing people that show up every f***ing day, because if they're the real Chicago f***ing fans, they can kiss my f***ing a** right downtown and PRINT IT!"

—Lee Elia, Cubs manager

"Fans don't boo nobodies."

—Reggie Jackson

*   *   *

UNCLE JOHN'S STALL OF SHAME

The Soap and Detergent Association's 2007 study of people's hand-washing habits at "major public attractions" in four major cities revealed some alarming results: Men wash their hands only 67% of the time (compared to women's 88%). Even more alarming, the research team found that the lowest occurrence of hand-washing by men happened at baseball stadiums, with only 57%.

THE ORIGINAL CLEVELAND INDIAN

Did you know that the Cleveland Indians' name was inspired by a real ballplayer? Here's the story of the greatest baseball player you've never heard of.

THE NATURAL

In the early 1880s, a Jesuit priest at the Indian school on the Penobscot reservation near Bangor, Maine, noticed that one of his students, a kid named Louis Sockalexis, had athletic abilities far above those of his peers. He ran faster than boys three or four years older than he was, he swam like he'd been born in the water, and he excelled at every sport the kids played on the reservation. Especially baseball.

The priest encouraged Louis to stay in school and develop his physical skills to their full potential. The boy took his advice— what kid wouldn't keep playing sports if he was better than all his friends? Sockalexis dominated his high-school football, baseball, and track teams, and then moved on to St. Mary's College in Van Buren, Maine. In 1894 he was recruited to play for Holy Cross in Worcester, Massachusetts. There he batted .436 his first season and .444 his second; he was also one of the fastest runners and hardest throwers in the country. At Holy Cross he smashed the national amateur distance record by throwing a baseball 393' 8".

GOING PRO

When the Holy Cross baseball coach moved on to Notre Dame in December 1896, "Sox," as he'd come to be known, followed. He distinguished himself as one of the best athletes on campus, but didn't last too long. Like a lot of college kids—then and now—Sox drank a lot more than was good for him, and on March 17, 1897, he was expelled from the school after he and a drinking buddy smashed up a brothel run by a woman known as Popcorn Jennie.

There have been 14 Native American ballplayers who were nicknamed "Chief."

CONSPIRACY?

To this day it isn't clear what caused things to get out of hand at Popcorn Jennie's that night. One version of the story was that it was just a party that went wild; another was that Sox and his friend busted up the place after Popcorn Jennie and her girls refused to serve an Indian.

A third, more sinister version of the story places the blame at the feet of Patsy Tebeau, the manager of a National League team called the Cleveland Spiders. The team had already signed Sox to play outfield as soon as the college season ended, but Tebeau wanted him to start right away. When Sox insisted on staying in school, Tebeau took him to Popcorn Jennie's, got him drunk, and then instigated the melee that got him thrown out of school. However the incident happened, Sox's formal education was over. He sat in jail for two days; then Tebeau bailed him out, settled the charges, and brought him to Cleveland.

THE MAIN EVENT

More than a century after the fact, it can be difficult to understand just how fascinated the American public was with Native Americans when Sox signed with the Spiders. General Custer's last stand at Little Bighorn had taken place just 21 years earlier; the Battle of Wounded Knee, only 7. The Wild West was still very fresh in the public mind. Sox wasn't just the first full-blooded Indian ever to play in the major leagues, he was already widely acknowledged as being one of the best players the game had ever seen. Signing him to the Spiders was a *big* deal. Fans poured in to Spiders games not just to see what for many was their first "Real Live Indian," but also to see what this amazing athlete could do.

Some fans, of course, were racists; they mocked Sockalexis from the stands whenever he took to the field, taunting him with war whoops and cries of "Get a tomahawk!" But they were soon outnumbered by Sox's many admirers. As the *Louisville Courier Journal* reported in April 1897, "Sockalexis was cheered at every move he made. He caught a long fly very prettily and the spectators remarked at his grace. The crowd tried to have some fun with Sox's name [Sockalexis! Sockalexis! Sock it to 'em, Sockalexis!] and imitated war whoops, to all of which the handsome Indian smiled good-naturedly."

In 2007 Alex Rodriguez became the 1st player since Roger Maris to lead in HRs, RBI, and runs.

Team nicknames were much more informal in those days than they are today, and it was common for a single team to be known by a number of unofficial names—the Spiders, for example, were also known as the Clevelands. Their spider nickname dated back to 1889, when a sportswriter complained that the team's scrawny, long-limbed players looked like spiders on the ball field. But they didn't remain the Spiders for long after Sox joined the team. By the first game of the regular season, the newspapers were already referring to the team as the Cleveland Indians.

THE SLUGGER

No doubt some of the sportswriters intended for the new name to be just as derisive as Spiders had been. But the negative connotation faded after the first few games, as Sox lived up to his reputation as one of the best players the game had ever seen. By the Fourth of July, the rookie already had a batting average of .328 (the third-highest in the league) and had scored 40 runs and batted in another 39 while also stealing 16 bases.

A number of people who saw Sockalexis play in 1897 never forgot the experience; many spent the rest of their lives comparing him to other, better-known greats of the game like Ty Cobb, Babe Ruth, and Joe DiMaggio. In such comparisons the other players almost always came up short. John McGraw, the legendary New York Giants manager who played baseball for 15 years and managed teams for another 33, thought Sox was the greatest player he had ever seen. As biographer Ed Rice writes in *Baseball's First Indian*, when former Red Sox manager Bill Carrigan sized up players in the 1930s, only one of them came close to measuring up to Sox. "Possibly the one player worthy of comparison is that young man Joe DiMaggio," Carrigan remarked. "He has a trace of Sockalexis' stuff, but I don't believe he can run or throw with the Indian."

FALL FROM GRACE

So how is it that DiMaggio, Ruth, Cobb, and others became baseball legends while Sockalexis ended up in the dustbin of baseball history? Because while the other greats had careers that lasted a decade or more, Sockalexis's glory days came to an abrupt end just two and a half months after he played his first major league game.

Joe McCarthy was the first manager to win pennants in both leagues.

DÉJÀ VU

Sox's career ended just as it had begun, in another drunken incident in a brothel. After spending the entire day of July 4, 1897, carousing in Cleveland's red-light district, Sox either jumped or fell out of the second-story window of a brothel and severely injured his ankle. The injury never healed properly, and although Sox limped through two more seasons, he never recovered the speed and agility that had made him such a great player.

Many early baseball players were a hard-drinking lot, and Sox was no exception. Before his injury, he kept his drinking under control and didn't let it interfere with his game. *After* his injury was another story: Sox began showing up for games hung over. At the end of July, he was suspended from the team and fined $175 for repeated instances of drunkenness. He played only 21 games in the 1898 season, and in 1899 he was released from the team just two weeks into the season, after playing only seven games.

Sox drifted for a year or two and spent time in jail for vagrancy before returning to the Penobscot reservation. There he worked odd jobs and, when he was up to it, umpired baseball games and coached youth teams in his spare time. He was working in a logging camp on Christmas Eve in 1913 when he suffered a heart attack and died. Just 42, he was still carrying around a pocketful of his old press clippings when he passed away.

OLD...AND NEW

As for the Cleveland Indians, when Sockalexis was released from the team in 1899, they reverted back to their old nickname, the Spiders...which, in retrospect, was probably a good thing. That season they plunged in the rankings to become the all-time worst team in major league history. They were so bad, in fact, that when the season ended the National League disbanded the franchise.

Cleveland didn't have to wait long for its next major league team, however, because Ban Johnson, president of a minor league called the Western League, had his eye on the majors. When the Spiders folded he moved his Grand Rapids team, the Blues, to Cleveland. In 1900 he renamed the Western League the American League, and then in 1901 announced that the American League would operate as a major league. Just two years after losing the Spiders, Cleveland had a major league team again: the Blues.

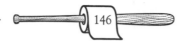

NAME GAMES

The Blues, also known as the Bluebirds and the Bronchos (among other things), became known as the "Naps" when legendary second baseman Napoleon "Nap" Lajoie signed with the team in 1902. The Cleveland team might still be called the Naps today, if not for two facts: 1) in 1915 Lajoie left Cleveland for the Philadelphia Athletics, and 2) whenever the Naps went into a slump, fans and sportswriters accused them of "napping."

Who wants to root for the Blues? After Lajoie left Cleveland, rather than revert back to the old names, team owner Charles Somers appointed a committee of local sportswriters to pick a new nickname for his team. There must have been a few old-timers in the bunch, because they passed over names like Hustlers, Youngsters, Leafs, Climbers, Eries, Euclids, Tip Tops, and Terriers to give the new team the old name of Indians. Was the name selected in the hope that the team would emulate the 1914 "miracle" Boston Braves, whose 60 victories in the last 76 games of the season brought them from last place to first and won them the National League pennant, and then the World Series? Or was it a nod to the short-lived Sockalexis era? Probably both.

"The Clevelands of 1915 will be the 'Indians,'" the *Cleveland Plain Dealer* wrote on January 18, 1915. "There will be no Indians on the roster, but the name will recall fine traditions. It is looking backward to a time when Cleveland had one of the most popular teams of the United States. It also serves to revive the memory of a single great player who has been gathered to his fathers in the happy hunting grounds of the Abenakis."

*　　*　　*

WHAT MAKES A WINNER?

"In the end it all comes down to talent. You can talk all you want about intangibles, I just don't know what that means. Talent makes winners, not intangibles. Can nice guys win? Sure, nice guys can win—if they're nice guys with a lot of talent."

—Sandy Koufax

First National League game: April 22, 1876 (the Red Stockings beat the Athletics, 6–5).

FUTURE BALL

Will there be baseball in the future? According to popular culture,
yes...sort of. Here are some takes on what baseball
might look like hundreds of years from now.

NINTENDO'S VERSION. In 1991 Nintendo came out
with a video game called *Base Wars*, depicting baseball as it
might be played in the 24th century: Human players have
been replaced by robots, and they play in a stadium that orbits the
Earth. Also, umpires are no longer necessary: In *Base Wars*, the
baserunner robot and the baseman robot fight it out with guns,
cannons, and missiles that shoot out of their arms. If the baseman
robot destroys the runner robot, he's out. If the runner annihilates
the baseman, he's safe.

VONNEGUT'S VERSION. Kurt Vonnegut's 1959 novel *The
Sirens of Titan* is about life in an Earth colony on Mars in the
22nd century. The main pastime on Mars is a sport called "German batball." It was invented by Winston Niles Runfoord, who
also led the colonization of Mars. It's roughly the same game as
baseball, but with a few adjustments. Instead of a pitched ball, the
batter balances the ball on one fist, strikes it with the other fist,
and then attempts to reach base before a fielder tags him out. The
ball is different, too. It's described as "a flabby ball the size of a big
honeydew melon" that is "no more lively than a hat filled with
rain water."

FUTURAMA'S VERSION. On the TV show *Futurama*, which
is set in the 31st century, baseball has been replaced by "blernsball" because the original game, according to blernsball's inven-
tors, was "as boring as mom and apple pie." In this sport, a long
piece of elastic tethers the ball to the field. If the batter hits it
with enough force to break the elastic and the ball hits the "hit
the ball here to win game" sign, his team automatically wins the
game. If a team hits the ball into a small hole in center field three
times, dozens of balls are shot at high speeds at the batter. Other
differences: relief pitchers take the mound by riding on a giant
tarantula, bases occasionally explode, and steroid use is mandatory.

Abraham Lincoln often delayed presidential business to play rounders (an early form of baseball).

TEST YOUR UMPIRE I.Q.

If you got a message on your answering machine informing you that you were needed to umpire Game 3 of the World Series, would you be up for the job? Take this quiz and find out.

1. Who decides whether the start of a game should be postponed due to bad weather or the poor condition of the field?
a) The manager of the home team.
b) The official scorer.
c) The head umpire ("umpire-in-chief").

2. If a ball hits the foul pole, does it count as a fair or a foul ball?
a) It always counts as a fair ball.
b) It always counts as a foul ball.
c) If it bounces off of the pole into foul territory, it counts as a foul. If it bounces into fair territory, it counts as a fair ball.

3. What happens when a fair ball lands on the field and then bounces over a fence or into the stands?
a) The batter and the runners advance one base.
b) The batter and runners advance two bases.
c) It counts as a home run—the batter and runners all run home.

4. True or false? If the batter hits a fair ball over the fence or into the stands, it always counts as a home run.

5. What happens if, while attempting to catch a fair fly ball, the fielder deflects it into the stands or over the fence into fair territory?
a) It counts as a single.
b) It counts as a triple.
c) It can count as a double or a home run, depending on the circumstances.

6. What happens when spectator interference prevents a fielder from catching a fly ball?

a) The umpire may, at his own discretion, eject the spectator from the game or order him to move to a seat farther from the field.

b) If the umpire can determine whom the spectator is rooting for, he can award an extra run to the other team.

c) If the fan is on the field or is reaching through a railing or other barrier to interfere with the catch, the batter is out. If the catcher is reaching through a barrier into the spectator area to catch the fly, he does so at his own risk—no interference will be called.

7. If a team manager is ejected from a game, is he allowed to stay in the park and watch the rest of the game?

a) No. He must leave the ballpark immediately.

b) Yes. He may watch the game on the TV in the clubhouse, but he may not step foot onto the field or into the stands.

c) Yes. He may watch the game from the stands, but only after he changes out of his uniform into his street clothes and takes a seat in the stands "well removed" from his team's bench or bullpen.

8. There are two outs and a runner on third. The batter hits a double; the man on third runs home and scores. If the batter forgets to touch first base on his way to second and is out on a throw to first base, does the run count?

a) Yes. "A run legally scored cannot be nullified by the actions of other players."

b) No. "No run shall score during a play in which the third out is made by the batter-runner before he touches first base."

c) In the American League, yes. In the National League, no. For interleague games, the two leagues toss a coin to see if such runs will count.

9. When a suspended game is resumed at a later date, is a player who was not a member of the team when the game was originally suspended allowed to substitute for a player who played in the game but is no longer a member of the team?

a) Yes.

b) No.

c) In the National League, yes. In the American League, no.

10. There's a runner on third when the batter hits a pop fly. The fly is caught, and after it's caught the runner on third leaves third base and runs home. After he scores, he fears he left third base *before* the fly was caught, so he tries to run back to third base...and is thrown out in the process. His run is deemed legal, but does it still count?

a) No. "A run legally scored can be nullified by subsequent action of the runner."

b) Yes. "A run legally scored cannot be nullified by subsequent action of the runner."

c) The run counts unless it's a tiebreaker at the bottom of the ninth inning or an extra inning.

11. A pitched ball slams into the catcher's face mask, gets stuck there, and remains out of play. What happens next?

a) Not much. The game just pauses until the ball is extracted or replaced with another ball.

b) Strike! The catcher's mask is by definition in the strike zone, so if a pitch hits his mask it's automatically a strike.

c) All runners advance one base.

12. What happens if a batter refuses to take his position in the batter's box when it's his time at bat?

a) The umpire calls "Strike!"

b) The umpire can call player interference (it interferes with the pace of the game) and eject the batter from the game.

c) The umpire moves to the next player in the batting order and refers the offending batter to the league president for discipline.

For the answers, turn to page 283.

*　　　*　　　*

"I made a game effort to argue, but two things were against me: the umpires and the rules."

—Leo Durocher

Only person honored in both the Baseball and Football Halls of Fame: umpire Cal Hubbard.

ONE FALSE MOVE

*Each of these players had a long, even storied, career.
But sadly, they'll forever be remembered for that
one error, one mistake, or one bad game.*

MICKEY OWEN

Going into the ninth inning of Game 4 of the 1941 World Series, the Brooklyn Dodgers led the New York Yankees 4–3. The Dodgers were poised to win the game and tie the series at 2–2. Then with two outs, the Yankees' right fielder, Tommy Henrich, came to bat. Dodgers pitcher Hugh Casey threw three strikes and struck him out. Game over, right? Wrong. The rules of baseball require the catcher to catch the third strike. If he doesn't, the hitter can attempt to take first base. If he beats the catcher's throw, he's safe. Well, Dodgers catcher Mickey Owen dropped the third strike, Henrich made it to first base, and the game continued. That started a seven-run Yankees rally and the Dodgers lost the game…and the World Series. Owen went on to play another 12 years (including three All-Star seasons), but he's still best remembered for dropping the ball that cost the Dodgers the 1941 World Series.

MITCH WILLIAMS

Going into Game 6 of the 1993 World Series, Toronto was ahead of Philadelphia, three games to two. By the ninth inning, the Phillies led 6–5, poised to force a decisive seventh game. Relief ace Mitch Williams took the mound for Philadelphia in the ninth. He needed two outs to win the game—and to prevent the two men on base from scoring. Toronto's Joe Carter came to bat. With a 2–2 count, Carter hit a home run and the Jays won, 8–6. (It's only the second World Series-ending home run in history.) Phillies fans' hopes of a World Series championship were over, and the blame was placed squarely on Williams (his late-inning pitching also blew a Phillies lead in Game 4). The team traded him a month later, and he was out of the game by 1997. In the few years after the World Series, Williams says he even received death threats.

Actor Charlie Sheen paid $85,000 for the ball Mookie Wilson hit…

DONNIE MOORE

It was Game 5 of the 1986 American League Championship Series. The California Angels led the Boston Red Sox three games to one. If the Angels won this game, they'd go to the World Series for the first time in team history. In the top of the ninth inning, the Angels led 5–4. The Red Sox had a runner on first base and power hitter Dave Henderson was at bat with a 2–2 count. One more strike and Henderson would be out, the Angels would win the game, and they'd go on to the World Series. The Angels sent in Donnie Moore, their top relief pitcher, even though he was battling a foot injury at the time. Moore wound up and threw the pitch straight down the middle...and Henderson smashed it out of the park for a two-run home run, bringing the score to 6–5. The Angels scored a run in the bottom of the ninth, but the Red Sox ultimately won the game in the 11th inning (with Moore on the mound) by a score of 7–6. The Angels proceeded to lose Games 6 and 7—and dashing their hope of a World Series. The devastating loss sent Moore into a deep depression, a problem he'd suffered from off and on for years. In 1989 his depression, along with a drug and alcohol problem, led him to attempt to murder his wife, after which he turned the gun on himself. Moore was 35.

BILL BUCKNER

Buckner is responsible for one of the most famous moments in baseball history, and easily the most famous error. In 1986 the 15-year veteran of the Dodgers and Cubs was now playing first base for the Red Sox in Game 6 of the World Series. If the Red Sox won this game, they'd win their first world championship since 1918, a drought thought to be caused by the "curse" of trading Babe Ruth away in 1920. In the 10th inning, the Mets' Mookie Wilson hit an easy ground ball to Buckner. As thousands of Red Sox fans watched in horror, Buckner reached down with his glove... and the ball *rolled between his legs*, past him, and into the outfield. Wilson reached base, runner Ray Knight scored, and the Mets won the game. And then the Mets won Game 7...and the World Series. Buckner became a pariah in Boston, his impressive lifetime statistics—2,715 hits and a .289 batting average over 21 seasons— forever overshadowed by that one costly error.

RICKEY BEING RICKEY

Rickey Henderson is the all-time stolen-base king (1,406), but he's almost as well known for his odd behavior and non sequiturs.

• In 1996 Henderson boarded the San Diego Padres team bus and was looking for a seat. Teammate Steve Finley said, "You have tenure, sit wherever you want." Henderson replied, "Ten years? Rickey's been playing at least 16, 17 years."

• In 2002 former Houston All-Star Ken Caminiti told a reporter than he thought 50% of major leaguers were taking steroids. Asked if it was an accurate representation, Henderson replied, "Well, Rickey's not one of them, so that's 49 percent right there."

• Henderson hit a home run in 2001 to break Ty Cobb's record for runs scored. After he did the usual slow trot around the bases, Henderson slid into home plate.

• Boston Red Sox officials reported that the morning after the Red Sox swept the St. Louis Cardinals in four games in the 2004 World Series, Henderson called the Red Sox front office trying to get tickets to Game 6.

• Henderson was the 5,000th batter struck out by Nolan Ryan. It doesn't bother him. "It's an honor. I'll have another paragraph in the baseball books. I'm already in the books three or four times."

• In 1997 San Diego Padres general manager Kevin Towers was trying to contact Henderson at a hotel. Since Henderson frequently used fake names to avoid the media and fans, Towers had a hard time finding him. After trying a few names, Towers finally found him registered under the name "Richard Pryor."

• In 1990 an Oakland A's teammate asked Henderson if he owned the then-popular Garth Brooks album *No Fences*. Henderson replied, "Rickey doesn't have albums. Rickey has CDs."

• Henderson played for nine teams in his career and a reporter once asked which one was his favorite. "Oakland," Henderson said. "They have a very colorful uniform."

- In 1989 the Yankees issued Henderson a $1 million bonus check. Three months later, an internal audit showed the check hadn't been cashed. A low-level Yankees employee called Henderson and asked if there was a problem with the check. Henderson replied, "I'm just waiting for the money market rates to go up."

- That wasn't the first time he didn't cash a check. In the early 1980s, the Oakland Athletics issued Henderson a $1 million bonus check. Six months later, an internal audit showed the team's books were off by exactly $1 million. It turned out that Henderson never cashed the check. He was so thrilled by his $1 million payday that he framed the check and hung it up in his house.

- On referring to himself in the third person: "Do I talk to myself? No, I just remind myself of what I'm trying to do. You know, I never answer myself so how can I be talking to myself?"

*　　*　　*

THE HECKLER'S HANDBOOK
Here are11 great heckling lines, compiled by the folks at Baseball Heckle Depot.

1. Hey, Dracula, wake up your bat!

2. You've had fewer hits than Vanilla Ice!

3. I'm gonna break your cane and steal your dog!

4. You couldn't even save anything at Wal-Mart!

5. How can you eat with those hands?

6. I thought only horses slept standing up!

7. You get hits than an Amish Web site!

8. I've seen better arms on a snake!

9. You couldn't throw a party!

10. You couldn't pitch a tent!

11. How's your Japanese?

Can't you see him in the jacket? James Dean lettered in high-school baseball.

ON THE BALL, PART II

*Here's the second installment of our look at how
modern baseballs came to be. (Part I is on page 68.)*

A WHOLE NEW BALL GAME
Major league batting averages remained low from 1914
until 1919. But by 1922, the number of home runs had
quadrupled and total runs scored had increased 40%. The shift
wasn't so much because of any change in the ball; it had more to
do with the way balls were *used* during the game.

As late as the 1920 season, professional teams still used baseballs until they were literally falling apart, no matter how dirty,
soggy, or misshapen they became. But this changed in 1920, when
the Cleveland Indians' Ray Chapman died (see page 63) after
being struck in the head by a pitched ball that was dark and dirty,
and may have been difficult to see in the bad light of that overcast
day. After Chapman's death, major league baseball decreed that
balls had to be replaced as soon as they became scuffed or dirty.

For the first time since the founding of the major leagues, players could count on being pitched a ball in near-perfect condition
every time they came up to bat. And after Babe Ruth emerged as
the greatest home run hitter the game had ever seen, players all
over the league followed his example and started swinging for the
fences instead of just trying to get on base. All of these factors
contributed to causing the number of home runs to soar.

UNRAVELING THE MYSTERY

That's the *official* story, anyway. But did new baseballs and the
Babe really cause the spike in home runs? Batting averages don't
remain constant from season to season. Some years they go up,
some years they go down. On more than one occasion they have
gone up right after baseball has emerged from a confidence-shak-
ing crisis, such as the 1919 Black Sox scandal and the 1994 players' strike, which forced the cancellation of the playoffs and the
World Series. Both of these events caused public interest in the
game to dip…and soon after the crises passed, batting averages
began to climb.

In 1919, for example, Babe Ruth hit 29 home runs. Then in 1920 he hit 54, and in 1921 he hit 59. Was it all those brand-new balls that did it, or was something sneakier at work? Many baseball fans have wondered whether in 1920, and again in 1995, and in other times of trouble, the balls were "juiced" somehow, perhaps by winding the yarn tighter than usual, to generate more interest in the game by increasing the number of home runs.

Both Major League Baseball and the companies that supplied the balls—Spalding until 1977 and Rawlings from 1977 to the present—have always denied that anything was done to alter the performance of the balls, but that hasn't stopped the speculation. Baseball manufacturing is a pretty secretive business, and the secrecy only fuels the rumors. How can we be sure the balls *aren't* being wound tighter when no one is allowed into the factories to see for sure? If league officials could sneak the first cork-centered baseballs into the 1910 World Series (see page 71), then what other tricky things are they capable of?

STRING THEORY

Two more changes occurred after 1911 to bring baseballs into the modern era: In 1931 the cork center was given a rubber coating to make it a little less lively, and in 1974 horsehide covers were abandoned in favor of cowhide. The supply of horsehides had dropped sharply over the years as workhorses were replaced by motorized vehicles and farm equipment. People still ate plenty of beef, so cowhide was an obvious substitute.

But the most significant change of all in recent years may have been unintentional and perhaps even unnoticed, both by Major League Baseball and Rawlings itself. Like the switch from horsehides to cowhides, it is due to changing lifestyles. When the number of home runs rose yet again early in the 2000 season, researchers at the University of Rhode Island decide to "autopsy" baseballs that had been used in major league games in 1963, 1970, 1989, 1995, and 2000 to see if anything about the balls provided any clues. One of the tests they performed was to ana-lyze the yarn by heating samples in a bleach solution. Wool fibers would dissolve completely in such a solution; synthetic fibers would not.

All the yarn in the 1963 ball dissolved, and so did nearly all of

the yarn in the 1970 ball. The yarns from the 1989, 1995, and 2000 baseballs were another story. They contained significant amounts of synthetic fibers, and the 2000 ball had the most of all—nearly 22%, or more than a third more than major league specifications call for. "The fibers were pretty much still intact," Linda Welters, one of the scientists involved in the study, told *Discover* magazine in 2001. "You could knit with it if you wanted to."

CALLED ON THE CARPET
So how did all those synthetic fibers get into yarn that was supposed to be no more than 15% synthetic? At the time, Rawlings got its yarn from a supplier that made it from "waste wool" recycled from old wool carpets. Years ago, 100% wool carpets were common, but in recent years they have all but disappeared in favor of synthetics and wool-synthetic blends. Did the suppliers use fibers they *thought* were 100% wool, but were actually wool blends? This could be the reason that the synthetic content has been rising in the yarn, and it's also possible that the higher content has affected performance. Wool absorbs moisture, especially in hot, humid air, and this moisture makes baseballs less lively. Synthetic fibers don't absorb moisture, so balls with a higher synthetic fiber content are likely to travel farther when hit...making home runs more likely.

So are synthetic-blend baseballs responsible for the rise in home runs in recent years (perhaps along with the use of anabolic steroids)? It's difficult to know for sure, but Rawlings isn't taking any chances—today its yarn is recycled from 100% wool *sweaters*. (People still wear plenty of those.)

* * *

WE'VE COME A LONG WAY, BABY
"In spite of their importance, we fear there are sections of the Official Rules that are somewhat less than exhilarating. So don't bother your pretty wits about them; simply race through the few pages assembled here and we guarantee that you'll end up knowing more about baseball than any man worth looking at!"

—*A Housewife's Guide to Baseball* (1958)

Vassar College fielded the first women's baseball teams, in 1866.

THE BABE SPEAKS

Babe Ruth was the greatest player of his time—not to mention an untamed and frequently uncouth spirit who often said whatever was on his mind.

"I learned early to drink beer, wine, and whiskey. And I think I first chewed tobacco when I was about five."

"I only have one superstition. Whenever I hit a home run, I make certain I touch all four bases."

"If I'd tried for them dinky singles I could've batted around .600."

"Don't ever forget two things I'm going to tell you. One, don't believe everything that's written about you. Two, don't pick up too many checks."

"Gee, it's lonesome in the outfield. It's hard to keep awake with nothing to do."

"I know, but I had a better year than Hoover."
> **—when a reporter pointed out that the salary he was demanding ($80,000) was more than that of President Herbert Hoover ($75,000)**

"I swing big, with everything I've got. I hit big or I miss big. I like to live as big as I can."

"I'll promise to go easier on drinking and to get to bed earlier, but not for you, $50,000 or $250,000 will I give up women. They're too much fun."

"If it wasn't for baseball, I'd be in either the penitentiary or the cemetery."

"Hot as hell, ain't it, Prez?"
> **—to Calvin Coolidge at Yankee Stadium**

"No thank you, ma'am. It makes my piss stink."
> **—after being offered asparagus at a society function**

"All ballplayers should quit when it starts to feel as if all the baselines run uphill."

*   *   *

"Wives of ballplayers, when they teach their children their prayers, should instruct them to say: 'God bless Mommy, God bless Daddy, and God bless Babe Ruth, who has upped Daddy's paycheck by fifteen to forty percent.'"
> **—Waite Hoyt**

The ivy at Chicago's Wrigley Field was the idea of Cubs owner Bill Veeck.

THE BIRTH OF BASEBALL, PART II

On page 39, we told you about the stick-and-ball games that most likely led to baseball. We pick up the story with the first organized teams.

THE CARTWRIGHT MYTH

In the years between 1837 and 1845, while playing games on whatever vacant fields they could find, William Wheaton and his fellow Gothams were busy changing and refining baseball's rules. Their first alteration: eliminating the practice of getting a runner out by throwing the ball directly at him. Instead, at each base they positioned a player whose job was to catch the ball and tag the runner out. In 1845, after Wheaton switched teams to the rival Knickerbockers (based in Lower Manhattan), he took those rules with him—and showed them to a Knickerbockers player named Alexander Cartwright.

Shortly after the Abner Doubleday origin was fully discredited, baseball historians turned their attention to Cartwright—the *new* "Father of Baseball." But they may have been a little too hasty: Recent findings now indicate that Cartwright's role was embellished by him, his son, and subsequent baseball writers. There were many men on the Knickerbockers (including Cartwright) who worked together to improve the game. What is generally agreed upon, however, is that the first prearranged "modern" baseball game took place on June 19, 1846, when Cartwright's Knickerbockers got trounced by the Gothams by a score of 23 to 1.

THE ADAMS REALITY

Much of what *had* been credited to Cartwright actually came from the Knickerbockers' first team president, Daniel Lucius "Doc" Adams. "It is ironic," says baseball historian Lindsey Williams, "that Cartwright, Spalding, and Doubleday are memorialized at Cooperstown while Adams is not—even though he devised all the modern rules of the game." Here's what Adams contributed.

• Arguing that baseball is a "gentlemen's game" (as opposed to

a children's game), Adams moved the bases from 45 feet to 90 feet apart and extended the pitching distance from 37.5 feet to 45 feet.

• Adams also turned baseball into a "fly game" by decreeing that an out would occur when a ball is caught by a fielder *before* it hit the ground, thus negating the "one-bounce" rule.

• Because the baseballs that Adams constructed for the team weighed so little, they couldn't be thrown very far. So he placed an extra player midway between the outfielders and the diamond. His job was to "stop" the "short" throws from the outfielder and relay them to the pitching spot (the mound would come later). Result: the shortstop. As the baseball became heavier, the shortstop moved to its present position between second and third base.

• Another player on that team, an attorney named Louis F. Wadsworth, disagreed with Adams's opinion that a baseball game should be seven innings; he thought it should be nine. Apparently, Wadsworth disagreed a lot, because he was thrown off the team three times. Still, he was able to successfully lobby for nine innings, adding another cornerstone to the foundation of modern baseball.

FINE-TUNING

In all, 20 new "Knickerbocker Rules" were put in place, establishing the "New York Game" as the way baseball would be played (as opposed to the "Massachusetts Game," which still included many features of town ball). Here are three other now-familiar rules that made it onto the Knickerbockers' list.

• Balls hit outside of first or third base are foul.

• On the third strike, the "striker" (batter) may run to first if the catcher does not catch the ball on the fly or on one bounce.

• "All disputes and differences relative to the game are to be decided by the Umpire, from which there is no appeal."

But the modern game wasn't completely set. The Knickerbocker Rules still included some holdovers from town ball, cricket, and other games. For example, foul balls were not yet considered strikes, there were no called strikes, and the game continued until one team scored 21 "aces" (runs), even if the full allotment of innings hadn't been reached. Other changes yet to come: Walks weren't a part of the game until 1863, and the number of balls it took to earn a walk changed from five to seven to nine before being permanently set at four in 1889.

A WALK IN THE PARK

Just as the game was taking shape, so too was the field. As early as the mid-1840s, baseball was already so popular that people began looking for permanent places for their home teams. Because the sport took on its modern form in cities and not in rural areas, people gathered in city parks to play and watch the game—hence the term "park" for a baseball field. The first baseball park was Elysian Fields in Hoboken, New Jersey. Businessmen from New York City took the ferry across the Hudson River to play baseball and cricket there, and it's where the Knickerbockers and Gothams played the first organized game, in 1846.

Elysian Fields was also where Henry Chadwick, a reporter who was supposed to be covering a cricket match for the *New York Times*, happened to see his first baseball game in 1856. "I chanced to go through the Elysian Fields during the progress of a contest between the noted Eagle and Gotham Clubs," he later wrote. "The game was being sharply played on both sides, and I watched it with deeper interest than any previous ball match between clubs that I had seen. It was not long before I was struck with the idea that base ball was just the game for a national sport for Americans." Chadwick spent the rest of his life championing the "National Pastime," a term coined that same year by the *New York Mercury*. (For Chadwick's contributions to the game, see page 11.)

GETTING ORGANIZED

The sudden popularity of the sport led to new problems: The Knickerbocker Rules were embraced by some ball clubs, but not all of them. Result: Opposing teams often found themselves arguing over how and where to play. Some regulation was needed. So in 1857, the Knickerbockers put out an open invitation to "all of the organized base ball clubs" around the region. To their surprise, 14 teams showed up to baseball's first set of meetings. And more teams were forming in cities such as Boston, Chicago, and even San Francisco, where a club was started by Alexander Cartwright. The consensus was that in order for baseball to thrive, it needed a governing body that presided over *every* club.

Those 15 teams formed baseball's first big league: the National Association of Base Ball Players. In 1858 the association decided to hold a tournament between the "best nines" from each region. This first "all-star game" (between the New York and Brooklyn regions) gave onlookers a look at the future of top-tier baseball: diving catches, pinpoint throws, and perfectly turned double plays. Already popular, baseball became *the* fad among the middle class in the United States. By 1860 the association boasted 60 teams.

That all-star series introduced something else to the game. Up until then, players played for free and crowds watched for free. This time, 4,000 fans showed up and paid 50 cents each to see the game. With that, the spirit of amateurism that had guided the association began to weaken. The business of professional baseball was born, and the game would never be the same again.

For Part III of the Birth of Baseball, turn to page 227.

Woodcut that appeared in the magazine Porter's Spirit of the Times, *1856. "The Eagles and Gothams playing their great match at the Elysian Fields on Tuesday, September 8th."*

Only designated hitter to be named World Series MVP: Toronto's Paul Molitor in '93.

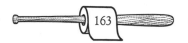

IT'S A WEIRD, WEIRD DIAMOND

Proof that baseball truth really is stranger than baseball fiction.

RUMORS OF MY DEATH

Many in the baseball world were saddened in August 2007 when the news spread that journeyman pitcher Bill Henry had died in Lakeland, Florida, at the age of 83. But no one was more surprised than Henry himself, who was alive and well and living in Texas (and he was 79). Thanks to a bit of digging by baseball historian David Allen Lambert, it was revealed that the Florida man, a retired salesman named Bill C. Henry, had been pretending to be the former pitcher, Bill R. Henry, for more than 20 years. Even his widow and pastor had thought he was the man who played for six teams from 1952 to '69 (and pitched in the '61 World Series for the Reds in a losing effort against the Yankees). The fake Bill Henry even gave a biannual lecture at Florida Southern College called "Baseball, Humor, and Society." When the real Henry heard about the fake Henry's ruse, he said from his home in Texas, "I've been right here this whole time."

IF YOU RETITLE IT, THEY WILL COME

In 1988 test audiences responded favorably to a new baseball fantasy film that was in postproduction. One thing they didn't like was the title, *Shoeless Joe*, the name of the book by W. P. Kinsella on which the film was based. (They said it sounded like the movie was about a bum.) So the producers changed the title to *Field of Dreams*. When Kinsella was asked what he thought about the change, he said he liked it. As a matter of fact, he hadn't even planned on calling the book *Shoeless Joe*—that was the name the publishing company gave it. Kinsella's original title: *Dream Field*.

IF WE TOLD YOU, WE'D HAVE TO KILL YOU

Bryan Hilferty is a volunteer Little League umpire living in Alexandria, Virginia. He's also an Army lieutenant colonel who

---

Don Drysdale led his league in hit batsmen in 5 separate seasons, a major league record.

works at the Pentagon. In 2007 Hilferty, in his capacity as an umpire, requested a copy of the Little League rule book in the hope of improving his umpiring skills. He was denied. Why? Because the Little League executives had decided that they would grant access to the official rules on a "need-to-know" basis only. They'd been sued by parents of kids who were injured in non-Little League games, and now kept the rules under wraps "so as not to invite any unnecessary litigation." Hilferty was still perplexed. "I have a secret clearance in the E-ring of the Pentagon," he said, "but I don't have clearance for the Little League rules?"

A MULTILAYERED STORY

It all started innocently enough. Sometime in the 1960s, a high-school student named Mike Carmichael was playing baseball for the Knox County Children's Home in Indiana. During a game, a baseball landed in a bucket of paint. After the ball dried, he was strangely intrigued by it. He decided to keep on painting it. Before long, the ball had grown to the size of a football. At that point he donated the paint ball to the local children's museum…but soon decided he wanted it back. The museum liked it so much that they refused to part with it. And that ended Carmichael's dream of owning the world's largest ball of paint. Or did it?

One day in 1977 Carmichael, married and now living in Alexandria, Indiana, decided to recapture his former glory. He hung a baseball from the ceiling of his shed and threw a layer of paint on it. Then he put on another layer…and another…and another. (Each layer was a different color.) By 2004 Carmichael's baseball was buried under an estimated 18,000 layers of paint—it was bigger than a beachball and weighed more than 1,300 pounds. "This took forever and it's a lot of work and a lot more money than people realize," he said. "I never thought it would come to this. It was just a little hobby."

Not so little any more—it's been honored by *Guinness World Records* as the largest ball of paint on Earth. Want to see it for yourself? It's a popular roadside attraction in Alexandria. Bonus: You can add a layer of paint to the still-growing ball yourself. (A few years ago, a man proposed to his wife by painting the proposal on the ball. She said yes.)

MORE NO-HIT WONDERS

On page 53 we gave you a brief history of no-hitters and perfect games, as well as some great no-hit stories. Well, we've got a lot more.

PERFECT RELIEF

In the history of Major League Baseball, there have been nine combined no-hitters (when a starting pitcher and one or more relief pitchers combine to no-hit the other team). But perhaps the strangest one happened on June 23, 1917. The Red Sox's ace pitcher, Babe Ruth, started the game against the Washington Senators. Ruth walked the first batter on four pitches, but thought that at least two of them were strikes. After arguing with umpire Brick Owens, Ruth was ejected. He charged the ump and took a swing at him, prompting police to escort Ruth off the field. Red Sox pitcher Ernie Shore hurriedly warmed up and went in to take over. Just after Shore took the mound, the runner tried to steal second, but was thrown out. Shore then went on to retire the next 26 Senators in order. Originally classified as a perfect game (all 27 outs were recorded while Shore was on the mound, and he didn't allow a runner to reach first), it's been subsequently reclassified as a combined no-hitter.

BUMPUS AND BOBO

• On October 15, 1892, the last day of the season, the Reds' Bumpus Jones made his major league debut. On the way to his 7–1 victory over the Pirates, he gave up four walks and an unearned run (thanks to an error), but didn't allow a hit. It was the highlight of Jones's brief career, which ended with a 2–4 record and 7.99 ERA. More than a century later, though, Jones is still the only pitcher in history to toss a no-hitter in his first major league game.

• After a few relief appearances for the St. Louis Browns in 1953, Bobo Holloman was awarded his first start on May 6 against the Philadelphia A's. Holloman didn't pitch very well; the A's made good contact all afternoon…but every ball went to the Browns defenders. Holloman also gave up five walks, three of them in the ninth inning, but not a single hit—making him the only pitcher

in the 20th century to throw a no-hitter in his first start after having begun his career as a reliever. Just like Jones's, Holloman's achievement came in an otherwise brief and unspectacular career. Holloman pitched in just 22 major league games, and that no-hitter was one of only three wins as a starter.

DIDN'T HAVE A LEG TO STAND ON

On July 15, 1973, in the game that would become Nolan Ryan's second of seven no-hitters, Tigers first baseman Norm Cash was due to bat with two outs in the ninth. After having struck out three times against Ryan, who was pitching for the Angels, "Stormin' Norman" left his bat in the dugout and walked up to the plate with a table leg. "You can't use that up here!" yelled umpire Ron Luciano. "Why not?" replied Cash, "I won't hit him anyway." Luciano held firm, and Cash went back to the dugout and got his bat. Good news: He didn't strike out. Bad news: He popped out to end the game. Ryan set a record that day for the most strikeouts in a no-hitter, with 17.

NO FANS AT THE GAME

Who has the least number of strikeouts in a no-hitter? The Cubs' Ken Holtzman—on August 19, 1969, he no-hit the Braves…without striking out a single batter.

I'M A LOSER, BABY

• On April 23, 1964, Ken Johnson of the Houston Colt .45s was two outs away from a no-hitter against the Reds when Pete Rose laid down a bunt in the top of the ninth. Johnson charged it but threw wildly to first, allowing Rose to reach safely. The official scorer ruled it an error, keeping the no-hitter intact. Next up, Chico Ruiz hit the ball right back to the mound; it ricocheted off Johnson's shin and bounced to the third baseman, who threw Ruiz out at first. On the play, however, Rose lived up to his nickname, "Charlie Hustle," and ran all the way to third base. With two outs, Johnson got Vada Pinson to hit a groundball to Houston's veteran second baseman, Nellie Fox, but he bobbled it, allowing Rose to cross the plate, making the score 1–0. Visibly upset, Johnson retired the next batter, keeping his no-hit bid alive. Unfortunately, the Colt .45's couldn't score in the bottom

of the ninth, making Johnson the first player to pitch a no-hitter... and *lose*.

• In 1990 the Yankee's Andy Hawkins no-hit the White Sox... but his team committed three errors in the eighth inning and allowed four unearned runs, making Hawkins the losing pitcher in his only no-hitter. "The guys clapped for him when he came in," Hawkins's teammate Dave Righetti said afterward, "but I don't think anybody really knows how to act."

TIT FOR TAT

In two bizarre days at San Francisco's Candlestick Park in September 1968, the Giants' Gaylord Perry no-hit St. Louis...and, just 15 hours later, the Cards' Ray Washburn avenged his team and no-hit the Giants. (Washburn's final two outs: future Hall of Famers Willie Mays and Willie McCovey.) It's the only time in history when two teams have no-hit each other on consecutive days.

THIS CHANGES NOTHING

Has there ever been a big-league game in which every batter on a team finished with the exact same average he had when he started? Yes, once. On Opening Day in 1940, Bob Feller of the Indians no-hit the White Sox. Chicago's batting average before the game: .000. After the game: .000. Feller would go on to pitch two more no-hitters in his Hall of Fame career.

OVERFLOWING WITH PERFECTION

July 18, 1999, was "Yogi Berra Day" at Yankee Stadium. In attendance was the original battery of the Yankees' 1956 World Series perfect game: pitcher Don Larsen and catcher Yogi Berra. Larsen threw out the ceremonial first pitch to Berra...and then the real game started, when Yankees pitcher David Cone stepped up to the mound and began retiring one Montreal Expo after another. Larsen, 69, had planned to watch only a few innings in the 95-degree heat before going back to his hotel room, but he couldn't bring himself to leave. Cone, meanwhile, didn't allow so much as a 3-ball count, let alone a man on base. Larsen stayed in his seat and watched Cone pitch a perfect game, just the third in Yankees history (Larsen's was the first). After the game, Larsen said, "David will think about this day every day of his life."

Pitcher Charlie Hough once broke a finger shaking hands with a friend.

UNCLE JOHN'S
STALL OF FAME

If you're a fan of the regular Bathroom Reader *series, you've seen our "Stall of Fame" articles, in which we salute the creative ways that people get involved with bathrooms, toilets, toilet paper, etc. Here is an all-baseball version.*

Honoree: The Hudson Valley (New York) Renegades, Class A club of the Tampa Bay Devil Rays
Notable Achievement: Creating bathroom-related team memorabilia
True Story: The Renegades are one of the many minor league teams owned by Mike Veeck, son of legendary owner Bill Veeck, who was known for putting on bizarre promotions (see page 17). In the Renegades' hometown of Fishkill, New York, the younger Veeck held one promotion in 2006 giving away toilet plungers bearing the Renegades logo, and one in 2007 giving away stadium seat cushions shaped like toilet seats. (Too bad Veeck doesn't own a team in Flushing, New York—who knows what that might inspire?)

Honoree: Glenn Davis, a slugger who hit 190 home runs for the Astros and the Orioles from 1984 to '93
Notable Achievement: Using the head to get his head into the game
True Story: While many players have had some odd pregame rituals, Davis's lands him in the Stall of Fame because he spent about 20 minutes before every game meditating alone in the clubhouse bathroom.

Honoree: The Frisco RoughRiders, the Class AA affiliate of the Texas Rangers
Notable Achievement: Turning the stadium restrooms into pleasing places to pass the time
True Story: At Dr Pepper Park in Frisco, Texas, team owners strive to make going out to the ballpark a pleasant experience for the whole family. "Families are a huge part of the RoughRiders

experience," boasts the team's official Web site. "And everybody knows that behind a good family is a good woman. So the RoughRiders became the first team in all of professional sports to hire an interior decorator to design nine unique women's restrooms at Dr Pepper Ballpark. For all you women out there...enjoy. For all you men out there...tough luck."

The RoughRiders aren't the only minor league club to spruce up their loos. At San Jose Municipal Stadium, the San Jose Giants have adorned both the men's and women's restrooms with painted murals. (The women's bathroom features scenes from the 1992 film *A League of Their Own.*) And on the walls of the ladies' rooms at the Brockton Rox ballpark in Massachusetts, soothing scenes of animals provide relief (so to speak) from all the action outside.

Honoree: The Milwaukee Brewers
Notable Achievement: Getting behind the health of their fans
True Story: Before the April 27, 2007, game at Miller Park in Milwaukee, male Brewers fans were invited to take "free, private, confidential rectal screenings in a mobile clinic vehicle next to the T.G.I. Friday's in the northeast corner of the ballpark." And what did the men get in return for bending over? Two free tickets to a future Brewers home game. To explain the promotion, Dr. William See of the Medical College of Wisconsin offered reporters this grim description: "If you picture six guys sitting at a Brewers game at Miller Park, one of them will be diagnosed with prostate cancer during his lifetime."

Honoree: Matt Elliott, reliever for the Mobile (Alabama) BayBears, the Class AA affiliate of the Arizona Diamondbacks
Notable Achievement: Losing a game because of a bathroom break
True Story: A reluctant entrant into the Stall of Fame, Elliot took the mound in the eighth inning of a June 2007 away game against the Devil Rays' Class AA club, the Montgomery Biscuits, with his team leading 4–3. Elliot retired the side, but not before giving up the game-tying run. Fuming mad, he stormed into the clubhouse bathroom and slammed the door shut. Only problem: He slammed it so hard that it broke and locked him inside. After the BayBears batters went down 1-2-3 in the top of the ninth, Elliot was supposed to go back to the mound...but he couldn't get

out of the bathroom. Elliot's teammates tried to pry open the door. Then his coaches tried. Then the stadium personnel gave it a shot. But the door stayed stuck. Meanwhile, the rest of the Bay-Bears' defensive team was waiting on the field, along with the Biscuits' leadoff batter. After nearly 10 minutes, the umpire told the BayBears to get a pitcher on the mound or forfeit the game. Another reliever hastily warmed up, went in, and promptly gave up a home run in the 10th, losing the game...all while Elliot had to listen to the play-by-play through the broken bathroom door. Forty-five minutes later, with the fire department en route, a stadium worker was able to pry the door open. Asked about his ordeal the next day, Elliot said that it was "a little hot in there."

Honoree: C. J. Wilson, relief pitcher for the Texas Rangers

Notable Achievement: Exposing the steamy underworld of big-league bullpen bathrooms

True Story: Wilson has spent a lot of time in American League ballparks. In 2007 he chronicled his day-to-day experiences in his blog, calling most bullpen bathrooms "terrifying." "Kansas City has a bathroom with no lock, no lights, and a two-foot-tall roll of TP," he says. "Anaheim has a creepy no-flush urinal. Oakland doesn't even have one, so you have to go to the dugout. And in Seattle your teammates barricade you in and slam fastballs (thrown baseball + metal door = explosion noise) into the door to kill your hearing. Toronto is actually decent, although you have to walk about 100 yards on slippery concrete to get there. Boston? Ha."

*   *   *

WELCOME TO THE BIGS

In his major league debut in 2002, Padres reliever J.J. Trujillo was called to the mound in the 10th inning of a tied game to face Orioles slugger Tony Batista. Trujillo, who had been called up from Double-A earlier that day, hung a slider...and Batista whacked it over the fence to win the game, marking the first and only time that a big-league pitcher ever gave up a game-ending home run to the very first hitter he faced. Trujillo's comment to the throng of reporters that awaited him after the game: "Nice debut, huh?"

Smallest American city with a major league team: Pittsburgh (population: 300,000).

UNIFORMS THROUGH THE AGES, PART II

The early 20th century was an era of change in baseball, not just for the game, but also for the uniforms, when many things we take for granted were tried for the very first time. (Part I of our timeline starts on page 25.)

1900–1904

• At the turn of the century, it was often the sportswriters, not the teams themselves, who invented the teams' nicknames. (They did it to make their stories more colorful.) Teams were often known by more than one nickname, and the names changed frequently. Because of this, most teams resisted displaying their nicknames on their uniforms. Not so with the Detroit Tigers: In 1901, their very first season in the major leagues, they wore baseball caps with tiger logos on them. It was the first time in major league history that a team wore a logo of their nickname anywhere on their uniforms.

• The practice of wearing white uniforms at home, and gray or darker uniforms for away games, was well established by the turn of the century. Some teams had road uniforms that were "negatives" of their home uniforms: Cleveland's 1902 home uniform, for example, was white with dark blue trim; their road uniform was dark blue with white trim.

• In 1903 the Detroit Tigers removed the word DETROIT from the front of their jerseys and replaced it with a simple, Roman-style "D" over the left breast pocket. In 1905, they changed the **D** on the road uniform to an Old English 𝕯. That 𝕯 is the oldest major league baseball logo still used on jerseys today. (The stylized "A" of the Oakland Athletics dates back to 1901, but it hasn't been used on jerseys since 1984—it's used only on the hat.)

1905

• In 1904 the Washington Senators finished with a 38-113 record, one of the worst ever. Looking for a fresh start for the 1905 season, the team renamed itself the Nationals. To avoid being associated with the previous year's team, they became the first major leaguers to display their team nickname—NATIONALS—on their jerseys.

Baseball card sets were made in Japan, Cuba, and Canada as early as 1912.

1906

• After their 1905 World Series victory, the 1906 New York Giants added the words "WORLD'S CHAMPIONS" to the front of their jerseys. They didn't make it to the World Series that year, and neither did the 1921 Cleveland Indians or the 1927 St. Louis Cardinals after they remade their jerseys following their World Series wins. It must be embarrassing for a team with the words WORLD'S CHAMPIONS emblazoned across their chest to end up losers, because in the more than 80 years since the last team did it, no other team has repeated the stunt.

• Another innovation the Giants introduced in 1906 did eventually catch on—they removed the folding collars from their jerseys and replaced them with…nothing. This first collarless jersey was ahead of its time; the Giants returned to collared jerseys in 1908.

1907

• In 1907 the Reading Red Roses, a minor league team in Pennsylvania, became the first team to put numbers on their jerseys. They wore 1 through 15, but not 13 (bad luck). The numbering concept didn't spread beyond Reading…yet.

• After buying the Boston Nationals, in 1907 new owner John Dovey added pinstripes to their road uniforms. By 1915 eleven of sixteen American and National League teams had pinstripes on at least one of their uniforms. Major league baseball hasn't had a pinstripe-free season since.

• Dovey never regreted adding pinstripes, but he did live to regret a second change he made in 1907: removing every trace of the color red from the team's uniforms, including their red stockings, even though the team had been nicknamed the Red Stockings when it was first organized in the 1870s.

For the previous few seasons, another Boston team—the upstart Americans—had been copying the Nationals' uniforms detail for detail…only in blue instead of red. (In black and white photographs of the era, the teams are virtually indistinguishable.) When Dovey abandoned red, the Americans pounced, remaking their uniforms *entirely* in red. They even adopted a red stocking logo for their jerseys, with BOSTON spelled out in white letters inside the stocking—the first jersey to feature a pictorial representation of a team's nickname. From then on, the Americans were

---

Only two Jewish players are in the Hall of Fame: Hank Greenberg and Sandy Koufax.

known as the Boston Red Sox. Dovey spent the next several years trying to reclaim red for his Nationals but didn't succeed. He sold the team in 1910, and in 1912 it was renamed the Boston Braves.

• In 1909, after years of wearing either a plain C or a C encircling a bat-wielding bear cub, the Chicago Cubs introduced their famous logo—a large C with the letters UBS inside of it—for the first time.

1910s

• In 1912 the New York Yankees introduced pinstripes to their home uniforms…only to dump them the following year. They put them back on in 1915, and they've been wearing them ever since. (The tale that the pinstripes were added to make Babe Ruth look slimmer is false; he didn't join the team until 1920.)

• In this decade, baseball teams began wearing pants with "belt tunnels"—wide belt loops that cover up large sections of the players' belts. This was reportedly done to make it more difficult for infielders to grab runners by the belt to prevent them from advancing to the next base.

• In 1916 the New York Giants experimented with purple *plaid* uniforms. The uniforms were abandoned at season's end. No big-league team has worn plaid since.

• Player numbers made their first major-league appearance in 1916, on the left sleeves of Cleveland Indians jerseys. But the team wore them for only a few weeks. In 1917 the Indians tried again (this time with the numbers on the right sleeves), but again for only a few weeks. Afterward they returned to numberless jerseys.

• In 1918 the St. Louis Cardinals became the first major-league team to use script lettering to spell out their team name across the front of their jerseys instead of the usual block letters. They abandoned the style after just two years.

• When New York Giants owner John McGraw disparaged the Philadelphia Athletics as "white elephants" in 1902, A's owner Connie Mack embraced the image. When the two teams met in the 1905 World Series, Mack presented McGraw with a white elephant toy, and soon after that the A's began wearing elephants on their team sweaters. 1918 was the first year than an elephant appeared on the jersey, on the left shoulder. Elephant logos have been a regular feature on A's uniforms ever since.

Part III of the baseball uniform story is on page 239.

Leroy Paige got his nickname, Satchel, from his childhood job of carrying bags at a railroad station.

BASEBALL IN REEL LIFE

Each of these are fine historical baseball films, but sometimes when Hollywood takes on history, history strikes out.

Film: *Eight Men Out* (1988)
In Reel Life: Dickie Kerr (played by Jace Alexander) tells former pitcher Kid Gleason (John Mahoney) about the time he saw him pitch a no-hitter against Cy Young.
In *Real* Life: Gleason never threw a no-hitter against Young...or anyone else.

Film: *The Pride of the Yankees* (1942)
In Reel Life: Lou Gehrig (Gary Cooper) concludes his speech at Yankee Stadium by saying, "Today, I consider myself the luckiest man on the face of the Earth."
In *Real* Life: Gehrig did say it, but at the beginning of his speech.

Film: *61** (2001)
In Reel Life: President Kennedy interrupts a press conference to announce that Roger Maris had hit his 48th and 49th home runs.
In *Real* Life: Kennedy never mentioned Roger Maris, Mickey Mantle, or their home-run chase in any of his press conferences.

Film: *A League of Their Own* (1992)
In Reel Life: Although this isn't supposed to be a straight history (Tom Hanks's character, Jimmy Dugan, is loosely based on Jimmie Foxx), the filmmakers did strive for accuracy on the ending title card, which states that the players were "the first women ever to be inducted into the Baseball Hall of Fame."
In *Real* Life: They weren't *inducted* into the Hall of Fame—they were only honored with an exhibit.

Film: *The Rookie* (2002)
In Reel Life: Jimmy Morris (Dennis Quaid) becomes a rookie with the Tampa Bay Devil Rays in 1999 at age 35. In Morris's debut, Alex Rodriguez is a member of the opposing Texas Rangers.
In *Real* Life: In 1999 A-Rod played for the Seattle Mariners.

MEMORIES

*Scattered pictures / Of the smiles we left behind /
Smiles we gave to one another / For the way we were*

Mickey Mantle *talks about a poignant moment after a game in which he struck out three times in a row:*

"When I got back to the clubhouse, I just sat down on my stool and held my head in my hands, like I was going to start crying. I heard somebody come up to me, and it was little Timmy Berra, Yogi's boy, standing there next to me. He tapped me on the knee, nice and soft, and I figured he was going to say something nice to me—you know, like, 'You keep hanging in there,' or something like that. But all he did was look at me, and then he said in his little kid's voice, 'You stink!'"

Floyd Rayford *played third base and catcher for the Orioles in the 1980s. He shared this story in the book* Baseball Confidential.

"I remember a game where I was catching Sammy Stewart and we had a 3–0 count on Dave Kingman with the bases loaded. I called for a fastball and Sammy shook it off. I put down another fastball and Sammy shook it off again. So I walked out to the mound and said, 'Sammy, what are we going to do?' He said, 'Let's go with the hard slider.' On my way back to the plate, I felt it was the wrong pitch, so I called for the fastball but he shook me off again. Finally, I put down the slider. Sammy threw it and Kingman hit it for a grand slam. I went back to the mound and before I could say anything Sammy said, 'You should have called for the fastball.'"

First baseman **Mickey Vernon** *spent more than 20 years in the big leagues, from 1939 to 1960. He won two batting titles with the Washington Senators, but his greatest thrill came on the first day of the 1954 season.*

"It was Opening Day at D.C.'s Griffith Stadium, and Allie Reynolds was pitching for the Yankees in the 10th inning. After he walked our leadoff man, Eddie Yost, he got the next batter out, and then I hit a home run to win the game. President Eisenhower sent a couple of Secret Servicemen out onto the field to grab me

---

Baseball terminology: A *sinker* is a fastball that breaks downward as it reaches the plate.

and take me to his box. He wanted to congratulate me. He said I was his favorite player. Now I played in a lot of games at Griffith Stadium, but I'll always remember that Opening Day game in '54, and being congratulated by Eisenhower."

*Third baseman **Jim Davenport**, who played his entire 12-year career for the San Francisco Giants, remembers his first and only All-Star Game.*

"The greatest thing to happen to me was making the 1962 All-Star squad. I remember taking a picture sitting between Stan Musial and Hank Aaron. It kind of made chills go up and down my arm—being a country boy out of Alabama sitting with these players. I was selected to play in the game by Reds manager Fred Hutchinson. Ken Boyer was first pick, I was second, and Eddie Mathews was the third. I remember I faced Dick Donovan of the Indians and hit the ball to left for a single. The game was a great experience. I got my chance to play in one with guys like Mays, Aaron, Musial, and Mantle, and I did okay."

*Brothers (and pitchers) Dizzy and Paul Dean had better arms than they had wits. St. Louis Cardinals catcher **Mike Ryba** talks about Paul's first start.*

"We used basically simple signs, one finger for the fastball, two fingers for the curve, and three fingers for the change of pace. The first inning was kind of long, but we got out of it alright. Paul didn't have too much. In the middle of the second, he called me out to the mound. 'What's the matter, Paul?' 'Mike,' he said, 'call for that two-finger ball more. I can get more on it.' Then I realized that Paul had been gripping the ball with the number of fingers I put down. On the one-finger grip, which called for a fastball, he had been throwing a one-finger pitch."

Willie Mays *says goodbye.*

"I remember the last season I played. I went home after a ballgame one day, lay down on my bed, and tears came to my eyes. How can you explain that? It's like crying for your mother after she's gone. You cry because you love her. I cried, I guess, because I love baseball and I knew I had to leave it."

Only player to hit a grand slam in both games of a doubleheader: Robin Ventura.

UNCLE JOHN'S PAGE OF BASEBALL LISTS

More random facts to chew on.

8 Rhyming Players
1. Ed Head
2. Mark Clark
3. Lu Blue
4. Heine Meine
5. Don Hahn
6. Greg Legg
7. Turk Burke
8. Hillbilly Bildilli

Ted Williams's Picks for All-Time Top 5 Hitters
1. Babe Ruth
2. Lou Gehrig
3. Jimmie Foxx
4. Rogers Hornsby
5. Joe DiMaggio

10 Nations and When They Formed Their First League
1. Netherlands, 1922
2. Mexico, 1925
3. Australia, 1934
4. Japan, 1936
5. Italy, 1948
6. Venezuela, 1945
7. Dominican Republic, 1951
8. Korea, 1982
9. Taiwan, 1990
10. Israel, 2007

5 Players Who Go By Their Middle Names
1. Lynn Nolan Ryan
2. Henry Louis Gehrig
3. George Thomas Seaver
4. Anthony Nomar Garciaparra
5. George Kenneth Griffey Jr.

4 Singers and Their Favorite Teams
1. Madonna: Tigers
2. Emmylou Harris: Braves
3. Tori Amos: Orioles
4. Britney Spears: Yankees

Only 3 Players to Hit 2 Home Runs in Their First Game
1. Bob Nieman, St. Louis Browns, 1951
2. Bert Campaneris, A's, 1964
3. Mark Quinn, Royals, 1999

7 MVPs Who Didn't Make the All-Star Team That Year
1. Don Newcombe, 1956
2. Dave Parker, 1978
3. Willie Stargell, 1979
4. Kirk Gibson, 1988
5. Robin Yount, 1989
6. Juan Gonzalez, 1996
7. Chipper Jones, 1999

4 Great Hitters' Pinch-Hitting Avg.
1. Ty Cobb, .217
2. Pete Rose, .250
3. Babe Ruth, .194
4. Jackie Robinson, .175

Tug McGraw's 4 Fastballs
1. Titanic (It sank.)
2. Bo Derek (A nice little tail)
3. Cutty Sark (It sailed.)
4. Peggy Lee (Is that all there is?)

Sen. Pete Domenici (R-NM) left the Dodgers farm system to become a high-school math teacher.

MASCOT CHRONICLES

Today almost every team has a furry foam-rubber creature who dances on the sidelines between innings or wanders through the stands during the game. Fun or annoying, they've become part of the ballpark experience.

MASCOT: Mr. Met

DESCRIPTION: A grinning 6'10" humanoid with huge feet and a head that's unmistakably a baseball, wearing a blue Mets cap and the number 00 on his uniform.

HISTORY: Mr. Met was among the first big league mascots. Introduced as an illustration in the Mets' 1963 yearbook, he morphed into live costumed form when the Mets moved to Shea Stadium in 1964. In the 1960s, team execs occasionally paired him with another baseball-headed humanoid mascot called "Lady Met" (or "Mrs. Met"), who wore an orange skirt to match her orange hair (Mr. and Mrs. Met also have three little "Met children"). Mr. Met also has a side job delivering safety messages on subways and buses for New York's Metropolitan Transit Authority.

MASCOT: The Swinging Friar and the San Diego Chicken

DESCRIPTION: The Friar is a bald monk, dressed in sandals and a dark robe with a rope belt; the Chicken is…the Chicken.

HISTORY: Surprise! The San Diego Chicken is *not* the official mascot of the Padres; the Swinging Friar is. He was chosen by fans in a contest in 1961. The Chicken was "born" in 1974 when a college student named Ted Giannoulas landed a $2/hour job from a radio station to wear the suit while giving out Easter eggs at the San Diego Zoo. He did so well that the station hired him to perform at Padres games. Giannoulas has worn the suit ever since…except when the station fired him in 1979, much to the dismay of Padres fans. So Giannoulas created a similar suit and was "reborn" at a Pads home game. Since then, the Chicken has made thousands of appearances at concerts, parades, and conventions…and has even seen his share of controversy: He was sued by producers of *Barney & Friends* after beating up a Barney look-alike (the Chicken won). Still, the *Sporting News* named him one of the "top 100 most powerful people in sports of the 20th century."

MASCOT: The Phillie Phanatic

DESCRIPTION: A furry, pear-shaped, neon-green creature with a tongue that juts out of a cylindrical bill.

HISTORY: The Phanatic debuted on April 25, 1978. During a game, he may be found roaming the stands, dumping popcorn on unsuspecting fans, plopping himself onto a fan's lap to watch the game, or shooting mustard-and-relish-laden hot dogs into the crowd with a four-foot-long Hot Dog Launcher. If you think being harassed by a 6'6", 300 lb. smelly green wacko is phun, you're a true phan. The Phanatic's costume was added to the National Baseball Hall of Phame's collection on July 27, 2002.

MASCOT: Chief Noc-A-Homa

DESCRIPTION: An "Indian chief" who emerged from a tepee to do a dance whenever the Braves hit a home run.

HISTORY: The chief first appeared with the Milwaukee Braves in the 1960s. When the team moved to Atlanta, he moved into a "tepee" in the bleachers at Fulton County Stadium. Strangely, every time the tepee was removed (when the Falcons needed the bleacher space), the Braves started losing. A superstition soon arose: no tepee, no wins. In 1982, with the Braves in first place, owner Ted Turner removed the tepee to add more seats...and the Braves lost 19 of their next 21 games. Lo and behold, when Turner put the tepee back, the Braves regained first place and won the division. In 1986, after years of complaints that Chief Noc-A-Homa was offensive (as well as a contractual dispute between the Braves and Levi Walker, who'd worn the suit for 17 years), he was replaced by Homer the Brave, a humanoid with a baseball head.

MASCOT: Wally the Green Monster

DESCRIPTION: A fuzzy green monster, named for the famous 37' left-field wall at Fenway Park.

HISTORY: The shy Wally, according to Red Sox lore, lived *inside* the Green Monster for 50 years before finally emerging in 1997. But the mascot's introduction did *not* delight fans: they practically booed him off the field. It took nearly 10 more years and the help of broadcaster Jerry Remy's amusing—and invented—Wally stories to make him the popular mascot he is today.

Former pitcher Turk Wendell brushed his teeth and chewed licorice between every inning.

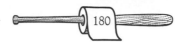

MASCOT MISADVENTURES

• The Pirates suffered an embarrassing blow in 1985 when Kevin Koch, the man who'd performed as the Pittsburgh Parrot for six years, was caught in a drug bust in 1985 and accused of connecting players with a cocaine dealer.

• In July 2000, Florida's Billy the Marlin accidentally hit a fan in the eye with a wadded-up T-shirt launched from a pressurized gun, knocking the man unconscious.

• "I hate the Phillie Phanatic," said Dodgers manager Tommy Lasorda. "In fact, I am not very happy about mascots in general." Why? In 1988 the Phanatic drove a four-wheeler over a dummy wearing a Lasorda jersey at Phillies home game. Lasorda was incensed: "I went right up to it and body slammed it to the turf."

• The rest of the National League mascots:

Colorado Rockies	Houston Astros	St. Louis
Dinger	Junction Jack	Cardinals
San Francisco	**Cincinnati Reds**	Fredbird and Redbird
Giants	Mr. Red and	
Lou Seal	Gapper	**Washington**
Milwaukee	**Arizona**	**Nationals**
Brewers	**Diamondbacks**	Screech the
Bernie Brewer	D. Baxter the	Bald Eagle
	Bobcat	

• The rest of the American League mascots:

Texas Rangers	Chicago White	Kansas City
Rangers Captain	Sox	Royals
Detroit Tigers	Southpaw	Sluggerrrr
Paws	**Baltimore Orioles**	**Los Angeles**
Seattle Mariners	The Oriole Bird	**Angels**
The Mariner	**Minnesota Twins**	Rally Monkey
Moose	TC	**Toronto Blue Jays**
Oakland Athletics	**Cleveland Indians**	Ace
Stomper	Slider	

• Only three teams don't have mascots: the New York Yankees, the Los Angeles Dodgers, and the Chicago Cubs.

Yankee Stadium was the first three-tiered sports facility in the United States.

THE TOOLS OF IGNORANCE

*The job of catcher is so risky that the catcher's mask, chest protector,
and shin guards are sometimes referred to as the "tools of ignorance,"
meaning that only a fool would agree to play the position. Imagine
what it was like when catchers wore no protective gear at all.*

THANKS...BUT NO THANKS

In 1876 the Harvard University baseball team began looking around for someone who could replace catcher Howard
Thatcher, who was leaving the team at the end of the season. An
obvious choice for the position was outfielder James Alexander
Tyng—he was one of the school's best all-around athletes. Tyng
had already played catcher in a couple of games...but his few
experiences behind home plate had convinced him that he never,
ever wanted to become a full-time catcher. He had two good reasons for refusing: He did not want to be maimed for life, and he
did not want to die.

CHOCK-FULL O' NUTS

In the mid-1870s the only "protective equipment" that some
catchers used was a hard rubber mouth protector, similar to the little mouthpieces that prizefighters wear today. Catchers wore nothing else to protect their face, chest, or hands—even catcher's mitts
were still more than a decade away.

Playing the position was so dangerous in those days that the
catchers stood a good 10–15 feet behind the hitter and caught
pitches on the bounce. Catching them on the fly wasn't required
by the rules of the day; strikes and foul tips still counted as long
as they were caught on one bounce. But even when catchers
positioned themselves that far back, they were still at risk of
injury from wayward pitches and foul tips that slammed into
their unprotected faces at 90 mph. Even the balls that *were*
caught could cause terrible injuries: Shaking hands with a veteran catcher, an old saying went, was like shaking hands with a
bag of peanuts.

He played more games with the A's, but Reggie Jackson wore a Yankees cap in his Hall of Fame picture.

DEAD MAN'S CURVE

As dangerous as the catcher's position was to begin with, it got worse with the invention of the curveball. A Yale pitcher named Charles Avery is believed to have been the first college player to master it; he started throwing curveballs in 1875. Now, after a summer of practice, Harvard's pitcher Harold Ernst had figured out how to throw it, too. What was good for the team was bad for the catcher: Because curveballs moved unpredictably, they were as difficult to catch as they were to hit.

In the few games in which Tyng had played catcher, he'd already been smashed in the face a couple of times. He knew that if he became the regular catcher it was probably just a matter of time before he was permanently disfigured or even killed. Fear had already begun to creep into his game, and that had team manager Fred Thayer concerned. "He'd become timid," Thayer remembered years later. "He was, by all odds, the most available man as catcher for the season of '77, and it was up to me to find some way to bring back his confidence."

SAVING FACE

The obvious solution was to improvise some kind of face protection that did not obstruct the catcher's vision. Thayer knew that fencers wore masks covered with sturdy metal mesh, but the mesh wasn't strong enough to protect against a baseball. Even so, they were a good place to start, so Thayer took a fencing mask to a local tinsmith and asked him to make a similar mask that could stand up to a baseball. The tinsmith came up with something resembling a birdcage that could be strapped to the face, with leather padding on the forehead and chin to help absorb the shock of a ball hitting the mask. After a few practices and a few adjustments to the mask, on April 12, 1877, Tyng wore it in a baseball game against a local semipro team called the Live Oaks. Harvard won the game 11–3, and Tyng committed only two errors, a very low number by the standards of the day.

Tyng made quite an impression that day, and while many sportswriters lauded the new device as an ideal solution to an obvious problem, many baseball purists derided it as a "rat trap," and an unnecessary one at that. "There is a good deal of beastly humbug in contrivances to protect men from things that don't

---

The first batting averages recorded were those of Boston and Cleveland, in 1871.

happen," one detractor complained, "There is about as much sense as putting a lightning rod on a catcher as a mask."

Thayer ignored the critics. He patented his catcher's mask in 1878, and that year Spalding began selling it in its mail order sporting goods catalog. Jim "Deacon" White of the Chicago White Stockings was the first professional player to wear a catcher's mask—after reading an article about Tyng, he had a metal-worker make him a steel-wire mask of his own. But it was still a very strange and unfamiliar device, and many players were reluctant to wear one. Spalding's model sold poorly for the first year or two...until the rules of baseball were changed to require that a two-strike foul tip had to be caught on the fly to count as the third strike. Catchers were going to have to move a lot closer to the hitter to catch those foul tips...and suddenly, wearing a mask didn't seem like such a bad idea. Over the next few years they came into regular use.

UNDER WRAPS

You'd think that once catchers had gotten used to playing baseball with birdcages and rat traps strapped to their faces, they'd be less inhibited about wearing gear that protected their chests, legs, and hands, but that wasn't the case. Some catchers did wear "breast protectors"—pads made of sheepskin stuffed with fur—and some fortified their socks with homemade shin guards made from strips of wood, cane, or rattan. But we don't know who these people were because they hid their gear under their uniforms, where it couldn't be seen or laughed at by fans and opponents.

Indeed, the man who is credited with being the first to wear a chest protector in a baseball game gets the credit only because he was the first one to get *caught*. In the mid-1880s, the wife of Charles Bennett, a catcher with the Detroit Wolverines, became so worried about his safety that she made him a padded vest that he could wear under his uniform. Bennett managed to keep it hidden for about a year. When his secret was revealed in 1886, rather than give it up, Bennett invited pitchers to throw fastballs at his chest, and the sight of the balls slamming into his ribs without causing injury helped speed acceptance of the device. Within a year or two, players were wearing them over the uniform in plain sight. By 1889 the first inflatable "body protectors" hit the market,

---

Roberto Clemente ended his career with exactly 3,000 hits.

a by-product of the invention of the pneumatic rubber tire several years before.

HANDS ON

By the late 1880s, baseball gloves had been around for about a decade, and catchers wore them just like anyone else. These gloves were little more than work gloves with the fingertips removed and a little extra padding sewn into the sensitive areas of the fingers and palms. The gloves provided some hand protection, but they were not designed to make it easier for players to catch the ball.

The first person to make a glove designed especially for catchers was Joe Gunson, who played for the Kansas City Blues. Gunson came up with the idea for his glove just before Decoration Day (Memorial Day) 1888, when he was faced with the prospect of catching both games of a doubleheader with a crippled finger and a swollen palm on his left hand, because the team's other catcher was even more injured than he was. Rather than submit himself to the risk of greater injury, Gunson decided to do something about it:

> I stitched together the fingers of my left-hand glove, thus practically a "mitt," then I caught both games. It worked so well that I got to work, took an old paint-pot wire handle, the old flannel belts from our castoff jackets, rolled the cloth around the ends of the finger, and padded the thumb. Then I put sheepskins with the wool on it in the palm and covered it with buckskin, thus completing the mitt, and the suffering and punishment we endured was all over.

MODERNIZING THE MITT

Gunson is credited with being the first person to invent a catcher's mitt, but the first person to actually *patent* one was Harry Decker of the Washington Statesmen. He is believed by many historians to have based his "Decker Safety Catcher's Mitt" on Gunson's design. Decker's glove was little more than a leather glove sewn to the back of a round leather pillow that covered the palm and fingers of the hand. The design of the catcher's mitt remained basically the same into the late 1930s, when the legendary Rawlings Sporting Goods "Glove Doctor," Bud Latina, improved on the original by creating the first mitt with a built-in pocket.

Curt Schilling buys a seat for his deceased father at every Red Sox home game.

But catchers still had to catch balls with both hands; that didn't change until the 1950s, when a catcher named Gus Niarhos cut a slit into the back of his catcher's mitt in a way that allowed him to close the mitt around the ball—now he could catch the ball with one hand while protecting his throwing hand by holding it behind his back. One-handed catcher's mitts, including some with spring-action hinges, have been available ever since.

LEG WORK

The last piece of the Tools of Ignorance ensemble was the simplest to come up with. When Roger Bresnahan decided in 1906 that he didn't want to spend another season being battered by bad pitches, thrown bats, or the cleats of runners sliding into home plate, he showed up for the first game of the season wearing protective gear that was already in widespread use in another sport. "I didn't invent anything," he remembered years later. "I simply got a pair of shin guards, such as cricket players wore." He got a lot of jeers that first day, but they didn't last long. "I guess they were a good idea," he joked, "they tell me catchers still wear 'em."

*   *   *

THE OVAL DIAMOND

"I couldn't see well enough to play when I was a boy, so they gave me a special job—they made me an umpire."

—Harry Truman

"They booed Ted Williams too, remember? They'll say about me, I knocked the ball over the fence, but they didn't like the way I stood at the plate."

—Lyndon Johnson

"When I was a small boy growing up in Kansas, a friend and I went fishing, and as we sat there in the warmth of a summer afternoon, on a riverbank, we talked about what we wanted to do when we grew up. I told him that I wanted to be a major league baseball player, a genuine professional like Honus Wagner. My friend said that he'd like to be President of the United States. Neither of us got our wish."

—Dwight D. Eisenhower

Only 14 players have ever hit four home runs in a single game.

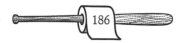
THE BARBECUE PIT

Forget the peanuts and Cracker Jack—
buy me some ribs and coleslaw!

LIFE AFTER BASEBALL

First baseman John "Boog" Powell needs no introduction to Baltimore baseball fans: He was with the Orioles from 1961 to '74, hit 339 career homers, played on four World Series and four All-Star teams, and won the 1970 MVP award. So what did he do after retiring from baseball? He opened Boog's BBQ in Oriole Park at Camden Yards in 1993, where he's been turning out hickory-smoked beef, pork, and turkey, served with beans or coleslaw, ever since. Boog's BBQ is now a staple at Camden Yards.

But Powell's not alone. Other enterprising players have hopped on the chuckwagon bringing food to the stadiums:

• Left-handed pitcher and Cy Young Award winner Randy Jones opened Randy Jones BBQ at the Padres' PETCO Park in 1992. He also sells a line of bottled sauces, which he says are based on an old family recipe.

• Four-time All-Star slugger Greg "The Bull" Luzinski has a stand called Bull's Barbecue at the Phillies' Citizens Bank Park, selling ribs and pulled-pork sandwiches with coleslaw and baked beans.

• "Stormin'" Gorman Thomas opened Gorman's Corner at the Brewers' Miller Park, offering BBQ sandwiches and grilled brats.

• Former Pirate catcher Manny Sanguillen runs (and signs autographs at) his outfield barbecue stand at PNC Park.

• Giants Hall of Famer Orlando Cepeda has Orlando's Caribbean BBQ at AT&T Park, featuring the signature Cha-Cha Bowl of chicken, black beans, rice, and vegetables.

• Former Red Sox pitcher Luis Tiant oversees a Cuban sandwich operation on Yawkey Way, bordering Fenway Park. The popular "Cubano" is ham, pork, pickles, and mustard on a roll, grilled crisp on a special press. (And yes, they also have barbecue.)

Wally Yonamine was the first American to play pro baseball in Japan after World War II.

THE HOUSE OF DAVID

One of the most famous and popular baseball teams in the early 20th century was a traveling team of bearded men who belonged to a religious cult. Here's the story of the House of David barnstormers.

NATIONAL PASTIME

In the early 1900s, there were only 16 major league teams in 10 cities, but there were countless regional minor leagues, and almost every town in America fielded some kind of amateur or semipro club. It was the era of barnstorming teams—independent baseball clubs that traveled the country and played local teams in exhibition games. And by far the most popular barnstorming team was the House of David.

The Israelite House of David was a religious commune formed in 1903 in Benton Harbor, Michigan, by a man named Benjamin Purnell. According to Purnell, the House of David's mission was to gather the 12 lost tribes of Israel and await the end of the world. Members were not allowed to have sex, eat meat, shave, or cut their hair. This gave the more than 1,000 male House of David members a distinctive bearded, mountain-man look, a very odd appearance in that era.

To pass time while waiting for the end of the world, Purnell suggested his followers play baseball. By 1915 the House of David team was so good that it joined the local Berrien County League—and won the league championship its first year. In 1916 team manager Francis Thorpe took the team on the road, playing exhibition games in southwest Michigan, northern Indiana, Wisconsin, and Chicago. Purnell fully approved—his top athletes could both spread the message of the commune…and bring in some money. By 1920 they were famous enough to warrant a pictorial spread in the *New York Times*. By 1925 the House of David was known all over the country.

THE GREATEST SHOW ON DIRT

When the House of David came to town, they brought with them a circus atmosphere. After the fifth inning, the game would pause and the House of David players would perform some

---

According to superstition, lending a bat to a fellow player is a serious jinx.

kind of show. One was an acrobatic version of the "pepper game" —one player would bat short grounders to a group of fielders, who would catch balls and throw them back as quickly as they could, all while doing somersaults and flips. Another fan favorite was the "donkey game," in which the team would play an inning of baseball while riding donkeys. They were like an early, long-haired baseball version of the Harlem Globetrotters, and like that team, they played at a very high level and made it look effortless. The House of David even beat the St. Louis Cardinals 8–6, led by female pitcher Jackie Mitchell.

Purnell's idea of using the baseball team to better the commune worked. The baseball team's revenues allowed the House of David to grow their own crops, generate their own electricity, live in huge mansions, and set up their own furniture and jelly factories. They also went into tourism, opening a hotel, restaurant, theme park and zoo, plus a ballpark, where a team was permanently stationed.

PLAY FOR TODAY

The House of David drew such large crowds that the commune sent out several teams at the same time in the 1920s. In addition to the home team, they had two road teams, a women's team, and a junior male team. In 1925, realizing that they didn't have enough talented players to field so many teams, they began recruiting ringers from outside the cult. The "Players for Hire" were required to grow beards to fit in, but didn't have to abide by any of the other commune rules. Most of the fake-Davids were undetectable, but others weren't asked to blend in...for a reason. Hall of Fame pitcher Grover Cleveland Alexander, for one, wasn't asked to grow a beard so the team could capitalize on his famous name and face. Alexander played for and managed the main House of David team from 1931 to 1935.

Along with retired major leaguers, Negro League stars and other famous athletes often signed on for a hitch with the House of David. Satchel Paige pitched with the team, as did Babe Didrickson Zaharias after she won three Olympic track and field medals (she later became a professional golfer).

END OF THE ROAD

Purnell died in 1927, not long after being tried in Michigan on charges of public immorality—a scandal that broke apart the House of David. A dozen young women had admitted to having affairs with Purnell—very much against commune rules—and as a result, the cult members had been forced to remove their own founder. The commune split into two factions—the Israelite House of David, and the City of David, led by Purnell's widow, Mary.

Both factions continued to stage "House of David" baseball teams, but the barnstorming era faded away after World War II. When the teams returned to the road in 1946 (they didn't travel during the war), America was on the verge of televised baseball and, eventually, an expanded version of the major leagues that muscled small teams out of the market. Regional leagues and traveling independent teams quickly became a thing of the past, and the last House of David team parked its tour bus for good in 1955.

*　　*　　*

SETH SWIRSKY'S COLLECTION

This author and songwriter (he wrote the jingle for Thomas's English Muffins) boasts one of the most impressive baseball memorabilia collections in existence. Among his unique treasures:

• A ball signed by the Beatles after their '65 Shea Stadium concert.

• Babe Ruth's first home-run ball, from May 6, 1915, signed by Jack Warhop, the pitcher who gave it up.

• Pete Rose's "Little Black Book" from 1987, which includes notes and the numbers of several women in several cities.

• The only known surviving ball from Johnny Vander Meer's record-setting second consecutive no-hitter in 1938.

• The third home-run ball that Reggie Jackson hit in game 6 of the 1977 World Series.

• Baseball commissioner Kenesaw Mountain Landis's original letter that banned "Shoeless" Joe Jackson from baseball.

• The ball that bounced off of Jose Canseco's head for a home run in 1993.

• Lefty Gomez's vanity license plate from 1956—it says "GOOF."

• Woody Allen's apology letter to Mel Allen for cutting all of the Yankees announcer's scenes from the 1987 movie *Radio Days*.

...Earle Combs wore No. 1; Mark Koenig, 2; Babe Ruth, 3; and Lou Gehrig, 4.

GETTING OUT OF TOWN

The Brooklyn Dodgers moved to California in 1957
because they couldn't replace their crumbling old stadium.
Here are the stories of why some other teams moved.

BOSTON...MILWAUKEE...ATLANTA BRAVES
The Braves had been in Boston since 1871, and they'd won
the World Series in 1914. But in terms of ticket sales, they
always trailed the crosstown Boston Red Sox. In 1935 owner Emil
Fuchs finally gave up trying to make ends meet and sold the team
to a construction tycoon named Lou Perini. The Braves didn't do
much better under Perini, winning the American League pennant
only once (1948), and suffering continually declining attendance.
To save his investment, in 1953 Perini moved the team to Milwaukee. Why Milwaukee? The Braves' farm team, the Brewers,
was located there, and drew more than a million fans per season—
more than the Braves drew in Boston. Perini made the right
choice. The Braves drew a record 1.8 million fans their first year
in Milwaukee. The team became lucrative, and in 1962 Perini
couldn't resist an offer to sell the team to a group led by Chicago
insurance executive William Bartholomay. The group wanted to
move the team to a bigger city and, coincidentally, Atlanta had
just begun building an $18 million, 52,000-seat stadium, hoping to
lure a professional sports team. It worked. Bartholomay moved the
Braves to Atlanta in 1966.

ST. LOUIS BROWNS...BALTIMORE ORIOLES
The St. Louis Browns entered the American League in 1902, com-
peting for fans (and fan dollars) with their National League rivals,
the St. Louis Cardinals. Despite the Browns almost always finishing near last place, they outdrew the Cardinals from 1902 to 1926.
But after the Cardinals upset the Yankees to win the 1926 World
Series, they dominated the local scene. Browns attendance dwindled, and the team planned a move to Los Angeles for the 1942
season. American League owners were expected to approve the
move at a meeting scheduled for December 8, 1941. But that was
the day after Pearl Harbor was bombed—the day the United

States entered World War II. The meeting was cancelled and the league postponed all major plans. So, the Browns remained in St. Louis and even shared their stadium, Sportsman's Park, with the Cardinals. Then Cardinals owner Fred Saigh was arraigned on charges of tax evasion and embezzlement, which nearly led *that* team to leave town, until a buyout by Anheuser-Busch brought in a much-needed cash infusion. The Cardinals continued to out-draw the Browns and in 1953, Browns owner Bill Veeck sold the team to a group of Baltimore businessmen, who moved the team there and renamed it the Orioles.

WASHINGTON SENATORS…MINNESOTA TWINS

The American League began in 1901 with eight teams. One of them was the Washington Senators. Owner Clark Griffith died in 1955 and left control of the team to his son, Calvin, who had no real interest in baseball and wanted to sell the team to someone who would move it out of town. After a proposed sale and move to San Francisco in 1956 fell through, Griffith decided to hold on to the team and move it to Minneapolis-St. Paul. American League owners rejected the move at the 1958 winter meetings (keeping the Senators in Washington was a sentimental decision), but Griffith and the league ultimately reached a compromise. The Senators would move (and be renamed the Minnesota Twins after the Twin Cities of Minneapolis and St. Paul) and Washington would get an expansion team to be called…the Washington Senators. The Twins, and the second incarnation of the Senators, began play in 1961.

WASHINGTON SENATORS…TEXAS RANGERS

When the American League invited offers to purchase the new Washington Senators team in 1960, the franchise went to a group of 10 investors led by Federal Aviation Administration official Elwood Quesada. But in 1967, the investors, unfamiliar with the business of baseball and unhappy that their investment was taking so long to show a return, sold their shares to trucking executive Bob Short. Short didn't have much experience in the baseball business, either (and he'd had to borrow most of the $9 million he paid for the team), so he sold a lot of the Senators' best players, including Gil Hodges, to bring in money to pay down the debt.

Ken Griffey Sr. and Jr. are the only father-son pair to play on the same team.

When the players left, the team got worse (the Senators' average won-lost record was 67–95), and ticket sales declined, putting the team in further financial jeopardy. In late 1970, Short gave up and put the Senators up for sale. But the mayor of Arlington, Texas, Tom Vandergriff, had another idea: Short could keep the team if he moved it to Arlington, an upscale suburb of Dallas. American League owners approved the move and in 1972, the second version of the Washington Senators became the Texas Rangers.

MONTREAL EXPOS...WASHINGTON NATIONALS

The Expos, the first major league club in Canada, entered the National League as an expansion team in 1969. They were usually mediocre (average season: 78–84) and often ranked last in the league in attendance. In 2001 their average home attendance dropped to 7,935 per game, one of the lowest rates ever. The team was losing so much money that in 2002, MLB owners authorized the league to buy the Expos and fold the team, along with the Minnesota Twins, who were also hemorrhaging cash. Lawsuits and injunctions prevented the league from doing anything with the Twins, which delayed eliminating the Expos as well. But the league still purchased the Expos with the intent of moving the franchise to a more profitable location. Commissioner Bud Selig considered offers from buyers in San Juan, Puerto Rico; Portland, Oregon; northern New Jersey; Norfolk, Virginia; Las Vegas; and Monterrey, Mexico. In late 2004, he decided to move the Expos to Washington, D.C. The new owners held a name-the-team contest for fans. The winner: the Nationals.

SEATTLE PILOTS...MILWAUKEE BREWERS

Today, Bud Selig is the commissioner of baseball, but in the mid-1960s, he was a Milwaukee car dealer and minority owner of the Milwaukee Braves. Selig was against the Braves' 1966 sale and move to Atlanta. The team went anyway, so Selig focused his attentions on trying to get an expansion team in Milwaukee. First, he formed an interest group called the Milwaukee Brewers Baseball Club (naming the future team after the city's old minor league franchise). Then, he convinced the Chicago White Sox to play a series of exhibition games in Milwaukee in 1967 and 1968. The games were wildly successful, attracting over 60,000

First player selected to an All-Star team as a write-in candidate: the Braves' Rico Carty (1970).

fans each. When Major League Baseball announced that four cities would get new teams in 1969, Selig thought Milwaukee was a lock. Instead, the franchises were awarded to San Diego, Montreal, Kansas City, and Seattle. Unable to keep the Braves in town and unable to get an expansion team, Selig shifted gears to trying to buy the Seattle Pilots (one of the 1969 expansion teams) and move them to Milwaukee. The Pilots had major stadium problems: Sick's Stadium, which had been built in 1913 for a minor league team, was falling apart and seated only 17,000 people, a violation of the Pilots' promise to expand the stadium to 30,000 seats before the 1969 season. It really didn't matter—on average, only 8,300 people attended each Pilots game. Selig bought the Pilots for $13 million. The sale got final approval from the league—and the banks handling the transaction—on April 1, 1970, just six days before the start of the season. The team's equipment was in storage in Provo, Utah, with truck drivers awaiting the word on whether to head to Seattle or Milwaukee.

PHILADELPHIA...KANSAS CITY...OAKLAND A'S

The Philadelphia Athletics were the early American League's most dominant team, winning nine pennants between 1902 and 1931. But during the Great Depression, team owner Connie Mack had to trade away or sell his best players to make ends meet. A lack of good players meant a bad team—the Athletics didn't have a winning record between 1933 and 1947—which meant low fan attendance and declining team revenues. After Mack's co-owner, Ben Shibe, died in 1922, Mack had taken sole control of the Athletics, but in 1950 the 88-year-old was forced out of the team by his sons Roy, Earle, and Connie Mack Jr. Attendance and revenues kept falling, and local fan loyalties switched permanently after the Phillies went to the World Series in 1950. With the team no longer making enough money to justify keeping it, the Macks sold the A's to businessman Arnold Johnson in 1955. The sale was pure business: Johnson owned Blues Stadium, a minor league ballpark in Kansas City. He sold the stadium to the city and then leased it back with a clause that said he could move the team to Los Angeles by 1958 if attendance dropped to under one million fans per season. Unfortunately for Johnson, that didn't happen—

the Kansas City Athletics had one of the highest attendance rates in the league. Johnson died in 1960 and Charles O. Finley, a Chicago insurance magnate, bought the team. He invested more than half a million dollars in stadium renovations, a farm club system, and even new uniforms, telling Kansas City that he wanted to keep the team in town. But he really didn't—he invested heavily to make the team more alluring to other cities. American League owners blocked a proposed move to Dallas in 1962, a move to Louisville, Kentucky, in 1964, and his initial attempt to move to Oakland in 1964. Finley persisted…and got the approval to move the team to Oakland in 1967.

*   *   *

THREE POP CULTURE INSPIRATIONS

• **Bama Rockwell**, a Boston Braves outfielder, made history in 1946 while playing the Brooklyn Dodgers at Ebbets Field. He smashed a ball that hit the Bulova clock perched above the scoreboard—shattering its face and causing glass to rain down on the field. A few years later, author (and Dodger fan) Bernard Malamud wrote that story into his book *The Natural*, which features Roy Hobbs hitting a home run off the light tower, causing glass to rain down on the field.

• **"Sudden" Sam McDowell**, a pitcher for the Indians in the 1960s, was among the best strikeout artists in the game. But after a trade to the Giants in 1971, his numbers began to dwindle, mostly due to alcoholism. He ended his career a shadow of his former self. McDowell's sad story became the basis for Sam "Mayday" Malone on the 1980s sitcom, *Cheers*.

• **"Steve Dalkowski** was the hardest thrower I ever, ever saw," said Orioles coach Cal Ripken Sr., who witnessed the young hurler throwing a ball through a backstop in 1958. Some have estimated Dalkowski's fastball at 110 mph. Sadly, he never found big-league success due to his lack of control, violent tendencies, and alcoholism. One of his teammates, Ron Shelton, went on to become a screenwriter. He modeled the character of hard-throwing, slow-thinking "Nuke" LaLoosh, played by Tim Robbins in the 1988 film *Bull Durham*, after Steve "White Lightning" Dalkowski.

Gene Autry, Bing Crosby, and Bob Hope were all ball-team owners.

MERKLE'S BONER & SNODGRASS'S MUFF

Were you one of the millions of fans who watched in horror as Bill Buckner let a ball roll through his legs in Game 6 of the 1986 World Series? (See page 152.) Well, it's just one of many major errors in baseball history.

FRED'S DREAD

In September 1908, the New York Giants were in the midst of a hotly contested pennant race with the Chicago Cubs. As the season drew to a close, the two teams met at the Polo Grounds in New York for an important three-game series. Playing first base for the Giants was 19-year-old rookie Fred Merkle.

During one of the crucial games, the score was tied 1–1 in the bottom of the ninth inning. The Giants were up, and already had two runners on base: Moose McCormick on third and Merkle on first. Al Bridwell came to bat and hit a single, driving in McCormick for what the Giants thought was the game-winning run. Giants fans streamed onto the field in celebration. Merkle, assuming the game was over, never touched second base and headed for the dugout.

Big mistake: For the run to count, Bridwell had to reach first, forcing Merkle to second. Chicago second baseman Johnny Evers, realizing that Merkle could still be tagged out—and the run nullified—yelled to his teammates in the outfield to throw him the ball. Evers, fighting off a base coach and a fan who'd figured out was he was trying to do, got possession of the ball and tagged second base, appealing to umpire Hank O'Day that he'd made a force out of Merkle at second, negating the winning run.

In the melee, O'Day couldn't make a decision. A fan got hold of the ball and threw it into the stands. Other fans began to riot, both teams' managers got into a screaming match with the umpires, and the police had to escort the Cubs players out of the hostile stadium. The question wasn't settled until the following day, when the league ruled that Merkle was out and the game would have to be replayed at the end of the season. The rematch turned out to be a one-game playoff for the National League pennant, since the teams

ended the season tied for first place. The Cubs won the rematch and, as a result, the pennant—and went on to win the World Series for the last time (to date) in their franchise's history. But if Merkle had tagged second before he went to the dugout, the Giants would have won the game…and the pennant.

SNODGRASS'S SLIP-UP

Four years later, another New York Giant became infamous for committing an error—only this time it was in the World Series. The decisive Game 8 against the Boston Red Sox (Game 2 didn't count because it was called on account of darkness) went into extra innings with the Giants leading 2–1 going into the bottom of the 10th. Red Sox pinch hitter Clyde Engle hit a pop fly to center field. Fred Snodgrass prepared to catch the ball and make the easy out. Instead, Snodgrass inexplicably dropped it. Engle reached second base.

But "Snodgrass's Muff," as the newspapers called it, didn't actually lose the game—it only put the game-tying run on base. He partially redeemed himself with a difficult catch on the very next play, making a running grab to put out Boston's Harry Hooper. The next batter, Steve Yerkes, walked, which meant the game-*winning* run was now on base.

On the next play, Boston's Tris Speaker hit a pop foul on the first-base side. It should have easily been caught for an out. Pitcher Christy Mathewson, catcher Chief Meyers, and first baseman Fred Merkle (yes, the same Fred Merkle) were all in position to catch it. Nobody called it, and they all stood and looked at each other as it fell to the ground. Still alive, Speaker hit a single. Yerkes advanced to third base and Engle scored, tying the game at 2–2. Mathewson intentionally walked the next batter to set up a force out. The next Red Sox hitter, Larry Gardner, hit a sacrifice fly to right field. Yerkes tagged third and scored. The Red Sox won the game 3–2, and the World Series along with it.

Snodgrass would unfairly take the blame for the Giants' late-game meltdown, and his error become known as "the $30,000 muff"—the difference between what the winning and losing players received. But it wasn't a total loss for Snodgrass. Giants manager John McGraw felt so bad that Snodgrass was blamed for the loss that he gave him a pay raise.

CALLING HISTORY

More famous plays…as told by the announcers who witnessed them.

"THE IMPOSSIBLE HAS HAPPENED!"

Situation: With two injured legs and a stomach virus, Dodgers slugger Kirk Gibson wasn't expected to play in the 1988 World Series against the Oakland A's. But in Game 1, down a run in the bottom of the ninth with a man on, manager Tommy Lasorda surprised everyone by calling on Gibson to face the game's best closer, Dennis Eckersley.

Sportscaster: Vin Scully, NBC-TV

The Call: "Look who's coming up!…Sax waiting on deck, but the game right now is at the plate. High fly ball into right field…she is…gone!" *Then Scully goes silent as Gibson limps around the base paths while the Dodger fans cheer. He finally says,* "In a year that has been so improbable, the impossible has happened!"

"GO CRAZY!"

Situation: In the 1985 NLCS, Ozzie Smith and the Cardinals were tied at two games apiece against the Dodgers. Smith, a switch hitter, had never homered from the left side of the plate during his seven-year career. The score was tied in the bottom of the ninth as the "Wizard of Oz" entered the box…batting lefty.

Sportscaster: Jack Buck, CBS Radio

The Call: "Here's the pitch. Smith corks one into right down the line! It may go…Go crazy, folks! Go crazy! It's a home run! And the Cardinals have won the game…by the score of 3 to 2 on a home run by…the Wizard! Go crazy!"

"OH, DOCTOR!"

Situation: In Game 4 of the 1984 NLCS, Steve Garvey of the Padres came up to bat with Tony Gwynn on first and the score tied 5–5 in the bottom of the ninth. San Diego had come back in the game to tie the score, but they were facing elimination against the Chicago Cubs' intimidating closer, Lee Smith.

Sportscaster : Jerry Coleman, Padres radio

A perfect game has been thrown, on average, once every 7.5 seasons.

The Call: "Pitch on the way to Garvey. Hit high to right field, way back! Going, going, it is…gone! The Padres win it! In a game that absolutely defies description, Steve Garvey, in the ninth inning, hit one over the 370 mark, and the Padres beat the Cubs 7 to 5! Oh, doctor! You can hang a star on that baby!"

"THE GIANTS WON THE PENNANT!"

Situation: The 1951 New York Giants battled back from a 13½-game deficit to force a three-game playoff against the Brooklyn Dodgers. After splitting the first two contests, the Giants were down by two runs in the bottom of the ninth at the Polo Grounds when outfielder Bobby Thomson came up to bat.

Sportscaster: Russ Hodges, Giants radio

The Call: "Bobby Thomson up there swinging. He's had two out of three, a single and a double, and Billy Cox is playing him right on the third-base line. One out, last of the ninth. Branca pitches. Bobby Thomson takes a strike called on the inside corner. Bobby hitting at .292. He's had a single and a double, and he drove in the Giants' first run with a long fly to center. Brooklyn leads it, four to two. Hartung down the line at third, not taking any chances. Lockman without too big of a lead at second, but he'll be running like the wind if Thomson hits one. Branca throws. There's a long drive! That's gonna be it, I believe! The Giants won the pennant! The Giants won the pennant! The Giants won the pennant! The Giants won the pennant! Bobby Thompson hits into the lower deck of the left-field stands! The Giants won the pennant, and they're going crazy! They're going crazy! Hey, ho! I don't believe it! I do not believe it! Bobby Thomson hit a line drive into the lower deck of the left-field stands, and the great place is going crazy. The Giants—Horace Stoneham has got a winner. The Giants won it by a score of five to four, and they're picking Bobby Thomson up and carrying him off the field!"

Preserving history: Because this game took place in the days before broadcasts were regularly taped, Hodges's call should have been lost forever. But an overconfident Brooklyn fan taped the broadcast because he wanted to record "Hodges crying" when the Giants lost. Even though his Dodgers got beat, the Brooklyn fan knew he had something special. The next day, he got ahold of Hodges and told him, "You *have* to have this tape."

Dave Winfield was born on October 3, 1951, the day "the Giants won the pennant!"

MORE RANDOM BASEBALL FACTS

Useless trivia…or essential information? You decide.

• Pitchers who win 20 games a season are rare, but pitchers who *lose* 20 games a season are even rarer. Since 1975, only five pitchers have done it. The last was Mike Maroth, who went 9–21 for Detroit in 2003.

• The Florida Marlins are the only team that travels north to spring training.

• Only two people to play for the Seattle Mariners who are in the Hall of Fame: Gaylord Perry and Goose Gossage.

• In 2003 the Detroit Tigers set the American League record for worst season: 43–119. But the all-time modern record holder is the 1962 New York Mets, who went 40–120.

• From 1992 to 1996, Los Angeles Dodgers players won the N.L. Rookie of the Year award a record five times. The winners: Eric Karros, Mike Piazza, Raul Mondesi, Hideo Nomo, and Todd Hollandsworth.

• Highest lifetime salary of all time (so far): Barry Bonds, with $188.2 million. Second place: Alex Rodriguez with $170.4 million.

• The four current teams that have never appeared in the World Series: the Tampa Bay Rays, Seattle Mariners, Texas Rangers, and Washington Nationals.

• In 2005 Ryan Howard of the Philadelphia Phillies was the N.L. Rookie of the Year. In 2006 he was the N.L. MVP. In 2007 he struck out 199 times, a record.

• Carl Yastrzemski hit .301 in 1968, but still won the American League batting title. It's the lowest highest average ever.

• Because of the wild-card playoff system, the Florida Marlins have appeared in and won the World Series twice, but have never won their division, the National League East.

First U.S. President to attend a major league game: Benjamin Harrison, 1892.

UNCLE JOHN'S ALL-TIME, ALL-CELEBRITY TEAM

After dusting off the old BRI time machine, we've traveled through the past 120 years to put together a group of players who—had they pursued another path in life—might have been known today for the numbers they put up instead of their acting roles, hit songs, novels, or military conquests.

Starting pitcher: HUGO CHÁVEZ

It was a childhood dream to become a major league pitcher that led Chávez into the Venezuelan Army in the 1970s, where he played in the National Baseball Championships. He was pretty good, too, though not quite overpowering enough to attract the attention of major league scouts...so he switched his focus to his military career. Two decades later, the controversial Chávez was elected president of Venezuela. (Appropriately, he's a lefty.)

Starting pitcher: KEVIN COSTNER

On the field as a boy, his dreams were of a life in baseball. And the kid from Ventura, California, certainly looked like he had the talent. As a Little Leaguer, Costner threw two no-hitters and once struck out 16 batters in a game. Although he excelled at sports in high school, Costner was too short (5'2") to have any real chance of playing in the bigs. Instead, he focused on acting. Over the next few years, Costner grew nearly a foot and could have gone back to baseball, but by then was well on his way to success in Hollywood.

Starting pitcher: BILLY BOB THORNTON

A self-described "junk pitcher" (one who throws with a lot of movement rather than great velocity), Thornton knew early on that he had a gift. "The first game I pitched in Little League, I struck out 10 batters. You're not supposed to really have a curve-ball when you're 12, but I did." Thornton's abilities took him all the way to a tryout with the Royals (although his dream was to pitch for the Cardinals). But that dream ended in his first at-bat

in spring training, when a wild pitch broke his collarbone. Thornton didn't jump straight into acting—here are some of his other jobs: stocking groceries, house painting, operating a drill press, playing drums in a soul band, driving a bulldozer, hauling hay, and working as a roadie with the Nitty Gritty Dirt Band.

Catcher: BILLY RAY CYRUS

The "Achy Breaky Heart" singer didn't buy his first guitar until he was 20 years old. Until then, the Kentucky native's most prized possession was his catcher's mitt. Determined to become the next Johnny Bench, Cyrus won a baseball scholarship to Georgetown College. Then, he says, "I just felt this voice inside saying, 'Buy a guitar and form a band and you'll fulfill your purpose. Trade in your catcher's mitt and buy a guitar.' And I did it."

First base: GEORGE H. W. BUSH

Bush attended Phillips Academy in Andover, Massachusetts, in the 1930s, where he played baseball under Patsy Donovan, a legendary big-league player and manager who in 1914 saw potential in a young pitcher named Babe Ruth. Donovan saw something in George Bush, too, and made him captain of the team. Bush later was captain of the baseball team at Yale as well. The talented lefty first baseman played in the first College World Series, when Yale lost to California. Bush certainly could have stayed in baseball after he graduated, but he moved to Texas and became an oilman, then went on to a successful career in politics. In the 1950s, Bush helped coach the Midland, Texas, Little League team that his son George W. played on. (George W. Bush is the first—and so far only—Little Leaguer ever to become president of the United States.)

Second base: BILLY CRYSTAL

Crystal's father was a pitcher at St. John's University and taught his son everything he knew about the game. Billy's dream: to play for the Yankees. The young infielder (and team captain) from Long Beach High in New York was awarded a baseball scholarship at Marshall University in West Virginia. But before he even got a chance to suit up, the sports program went defunct. So the charismatic Crystal stayed in school to pursue his other love—entertaining people. He went on to direct the classic baseball film *61**, about

Joe DiMaggio beat Ted Williams for the MVP award twice: 1941 (by 37 votes) and 1947 (by 1).

the trials and tribulations of Roger Maris's record-breaking season. In 2008, a day before his 60th birthday, Crystal played with the Yankees in an exhibition game...and struck out in his only at-bat.

Shortstop: NELLY

Born Cornell Iral Haynes Jr. in 1974, Nelly grew up in St. Louis, Missouri, before becoming one of the top-selling rappers in the world (he's sold over 40 million albums). Nelly's parents split up when he was seven, forcing him to move from home to home and school to school, where he got expelled for fighting. Good thing for Nelly that he found baseball. It gave him a purpose and a constructive outlet for his frustration. Maturing into a star high-school shortstop with good range and a strong arm, Nelly garnered the attention of scouts from the Pirates and Braves, but decided, while still at high school, to turn to music instead.

Third base: HECTOR ELIZONDO

Elizondo was a sickly child growing up on New York's Upper East Side in the 1940s. But, determined to improve himself, he started exercising and by the time he was 10, he was dancing, singing, and acting on local television. When high school rolled around, however, Elizondo wasn't sure what he wanted to be: dancer, jazz musician, gangster, or major league ballplayer. He showed aptitude at all of them, but it was baseball that the teenager cared most about—scouts from both the Pittsburgh Pirates and New York Giants came out to see him play. Unfortunately, a knee injury put an end to careers in both baseball and dancing, so, after a brief stint as a history teacher, Elizondo decided to pick up acting again. With over 80 film and TV roles roles to his credit (*Pretty Woman*, *The Princess Diaries*, *Chicago Hope*), Elizondo hasn't stopped working since 1960.

Left field: GARTH BROOKS

A star high-school athlete, Brooks played baseball, football, and track and field. After receiving a scholarship from Oklahoma State to throw the javelin, he got a degree in advertising before pursuing a music career. Result: Brooks has sold more records than Elvis Presley. But the sports bug never left him. In 1998 he pulled some strings and landed a tryout with the San Diego Padres. How'd he do? Not bad for a 36-year-old who hadn't played organized ball for nearly 20 years. Brooks's biggest thrill came when he was put in as a pinch runner in a spring training game against the Cubs. After twice nearly getting picked off at first (Brooks hugged the ump the second time he was called safe), the batter grounded into a double play, thus ending Brooks's brief baseball career. "It was great," he said. "It was a piece of Americana going right down my throat."

Center field: ZANE GREY

A promising pitching career was literally cut short when the distance between home plate and the pitching spot was increased by 10 feet, 6 inches in 1893. Grey couldn't make the transition, but he was a good enough hitter to stay in baseball. Moving to the outfield, the minor leaguer from Zanesville, Ohio, was still on his way to a major league career…except that, more than anything else, Grey wanted to be a writer. He replaced his bat with a typewriter, but he never abandoned baseball—he would go on to write some of the best baseball fiction of the 20th century, including *The Young Pitcher* (1911) and *The Redheaded Outfield and Other Baseball Stories* (1920).

Right field: DENNIS HAYSBERT

Baseball fans know this actor as Pedro Cerrano, the Cuban slugger who had a penchant for voodoo in the 1989 film *Major League*. The role wasn't a stretch, as Haysbert has always been a talented athlete and could have pursued a career in either baseball or football. He even contemplated trying out for the Olympics at one point. But it was the acting bug that won out. Good thing, too, because Haysbert has given us classic lines like "I cannot hit curveball. Straightball I hit it very much. Curveball, bats are afraid. I ask Jobu to come, take fear from bats. I offer him cigar, rum. He will come." (For the record, Haysbert *was* a pretty good curveball hitter. "The only reason I missed those curveballs in the film was because it was in the script," he said.)

Designated hitter: EDWARD JAMES OLMOS

Olmos, the star of such films as *Talent for the Game* and *Stand and Deliver*, was born in East L.A. in 1947. He was a poor kid from the *barrio*, but while many of his friends joined gangs, Olmos focused on baseball. By high school, he had developed into a great hitter,

winning the Golden State batting championship when he was 14.
But when Olmos turned 15, he found a new love: rock 'n' roll.
After a few years as a moderately successful rock musician, touring
California in a band called Pacific Ocean, Olmos decided to try
acting because his friends said he had a "flair for the dramatic."

Reliever: ROBERT REDFORD
Redford was a star pitcher at Van Nuys High School in Southern
California (Don Drysdale played second base on the team). In 1955
Redford won a baseball scholarship to the University of Colorado,
where his strong arm and better-than-average control made him a
pretty good prospect. But just as tragedy ended Roy Hobbs's
dreams in *The Natural*, Redford's baseball dreams were sidetracked
when his mother died suddenly while he was away at college.
After that, Redford lost interest in both sports and school, and
was soon out of both. He skipped around Europe as a painter for
year, and then returned to the United States to take up acting.

Closer: CHARLIE SHEEN
The main reason that Sheen was chosen for the role of Rick "Wild
Thing" Vaughn in the 1989 film *Major League*: His Hollywood
bad-boy persona fit the character perfectly. It also didn't hurt that
in high school Sheen had been a hard-throwing pitcher with a
fastball that approached 90 mph (his high school won-lost record
was 40–15). The experience came in handy for his *Major League*
scenes on the mound. Many players have called it one of the most
accurate portrayals by an actor in the history of baseball films.

*   *   *

A NICKNAME IS BORN

"You know who gave it to me? Bobby Hoffman, who played with
the Giants. We played on the same American Legion team. And,
you know, we didn't have no dugouts when we played. We sat on
the ground, or a bench was full with the players. And I was sitting
on the ground with my legs crossed and my arms crossed. And he
says, 'You look like a Yogi.' And that stuck."

—Lawrence "Yogi" Berra

First major league team pictured on a Wheaties box: The 1987 Minnesota Twins.

"FAN"-ATICS

*Most of us merely pledge lifelong devotion to our favorite
baseball team. Compared to these folks, we're wimps.*

IF YOU BIRTH IT... Paul and Teri Fields are die-hard Cubs
fans. How die-hard? When their son was born in 2007, they
named him Wrigley. (Get it? Wrigley Fields.) Said Teri: "We
thought if we called him 'Wrigley,' the Cubs would surely go to
the World Series." Unfortunately for the Fieldses, they didn't.

TAKE THAT! An especially tense moment came in the Chicago
stands during a 2005 World Series game between the White Sox
and Astros. A Sox fan who'd been loudly teasing Patty Biggio,
wife of Houston's Craig Biggio, somehow entered the Astros' family
section, slapped Patty, and ran away. An innocent prank? Not to
Patty. "She ran after him," said Craig Biggio after the game. "My
brother-in-law ended up putting him against the wall. You don't
slap a New Jersey girl and get away with it!"

A SHINING EXAMPLE. A 40-year-old Mets fan named Frank
Martinez was once evicted from his apartment for his habit of running down the hallway when his team won, yelling "M-E-T-S!"
He was also was evicted from the Mets' ballpark, Shea Stadium,
for *three years.* Why? In 2007 he brought a high-beam flashlight to
a game against the Braves and, from his seat behind home plate,
shone it into the eyes of the pitcher and infielders. After the
Braves complained, security confronted Martinez and found the
flashlight in his bag. (It wasn't just mean, but dumb, too: The Mets
were down by seven runs...in a game in April.)

A NIGHT TO REMEMBER. In 2004 seven Red Sox fans road-
tripped 1,500 miles to the ballpark in Fort Myers, Florida. Still
feeling the sting of their team's heartbreaking loss to the Yankees
in the 2003 playoffs, they *had* to be there for the first rematch. So
they waited outside the stadium all night to get tickets...to a
spring training game. "Hopefully, we'll remember this night when
we win the World Series this year," said fan Sam King. "We'll look
back and say, 'That's where it all began!'" Turns out, he was right.

The term "fan" was first used to insult baseball "fanatics" in the late 1800s.

MORE TEAM NAME ORIGINS

On page 13, we told you the stories of how some MLB teams got their names. Here's the rest of the league.

SAN DIEGO PADRES. The Padres took their name from an old minor league team, which was inspired by the *padres* (Spanish for priests) in the area's Catholic mission, Basilica San Diego de Alcala.

NEW YORK METS. Team executives considered Bees, Jets, Skyliners, Skyscrapers, Burros, Continentals, and Meadowlarks but ultimately decided on Mets. It references the organization that successfully lobbied Major League Baseball for the expansion team: the New York Metropolitan Baseball Club.

BALTIMORE ORIOLES. The Baltimore Oriole is the state bird of Maryland. Several 19th century teams used the name Orioles and when the St. Louis Browns moved to Baltimore in 1954, the name was readopted.

COLORADO ROCKIES. Named after the majestic mountain range. They're not the first team to use it—an NHL team was called the Colorado Rockies until they moved to New Jersey and became the Devils.

ARIZONA DIAMONDBACKS. Diamondbacks are rattlesnakes indigenous to the Arizona desert. It was the winning entry in an *Arizona Republic* team-naming contest, which was held a few months before Phoenix, where the team is based, was actually awarded the franchise.

NEW YORK YANKEES. First called the Highlanders because their ballpark was located at the highest point in New York. Sportswriters hated the name because they couldn't fit it into headlines. In 1909 one writer arbitrarily substituted "Yankees"—patriotic slang for "Americans." The name became official during World War I.

First player to win the MVP Award on a last-place team: Andre Dawson, with the Cubs (1987).

MILWAUKEE BREWERS. The Brewers were a minor league team in the area in the 1890s, and a major league team for the 1901 season. Then the team moved and became the St. Louis Browns. Both in the 1800s, and in 1970 when the modern Milwaukee Brewers were formed, the city was the beer-brewing capital of the United States.

TAMPA BAY RAYS. In 2007 the team changed its name to just "Rays," but was originally called the Devil Rays after the many native devil rays and manta rays in the local waters.

TEXAS RANGERS. Named after the legendary state police force, the Texas Rangers.

ATLANTA BRAVES. The team started in Boston in the mid-1800s as the Red Stockings…then the Beaneaters, the Doves, and the Rustlers before becoming the Braves in 1912. Why Braves? The team's owner, James Gaffney, was a member of New York City's political machine, Tammany Hall. The symbol of Tammany Hall was an Indian chief, or brave, named Tammany.

ST. LOUIS CARDINALS. In 1899 the team changed names and colors from the Brown Stockings to the red-uniformed Perfectos. Legend says "Cardinals" came about when a female spectator commented that the new red uniforms were "a lovely shade of cardinal."

CINCINNATI REDS, BOSTON RED SOX, and **CHICAGO WHITE SOX.** In the 1880s, it was fashionable for teams to take a nickname based on the color of their uniform (like the Toledo Blue Stockings or St. Louis Brown Stockings). Over time, the "stockings" got modernized to "sox," or dropped altogether.

❊   ❊   ❊

"Catching a flyball is a pleasure, but knowing what to do with it after you catch it is a business."

—**Tommy Henrich**

Only 17 Negro League players are members of the Hall of Fame.

GLOVE STORY

It's hard to imagine baseball without baseball gloves—they go together like, well, a hand and a glove. But, believe it or not, players fought against wearing them for more than 30 years.

TOUGH GUY

Who was the very first baseball player ever to play the game while wearing a glove? Nobody knows for sure, and one of the reasons for this is because the player, whoever he was, didn't *want* us to know he was wearing it. In the mid-1800s, wearing protective equipment, even when injured, was frowned upon as "unmanly." Protective equipment wasn't really even needed when baseball was invented in the mid-1840s. At the time, it was played by stockbrokers and insurance salesmen in their free time; these gentlemen prided themselves on *not* playing the game very hard, and the balls were lighter and softer than they are today.

By the early 1860s, however, the game had changed dramatically. The gentlemen's diversion had evolved into a professional game populated by ex-miners and longshoremen, and the style of play had gotten much rougher. The pitching was faster, and the baseballs were harder. Catching them with bare hands had really begun to *hurt*—broken fingers and smashed palms were common; so were blisters, bruises, and open wounds caused by the skin of the hand splitting open on impact with the ball. If your injuries didn't heal in time for tomorrow's game, that was your problem. You played injured…and your bashed hands ended up hurting even more.

UNDER COVER

As early as 1860, a few players did begin to trade the pain of pain for the pain of public ridicule. They began wearing leather workmen's gloves or even their old winter mittens—nicknamed "mitts"—to protect their injured hands. These gloves didn't have any padding, so some players improvised by stuffing feathers, old rags, or even raw steaks into the palms. Some people wore two gloves on each hand: a small glove inside a larger one, with

padding stuffed in between. These players were invariably taunted by fans (and other players), and because of this the practice remained rare. Players wore gloves as a last resort and discarded them as soon as their injuries healed enough to allow them to resume playing barehanded.

The beginning of the end of baseball's barehanded era can be traced to an afternoon in 1875, when Albert Spalding, star pitcher of the Boston Red Stockings, spotted a New Haven, Connecticut, first baseman named Charles C. Waite sheepishly wearing flesh-colored gloves at a game in Boston. As Spalding wrote in his 1911 memoirs, it was the first time he'd ever seen a player wear gloves:

> Now I had for a good while felt the need of some sort of hand pro-tection for myself. In those days clubs did not carry an extra car-load of pitchers. For several years I had pitched in every game played by the Boston team, and had developed severe bruises on my left hand. When it is recalled that every ball pitched had to be returned, and that every swift one coming my way, from infielders, outfielders or hot from the bat, must be caught or stopped, some idea may be gained of the punishment received.
>
> Therefore, I asked Waite about his glove. He confessed that he was a bit ashamed to wear it, but had it on to save his hand. He also admitted he had chosen a color as inconspicuous as possible, because he didn't care to attract attention.

Like other players who'd taken to wearing gloves in the game, Waite wore them on both hands. He cut the fingers off of the right glove so that it wouldn't interfere with his throwing, and cut a large opening into the back of each glove for ventilation.

GIVE HIM A HAND

Spalding was impressed—and besides, his hands *really hurt*—but the stigma against gloves was still so great that it took him two years to work up the nerve to join the "kid-glove aristocracy," as he called it, and finally start wearing gloves. Was it because he was one of the biggest stars in baseball? Or, more likely, was it because he had founded the sporting goods company that would bring him even greater fame and fortune? Perhaps Spalding had already figured out that if the stigma surrounding protective gear could be removed, there was big money to be made in selling it to

the baseball-loving masses. Whatever the case, when Spalding finally stepped out onto the ballfield in 1877 wearing a glove, it wasn't flesh colored—it was made of shiny black leather, the color that stood out the most against the light fabric of his Chicago White Stockings uniform (he'd switched teams in 1876).

Almost overnight, Spalding's star power made wearing a glove not just acceptable, but fashionable, as he wrote in his memoirs:

> Happily, in my case, the presence of a glove did not call out the ridicule that had greeted Waite. I had been playing so long and had become so well known that the innovation seemed rather to evoke sympathy than hilarity. I found that the glove, thin as it was, helped considerably, and I inserted one pad after another until a good deal of relief was afforded.

SPITTIN' IMAGE

As late as 1919, baseball gloves weren't all that different from regular gloves. They looked a lot like golfing and bicycling gloves do today, and were designed solely to protect the hand from injury, not to aid in the catching of baseballs. That year "Spittin'" Bill Doak, a pitcher with the St. Louis Cardinals, hit on the idea of connecting the index finger of the glove to the thumb with lacing or leather strips "to form a pocket which will conform or adjust itself automatically to a ball caught by the glove." The modern baseball glove was born. All that remained was to lace the four fingers of the glove to each other, a step taken in 1949 that turned the entire glove, not just the area between the thumb and index finger, into one big ball-catching device. This development, along with the rapid increase in glove size that occurred during the 1950s, has been credited with bringing the era of the .400 hitter to an end. A lot of balls that would have been impossible to catch using the gloves of the 1940s can be easily caught using gloves made today.

ANATOMY OF A BASEBALL GLOVE

• Major league baseball gloves are made from only the finest steer hides—if the skin is marked with brands, scars, punctures, or barbed wire scratches, or any other blemishes, it is rejected. Steerhide (from male cattle) is preferred over cowhide (female) because it's tougher, and hide from steer slaughtered in the summer months

is preferred over winter hides because cold weather makes the hides *too* thick and tough.

• It takes about six square feet of hide to make the 20 pieces of leather and nine feet of lacing that are used to make a single glove. The hide from one steer can provide enough leather to make as many as eight gloves.

• Different parts of the hide are used to make different parts of a glove. The "heart of the hide," the area that runs along the backbone, is the toughest part because it's the area that stretches the least as the steer grows. The heart of the hide is used to make the part of the glove that receives the most abuse: the palm or pocket.

• The fingers and the back of the glove are made from a softer part of the hide called the flank.

• The steer's belly is the softest part of the hide; leather from this area is used to make the inner lining of the glove.

• Small pieces of leather from the neck and other parts of the hide are used to make the web of the glove.

• Baseball glove technology has changed a lot over the last 50 years. Today's gloves come with everything from air pumps (for a perfect fit) to detachable sponges (for wiping the sweat off your face) to shaded plastic in the webbing (to protect your eyes from the sun when you're looking up at a fly ball). In the 1980s, Mizuno, a Japanese glove manufacturer, even made a pair of "wireless" gloves, one for the pitcher and one for the catcher, that allowed them to signal each other electronically without resorting to— *gasp!*—hand signals. (It bombed.)

* * *

TO THINK OR NOT TO THINK

"Don't think, just throw."
> —Crash Davis (Kevin Costner), *Bull Durham* (1988)

"Think, Billy, don't just throw."
> —Billy Chapel (Kevin Costner), *For Love of the Game* (1999)

TEST YOUR UMPIRE I.Q.

*Here's a little more mental batting practice for all you
armchair umpires out there. Batter up! Play ball!*

**1. What happens when a batter fails to bat in his proper turn in
the batting order?**

a) As soon as an improper batter swings at a pitch in the proper
batter's place, the umpire must call the original batter out.

b) The rules require that the umpire do nothing on his own initiative. The defending team must call the violation to the umpire's
attention, and they must do so before a pitch is made to the next
batter. As soon as a pitch is made to the batter that follows the
improper batter, the improper batter is considered a proper batter
and the results of his at-bat become legal.

c) The defending team has 24 hours after the end of the game to
call an improper batting order to the umpire's attention. If the
game has a bearing on the league championship, it must be replayed
from the point where the improper batter comes up to bat.

**2. If a ball is hit in the direction of the dugout, can a fielder
enter the dugout to catch it?**

a) Yes.

b) No, but if a player already in the dugout catches the ball, even
if he's on the batter's team, the catch counts and the batter is out.

c) No. The fielder can reach into the dugout to catch the ball, but
if he steps foot inside the dugout, the catch doesn't count.

**3. What happens if the batter hits a ball while one or both feet
are entirely outside the batter's box?**

a) Strike!

b) Out!

c) The umpire gives him a warning; if the batter does it a second
time, he is ejected from the game.

**4. When can an umpire penalize a batter for using an illegal
altered bat?**

In 2007 Ichiro Suzuki hit the first inside-the-park home run in All-Star Game history.

a) *Any time* the umpire discovers that a player owns such a bat or has one in his possession, even if the discovery is made between games or on days off.

b) If the player brings one into the ballpark during a game. This rule applies even if he leaves it in his car in the parking lot.

c) When he carries the altered bat into the batter's box for his turn at bat.

5. There are two outs and the bases are loaded. The batter is walked to first and the runner on third walks home. But the runner on second, instead of stopping at third, runs for home and is tagged out on the attempt. Does the run walked in by the the runner on third still count?

a) Yes.

b) No.

c) In the National League, yes; in the American League, no. In the World Series and the All-Star Game, it's decided by a coin toss.

6. What's the penalty if a fielder deliberately throws his glove at a fair ball or touches a fair ball with his cap, mask, or "any part of his uniform detached from its proper place on his person?"

a) Each runner, including the batter-runner, may advance two bases.

b) Each runner, including the batter-runner, may advance three bases.

c) The fielder is ejected from the game. The batter-runner and other runners do not advance any bases.

7. It's the bottom of the ninth inning, the score is tied, and there's a runner on first. The batter hits a ball out of the park for the winning run. The runner on first, thinking that the game is over, walks directly toward the dugout and is called out "for abandoning his effort to touch the next base." Does the home run still count?

a) Yes.

b) No.

c) Maybe. If there are fewer than two outs, yes. If there are two outs, the runner's out makes three outs. The inning is over and the score is still tied.

8. There are two outs when two runners cross home plate. If the first runner fails to touch home plate and is called out, or is tagged out when he attempts to return and touch the base, does the second runner's run count?

a) Yes.

b) No.

c) Maybe—it depends on the circumstances.

9. After receiving the ball, how much time does the pitcher have to deliver his next pitch when the bases are unoccupied?

a) There's no set time limit, but if he delays for too long the umpire will tell him to hurry up.

b) 12 seconds.

c) One minute.

10. What happens when the pitcher accidentally drops the ball while he's got his foot on the pitching rubber?

a) It counts as a "balk" and all runners may advance one base.

b) It counts as a ball. If it's the fourth ball, the batter walks to first base.

c) Nothing—the pitcher just picks up the ball and prepares for his next pitch.

For the answers, turn to page 284.

*   *   *

MR. MODESTY

Ted Williams was one of the best all-around baseball players in history. He was also a decorated pilot in World War II, and even a champion fisherman. In an interview with Williams, sportscaster Bob Costas asked him if he realized he was "in real life, the type of American hero John Wayne portrayed in his movies." Williams's response: "Yeah, I know."

The right-field wall in PNC Park (Pittsburgh) is 21' high, a tribute to Roberto Clemente, #21.

BRAINIACS

*Some are funny on purpose, others by accident—
but they'll all make you scratch your head.*

"The ball became the same color as the sky, so I wasn't able to see it. I was sending mental signals for the ball not to come my way, because during that time of day it's impossible for me to see the ball. So I lacked mental signals. Usually, I don't send mental signals, so because this is the first time, I thought, please don't come my way."

> **—Ichiro Suzuki, after missing a routine fly ball**

"I lost it in the sun."

> **—Billy Loes, Brooklyn Dodgers pitcher, after fumbling a grounder**

"Therapy is a good thing. It can be therapeutic."

> **—Alex Rodriguez**

"I don't get upset over things I can't control, because if I can't control them there's no use getting upset. And I don't get upset over the things I can control, because if I can control them there's no use in getting upset."

> **—Mickey Rivers**

"Most people are dead at my age, anyway. You can look it up."

> **—Casey Stengel**

"Any time I've taken the mound, it's always been the same old Samson-and-Goliath story written about me."

> **—Randy Johnson, Arizona Diamondbacks**

"They've got so many Latin players we're going to have to get a Latin instructor up here."

> **—Phil Rizzuto**

"It's better than my wedding ring! You can always get wedding rings."

> **—Johnny Damon, Red Sox, on his World Series ring**

"The good Lord was good to me. He gave me a strong body, a good right arm, and a weak mind."

> **—Dizzy Dean**

"I thank God for giving me lots of stuff."

> **—Manny Ramirez, Red Sox**

Most strikeouts thrown in one game: 21, by Washington's Tom Cheney, in 16 innings (1962).

LITTLE-KNOWN FIRSTS

Our second list of baseball firsts that don't always make the record books.

• First spring training game broadcast on national television: March 5, 1988, when NBC aired a Dodgers/Yankees game from Fort Lauderdale, Florida.

• Who's the first (and so far, only) player to hit a homer into three different bodies of water? Luis Gonzalez. In April 2000, he hit one into the pool of Phoenix's Bank One Ballpark. Three months later he landed one in McCovey Cove in San Francisco. And seven years after that, he clubbed one into Tampa Bay's ray pool.

• First home run of the 20th century: Phillies shortstop Monte Cross hit a three-run blast against the Boston Beaneaters on April 19, 1900. (The last homer of the century was hit by the Yankees' Jim Leyritz on October 27, 1999.)

• First time a 700+ home run hitter faced a pitcher with 300+ wins: August 14, 2006, when the Giants' Barry Bonds went 0 for 3 against the Dodgers' Greg Maddux.

• First time fans could watch an entire major league game live on the Internet: August 26, 2002, at 1:00 p.m. EST (Rangers at Yankees).

• First U.S. president to witness a triple play: President Richard Nixon, on July 15, 1969. The Tigers pulled it off against the Washington Senators.

• In 1971 a computer programmer named Don Daglow created the first baseball game for the computer. It was called *Baseball* and is now on display at the Baseball Hall of Fame.

• What's so quirky about July 28, 2006? It was the first time a hitter whose last name starts with "Q" (Carlos Quentin of the Diamondbacks) homered off of a pitcher whose last name also starts with "Q" (Chad Qualls of the Astros).

• First player to earn $100,000 a year: Hank Greenberg (1947). First player to earn $500,000 a year: Mike Schmidt (1977). First $1 million man: Nolan Ryan (1979).

Pete Rose played 500 or more games in each of five positions, the only player to do so.

BASEBALL
BY THE LETTERS

Trivia, jargon, odd facts, and more…from A all the way home to Z.

A **is for…ACE**, or a team's best starting pitcher. Most people think the term is derived from the highest-value card in a deck of playing cards, but according to baseball legend, it's not. In 1869 the Cincinnati Red Stockings became the first all-professional baseball team and went on a nationwide tour to promote themselves, playing any challengers from the amateur leagues. They had an amazing record of 57–0, largely on the strength of their best pitcher, who pitched more than 70% of the team's innings. His name: Asa Brainard. Legend has it that other teams began to referring to their best pitchers as "their Asa's," and that that was eventually shortened to "Ace."

B is for…BATTING CAGE, the screen placed around the back and sides of home plate during batting practice. The Baseball Hall of Fame gives credit for its invention to minor league catcher Willington Titus, who constructed a simple backstop in 1907 so he wouldn't have to chase foul balls and wild pitches during practice. (It wasn't called a "batting cage" until 1952.)

C is for…CHARLEY HORSE, coined by baseballers around 1885. It refers to a painful cramp, usually in a thigh muscle, but also used generally for any leg or arm cramp. One theory says it refers to a horse named Charley—presumably bet on by baseball players—who suffered a leg injury during a race. Another says it refers to Hall of Fame pitcher Charley Radbourne, nicknamed "Old Hoss." He regularly suffered cramps, and charley horse was somehow derived from "Charley" and "Hoss."

D is for…DIAMOND, the term for the infield formed by the four bases, although some people will tell you that it's really a square (a square on its side is still a square). It was first called a "diamond" in 1875, long after the sport was invented—it was

---

On October 2, 1920, the Reds took 2 of 3 games in the only tripleheader of the 20th century.

just a "field" before that—because it resembles the diamonds on playing cards.

E is for...EEPHUS PITCH, developed by pitcher Truett Banks "Rip" Sewell of the Pittsburgh Pirates in 1941. He hurt his foot in a hunting accident that year and lost a lot of speed in his pitches, so he added to his arsenal a very high, slow, blooper pitch that would sometimes reach a height of 25 feet. It so upset the batters' timing, and so tempted them to try to knock it out of the park, that Sewell actually did quite well with it. He used it hundreds of times over the rest of his career—and it was taken for a home run only once (by Ted Williams in the 1946 All-Star Game...and only because Sewell announced that he was going to throw it again after Williams had just whiffed on one). Why was it called the "Eephus pitch"? After the first time he used it manager Frankie Frisch asked Sewell what he called it. Teammate Maurice Van Robays said, "That's an Eephus pitch." Frisch asked him what an eephus was. "Eephus ain't nothin'," Robays replied—and the name stuck. A few other pitchers have used the Eephus through the years, including Bill "Spaceman" Lee in the 1970s, and Dave LaRoche in the 1980s (although LaRoche called his "LaLob").

F is for...FOUL TIP, a term often used incorrectly by fans and sportscasters alike. According to the official rules, a foul tip is a ball that goes sharply and directly from the batter's bat to the glove or hand of the catcher and is caught. If it's dropped, it's simply a foul. Unlike any ordinary foul ball that's caught by a catcher (or anyone else), it is not automatically recorded as an out. If there are no strikes on the batter, or just one, it's a strike. If it's the third strike—then it's an out. Also, it remains a live ball, so runners may attempt to advance, but, as is more often the case, the catcher may use it to try to throw a runner out.

G is for...GOLDEN SOMBRERO, a slang term for striking out four times in a single game, as in, "He gets the golden sombrero tonight." It comes from the hockey term "hat trick," referring to a feat repeated three times. Since four is more than three, a *large* hat is used for the baseball feat. A five-strikeout game is a "platinum sombrero"; six-strikeouts make a "titanium sombrero," which has happened only eight times in history—all in extra-inning games.

H is for...HOMER. No, not Homer Simpson, and not the nickname for a home run. This term refers to any baseball announcer who breaks the unspoken rule that they remain neutral and not favor their team. (Though it's meant as a pejorative, many fans actually prefer homers to more impartial announcers.) Famous homer moment: On October 8, 2007, while covering the New York/Cleveland division series, Yankees radio announcer Suzyn Waldman lost her cool when the Yanks lost, 3 games to 1, and cried on the air.

I is for...INNING. It comes from the Old English verb "to in," meaning "to put in, enclose, or include." It came into sports use around 1735 in the British game cricket, and referred to a player's turn at bat, or a player's "in." Baseball's original 1845 rules contained neither the word "inning" nor a rule about how many must be played in a full game. In 1857 the rules changed, and nine innings of play were required for a complete game.

J is for...JENNINGS, as in Hughie Ambrose Jennings, who holds the most painful record in baseball history: the most times hit by a pitch. Over a 17-year career between 1891 and 1918, Jennings faced a pitcher 4,904 times...and he got beaned 287 times. That's a .171 hitting average—*getting* hit, that is. Best part: His nickname was "Ee-Yah" (probably because he yelled it so often).

K is for...K. Why do they use the letter K to represent strikeouts? Because the letter Z was too tired (Ba-dum). Actually, in 1861 baseball writer Henry Chadwick (see page 11) developed the "box-score" system we know today, where "1" denotes a pitcher, "2" a catcher, "3" the first basemen, and so on. He also came up with "HR" for home run, "BB" for base on balls—and "K" for strikeout. Why? Because "S" was already being used for "single." The word "strikeout" didn't come into existence until 1887; before then the term was "struck," making his choice of its last letter—"K"—a little more understandable.

L is for...LINEUP, another word invented in baseball. It's been used to refer to a team's nine players for a specific game since at least 1889 (*before* police departments started using it).

Davy Force of the Philadelphia Athletics is credited with the first assist, in 1876.

M is for...MURDERER'S ROW, the nickname of the Yankees teams of the late 1920s, more specifically the 1927 team that included Babe Ruth and Lou Gehrig, considered one of the greatest teams in the sport's history. Gehrig hit 47 home runs that year and Ruth hit 60, and they were only two of the five players on the team who batted over .330 that year. They won 110 games (still fifth on the all-time list), won the American League pennant by 19 games, and swept the Pittsburgh Pirates in the World Series. But the term was actually coined when Ruth still played for the Red Sox—and Gehrig was just 15 years old. In 1918 a sportswriter used it to describe that year's Yankee team, which included mostly forgotten stars like Frank "Home Run" Baker and Wally Pipp—a team that won only 60 games and didn't make it to the Series.

N is for...NICE GUYS FINISH LAST, a phrase coined by Brooklyn Dodgers manager Leo Durocher on July 6, 1946, and familiar worldwide today. His actual quote, according to his autobiography: "Take a look at them. All nice guys. They'll finish last. Nice guys. Finish last." (He was referring to the 1946 New York Giants. They finished last.)

O is for...ON THE INTERSTATE, a term that refers to someone batting between .100 and .199, because the numbers, especially when listed on older-style scoreboards, look like the common abbreviations for interstate highways, such as I-40 or I-95. It is not, of course, a compliment to be "on the interstate," and players who stay there too long may be literally on the interstate...to a minor league team.

P is for...PICKOFF, describing when a pitcher throws an on-base player out, usually a man on first base. The term has been in use since at least 1939. A pickoff move is generally easier and more successful for left-handed pitchers, who don't have to twirl to throw to first base, as shown by the fact that the all-time pickoff leader (since record-keeping began in 1957) is Steve Carlton—also known as "Lefty"—with 144 in his career. The next four pitchers on the list are Jerry Koosman, Mark Langston, Andy Pettitte, and Kenny Rogers, all lefties.

Q is for...QUINN, as in Paddy Quinn, the first person in the history of professional baseball...whose last name started with the letter "Q." Quinn started his pro career on July 26, 1871, as a catcher for the Fort Wayne Kekiongas and finished with the Chicago White Stockings in 1877. (Number of baseball players in major league history with names ending with the letter "Q": 42, including five Quinlans, three Queens, two Quirks, two Quicks, one Quest, and one Quisenberry.)

R is for...ROOT! as in "Root, root, root, for the home team..." It was coined by a baseball writer in 1889 and is believed to come from another meaning of root: "to work or study hard," which dates back to the 1850s. **Extra:** R is also for "rhubarb," which used to be a common term for a baseball fight or argument. The origin is uncertain, but it dates back to at least 1938 and may be related to the practice of stage actors repeating the word "rhubarb" to mimic the sound of a murmuring crowd.

S is for...SECOND-GUESSER, coined in the 1930s to refer to any baseball fan who questions the actions of players, managers, or umpires. By the 1940s, it had evolved into the commonly used verb "to second-guess," meaning to criticize someone's actions after the results of those actions are known.

T is for...TAG UP, referring to when a base runner returns to the base he occupies after a fly ball is hit, and, in accordance with the rules, gets ready to run after the ball is caught. Example: "Pujols tags up on third and gets ready to take off for home plate." The word "tag" alone can also mean to get an out by touching a runner with the glove or hand with the ball in it. Its use goes back to at least 1907.

U is for...UNCLE CHARLIE, a nickname for a very well-executed curveball. The exact origin is unknown, but according to etymologist Paul Dickson it came from CB radio lingo in 1970s. He says the "c" sound in "uncle" and the "r" sound in 'Charlie" suggested the "c" and the "r" sounds in "curve."

V is for...VORP, or *Value Over Replacement Player*, a statistics

system for hitters and pitchers invented by baseball writer and mathematician Keith Woolner in the 1990s. Very basically: A player's value is determined by comparing his actual stats to the stats of an imagined "replacement-level" player. According to Woolner, "replacement level is the expected level of performance the average team can obtain if it needs to replace a starting player at minimal cost." It's complicated, but it has become a very popular system of player rating for fans and for teams. Top VORP hitter in 2007: Yankee third baseman Alex Rodriguez, with a rating of 96.6, which means that in hitting and base-stealing terms, he was 96.6 runs better than a replacement-level third baseman in the major leagues. (*Worst* VORP hitter in 2007: Twins third baseman Nick Punto, with a rating of -27.1.)

W is for…WW. Onetime Yankee shortstop Phil Rizzuto is now better known for his 40-year career as a Yankees announcer. After one game he called, someone noticed a strange entry in his scorecard…the letters "WW." What did that stand for? Rizzuto's answer: "Wasn't Watching." He is said to have used it on numerous occasions, and it's now regularly used by non-official scorekeepers when they miss a play.

X is for…XEROPHTHALMIA, which, according to the U.S. National Library of Medicine, is defined as "dry-eye syndrome," characterized as a deficiency of tear production attributed to a lack of vitamin A. Some experts say it's the reason there's no crying in baseball. (Okay, we made that last part up—but there aren't a lot of baseball words that begin with "X.")

Y is for…YELLOW HAMMER, jargon for a curveball that drops sharply. It's said to be named after the yellowhammer, the state bird of Alabama, which is known for its quick darting and diving flight movements.

Z is for…BARRY ZITO. The three-time All-Star once said, "When I'm pitching, it's like I'm in a nice little ballet. Everything is going slow all around me. It's very peaceful." Ahhh.

Barry Zito's uncle is actor Patrick Duffy, who starred in *Dallas*.

AY, THERE'S THE RUBE

One of baseball's early stars, Rube Waddell had pitching abilities that were matched only by the great Cy Young. Yet today Waddell is mostly forgotten. Here's the story of one of baseball's best athletes—and strangest characters.

POSTER BOY

The 1902 Philadelphia A's drew twice as many fans as the previous year's team. One of the biggest attractions was the team's newest acquisition—a hard-throwing, unpredictable pitcher named Rube Waddell. A few days before he was scheduled to start, posters went up all over town advertising his odd exploits, enticing fans to go out to the park just to see what "the Rube" would do next. Maybe he'd run through the stands begging for candy and picking fights with fans. Or maybe he'd be found on the sidewalk outside the ball park playing marbles with a group of kids. Or perhaps he'd perform cartwheels on his way back to the dugout after striking out the side.

No one quite knew what to make of George Edward Waddell. Born in Bradford, Pennsylvania, in 1876, he's been described by historians over the years as "autistic," "mentally retarded," "Peter Pan," and even "a drunk Forrest Gump." Or as A's manager Connie Mack put it: "The Rube had a two-million dollar body and a two-cent head." And connected to that two-million dollar body was one of the best left arms in the history of the game.

A LOOSE CANNON

During the dead ball era, most pitchers were just throwers, tasked with getting the ball over the plate so the batters could slap it into play. Not Waddell. At 6'1" and 200 pounds, he frightened hitters. He'd yell animal noises and then blast the ball right by them. In Waddell's minor league days, he once told his defensive team to stay on the bench, then went out alone...and struck out the side. He tried it again at an exhibition game in the majors, but because the rules dictated that nine players must be on the field, Waddell told his teammates to sit down in the grass...while he struck out the side.

Waddell's impressive arsenal included a blistering fastball, a

---

In 1970 Don Drysdale appeared on *The Brady Bunch*—he taught Greg how to throw a fastball.

screwball, and a sharp-breaking curve that was way ahead of its time. He used what Mack described as "the most perfect overhand delivery I have ever seen on a lefthander" to rack up a career 2,316 strikeouts, a 2.16 ERA, and 50 shutouts. He led his league in strikeouts for six consecutive years. To this day, Waddell holds the A.L. single-season strikeout record for a lefty, with 349. The only pitcher in either league who equalled him in strikeout power was Cy Young (when Young threw his perfect game in 1904, Waddell was the opposing pitcher and lost 3–0).

So if the Rube was so dominating, how come it's called the Cy Young Award and not the Rube Waddell Award? And how could a pitcher who specialized in strikeouts lose so many games? (His career record was 193–143.) The problem was that, between his childlike qualities and legendary thirst for alcohol, Waddell was nearly impossible to manage. Only one man, Connie Mack, was (somewhat) able to keep the Rube under control.

RUBE AND MACK
Mack first managed Waddell briefly in Milwaukee in 1900, but just as with the Rube's previous coaches, Mack had trouble putting up with his quirks. Two years later, though, Mack was so desperate for good pitching in Philadelphia that he sent two Pinkerton detectives to find Waddell (who had walked out on the Chicago Orphans to play baseball with a group of traveling barnstormers) and bring him to Philadelphia. The agents found Waddell in California, pitching for the Los Angeles Loo Loos, and put him on a train to Philadelphia.

Under Mack's watchful eye, Waddell helped the Athletics win the 1902 American League pennant by striking out 210 batters on his way to a 24–7 record in only 33 starts. Waddell had his best years in Philadelphia, becoming a fan favorite and adding the spark to a pitching rotation that also included future Hall of Fame pitchers Eddie Plank and Chief Bender. But Mack had his hands full keeping Waddell focused on pitching.

• Waddell loved fishing. After he'd pitched (and won) a 17-inning game, the first game of a doubleheader, Mack convinced him to pitch in the second game (a shortened 5-inning game) by promising an all-expenses-paid, three-day fishing trip. Result: Waddell went out and pitched a one-hit shutout.

• Mack could deal with the Rube's fishing mania; it was the alligator wrestling that scared him. Waddell discovered the "sport" during spring training in Florida…and was reportedly very good at it. But instead of trying to bribe him into giving it up, Mack simply threatened to fire Waddell if he didn't quit. (He quit.)

• Dealing with Waddell was often less like managing and more like keeping tabs on a toddler. For example, the only safe way to keep Waddell close to the team was to pay his salary in small installments. When Ossie Schreckengost, Waddell's catcher and roommate, threatened to quit unless Waddell stopped eating Animal Crackers in bed (teams saved money by making players share a bed on the road), Mack added an "Animal Crackers clause" to Waddell's contract, forbidding the pitcher to eat cookies in bed.

• Another constant concern for Mack: Waddell's desire to be a hero   which was fine, except that he often had no regard for his own safety. In the space of three days in 1905, Waddell stopped a fire in a crowded department store by picking up a flaming oil stove and carrying it outside, assaulted his father-in-law with an iron, saved the life of an injured teammate by carrying him all the way to the hospital, and was arrested for bigamy (he "forgot" to divorce his first wife before marrying his second).

A HERO'S DEMISE

But it wasn't an alligator or a collapsing building that led to the end of Waddell's career; it was a playful wrestling match for a teammate's straw hat in 1905. Waddell fell on his throwing arm and it immediately stiffened up. The timing couldn't have been worse—the A's were about to play in the World Series, which Waddell was forced to sit out. After the New York Giants trounced the A's, rumors began circulating that Waddell had faked the injury after accepting a $17,000 bribe from a gambling ring. Mack vehemently denied this for the rest of his life: "Money meant nothing, glory everything, to him."

Waddell's shoulder never fully healed and his pitching career steadily dwindled. Reluctantly, Mack released him in 1908. (The A's home attendance dropped 30%.)

Waddell's youthful spark briefly returned in 1911 when the 34-year-old pitcher joined the minor league Minneapolis Millers and won 20 games. Still too erratic to find a job on a major league

Actor William Bendix (Babe Ruth in *The Babe Ruth Story*) was once a batboy for the Yankees.

team, Waddell was living on his manager's farm in Hickman, Kentucky, in January 1913 when a dike holding back the Mississippi River broke and released floodwaters into the small town. Waddell stood in nearly freezing water for 13 hours, stacking sandbags in an effort to rebuild the dike. He helped save the town but contracted a severe cold, which led to pneumonia, and then to tuberculosis. Waddell never fully recovered. He tried to keep on pitching, but by this point was only a shadow of his former self. On April Fool's Day 1914, Waddell, down to 130 pounds and living in a tuberculosis sanitarium, died at the age of 37.

A decade later, Waddell's impact on the game was put into perspective by the *Sporting News*: "No player that ever lived, not even Babe Ruth, has so captured the affections of the fans of his day as did Waddell." He was inducted into the Baseball Hall of Fame in 1946.

*   *   *

A FEW MORE OF RUBE WADDELL'S ANTICS

• One time during spring training in Jacksonville, Florida, the Rube went missing on his pitching day. He was found a few hours later leading a minstrel parade down Main Street.

• Opposing teams would sometimes bring toys—such as those little drumming monkeys—and play with them in the dugout while Waddell was on the mound, trying to distract him and take his focus off the game. (The tactic often worked.)

• After being fined $100 on a road trip, Waddell demanded to know why. He was told it was for that "disgraceful hotel episode in Detroit." To which Waddell responded, "You're a liar! There ain't no Hotel Episode in Detroit!"

• After besting Cy Young in a 20-inning game in 1905, Waddell traded the "game ball" for free beers at a local bar. A few weeks later he traded another "game ball"—from the same game—for free beers. Legend has it that there are more than 50 scuffed-up baseballs out there, all claiming to be the genuine Cy Young vs. Rube Waddell game ball.

THE BIRTH OF BASEBALL, PART III

By 1860 the basic rules for baseball had been set (see page 159). After that, most changes in the game took place not on the field, but behind closed doors.

THE WAR YEARS

Even though baseball was growing more popular among the middle class in the Northeast and Midwest, it wasn't the foremost thought on most Americans' minds as the 1850s drew to a close. The United States was in crisis—the Southern states were threatening to secede, and the Civil War was imminent. But instead of fading away, baseball became even more popular during the war. At prisoner-of-war camps in the North, Union soldiers taught the game to Confederates, while Yankee prisoners in the South taught it to their Rebel captors.

This introduced baseball to a whole new class of players. Up until then, teams were primarily made up of doctors, lawyers, and shopkeepers who could afford to take afternoons off. During the war, almost everyone had time to play, regardless of economic status. Even out on the front lines, troops played baseball during long days of waiting for their next battle. In a letter home to his family, Union soldier Alpheris B. Parker of the 10th Massachusetts wrote: "The parade ground has been a busy place for a week or so past, ball-playing having become a mania in camp. Officer and men forget, for a time, the differences in rank and indulge in the invigorating sport with a schoolboy's ardor."

BA$EBALL

Even before the Civil War ended in 1865, a few players were getting paid—the first may have been A. J. Reach, who played second base for the Brooklyn Eckfords at the Union Grounds in New Yok City, the first enclosed ballpark that charged admission. But people weren't accustomed to the concept of paying athletes to play a game—amateurism was considered "noble." So those first payments were made in secret...but not for long. "In the late 1860s, advancing skills led to heightened appetites for victory," writes John Thorn in his book *The Game for All America*, "which inevitably led to *sub rosa* [secret] payments and, by 1870, rampant professionalism." The first openly salaried team was the 1869 Cincinnati Red Stockings, who went undefeated and made it no secret that their players were paid.

And just as increased skills had led to salaries, the salaries, in turn, resulted in to an even *more* competitive game on the field. Batters started hitting the ball harder, base runners started stealing bases, and a few pitchers even started trying to strike hitters out. Off the field, however, baseball was being transformed in smoke-filled rooms by wealthy men, some of whom loved the game, and some of whom just saw dollar signs.

THE ASSOCIATION IN CHAOS

This "rampant professionalism" rendered the National Association of Base Ball Players obsolete—most teams were going pro. So in 1871, a new league was formed, the National Association of *Professional* Baseball Players, and it had problems from the very beginning. Without a central governing body, the individual teams couldn't maintain control over basic necessities of the game such as consistent rules, schedules, and venues. And the teams didn't even have to be that good—they just needed to pay the $10 entrance fee, giving many cities multiple teams of varying quality.

It was a mess…but it wasn't a failure. "It's easy now to criticize the way the N.A. was set up," says sports historian Ralph Hickok. "But it must be remembered that this group of clubs was trying to do something totally new, so it's not surprising that this first attempt was far from perfect. When the National League replaced the N.A. in 1876, it avoided many of the mistakes that the association had made. But it also built on the foundation that the association had laid down." The man who had the biggest part in building upon that foundation was the president of the Chicago White Stockings, William A. Hulbert.

DEAD ENDS

Hulbert was a no-nonsense oil baron who wanted to construct a strong—and profitable—team in Chicago, which was still rebuilding after the great fire of 1871. Yet he met resistance at every turn.

He was frustrated by eastern teams that were out of the pennant race deciding at the last minute not to make the trip to Chicago—or, worse, not showing up after Hulbert's team had traveled all the way to *their* towns. As Hulbert's complaints were repeatedly ignored by his eastern counterparts, he surmised—correctly—that they were conspiring to keep the best players in the N.A.'s four main cities: New York, Philadelphia, Boston, and Hartford. When Hulbert's star shortstop, Davy Force, announced that he was leaving to play for the Philadelphia Athletics, Hulbert demanded that the N.A. put a stop to "contract jumpers"—players who sold their services to the highest bidder. Again, he received no response.

That was the last straw. Hulbert needed more power to fight the system, and to get that, he needed a powerful ball team. So he did some back-door dealing of his own and stole Cap Anson, the game's first great hitter, from Philadelphia. Hulbert then acquired four players—including pitcher Al Spalding—from the Boston Red Stockings, the reigning dynasty that had monopolized the best talent and won four straight N.A. pennants.

MAJOR LEAGUE BASEBALL

Hulbert had an ulterior motive: He wanted to end the reign of the N.A. and form a new league, one run by a central governing board that would preserve the integrity of the game. In what amounted to a coup d'etat, Hulbert first secured the support of three other western teams—the Cincinnati Red Stockings, the St. Louis Brown Stockings, and the Louisville Grays—and then called for a meeting with the owners of the New York Mutuals, the Philadelphia Athletics, and the Boston Red Stockings. On February 2, 1876, at the Grand Central Hotel in New York City, the other owners gave in to Hulbert's demands, marking the beginning of the National League of Base Ball Clubs (note the substitution of "Clubs" for "Players").

The N.L. began with four eastern and four western teams, and for the first time their schedules were actually set before the season started. No city with fewer than 75,000 people could join the league, and only one team was allowed per city. Hulbert strove to keep the new league "pure" by turning down invitations to play games against "minor league" teams. He also banned drinking, gambling, and playing on Sundays.

Perhaps most importantly, Hulbert played a major part in creating baseball's first "reserve clause." This was designed to put a limit on salaries—each club's largest expense, and one that made it difficult for them to keep solvent. But the reserve clause also put an end to contract jumping. If a player was named in his team's reserve clause, the only way he could switch teams was to be traded or released. No other team could sign him, ensuring that a club's best talent would remain with that club for years. When it was enacted in 1879, only five players per team were given a reserve clause, but that number soon rose. The players didn't like it (some even compared it to slavery), but without the reserve clause the National League might not have lasted into the new century.

OFF AND RUNNING...

With that, the foundation of major league baseball was laid. It was off to a rocky start, as gambling scandals, inconsistent rules, and umpire abuse marred the first 25 years of the National League. But the league was able to weather those storms—as it would when, in 1902, the upstart American League threatened the "Senior Circuit" for baseball supremacy. After a tense season, the first World Series took place in 1903...but few people acknowledged its validity. After two more tense years of threats, boycotts, and lawsuits, the first *actual* World Series took place in 1905. The N.L. New York Giants defeated the A.L. Philadelphia Athletics. And with *that*, Major League Baseball—as we know it today—was born.

That's been the cycle of baseball ever since: Rule changes and subsequent realignments shake things up, but the game keeps going. Scandals come and go, and some even leave a nasty stain, but none has been catastrophic enough to put an end to baseball altogether. It just goes to show that no matter how much the less-savory aspects of baseball threaten to kill the game, it's impossible to stop a bunch of grown men from hitting a little ball with a stick and then chasing it around a field...while thousands of people cheer them on.

*   *   *

"Baseball never had no 'fadder'; it jest growed."

—Henry Chadwick

Honus Wagner was the first player to have his signature branded into a Louisville Slugger (1905).

THE STRANGE FATE OF TED'S HEAD

Ted Williams's lifelong dream was to be known as "the greatest hitter who ever lived." It's sad, then, that today many people know him as "that baseball player who got cryonically frozen."

HEADING FOR HOME

In the summer of 2001, some old friends went to Hernando, Florida, to pay a visit to Ted Williams, the legendary Red Sox slugger and the last major league player to bat over .400. The "Splendid Splinter" was 83 years old and in poor health; in recent years he'd battled heart disease, strokes, and a broken hip. Now nearly blind, Williams required round-the-clock nursing care and could only get around with the aid of a walker. But his spirits were high as he visited with his friends, and when one of them pointed to a photograph of Slugger, a beloved Dalmatian that had died in 1998, Williams told them that he was saving the dog's ashes so that when he died, they could be scattered together in the waters at one of his favorite fishing spots.

The old ballplayer's health deteriorated further over the next year, and on July 5, 2002, he died. Just as he'd told his his friends, his will instructed that his remains "be cremated and sprinkled at sea off the coast of Florida where the water is very deep."

COLD STORAGE

It wasn't to be. Even as Williams lay dying, a "standby team" dispatched by an organization called the Alcor Life Extension Foundation was at his bedside, waiting patiently for him to breathe his last. Within moments of his being declared dead at 8:49 a.m., the team sprang into action, pumping his body full of blood thinners and packing it in a body bag filled with dry ice for the trip to a nearby airport, where a chartered jet stood by to take it to Alcor headquarters in Scottsdale, Arizona. By 11:30 p.m. Williams's body was stretched out on the Alcor operating table. There, in a procedure lasting 37 minutes, a surgeon decapitated the corpse so that head and body could be frozen separately in "dewars," high-tech

steel thermoses filled with liquid nitrogen. Over the next several days, his head and body were slowly chilled to -320°F, and they've been floating in what Alcor calls "long-term storage" ever since. Williams's head reportedly sits in a dewar on a shelf; the rest of his body floats in a much larger dewar several feet away.

CRYONICS 101

The purpose of freezing bodies "cryonically," as advocates call it, is to halt decay and preserve the body in as intact a form as possible, in the hope that someday medicine will be able to cure the dead person's illnesses and reverse the aging process. When that day comes, the person can be thawed out, resuscitated, and restored to a second youthful, vigorous life.

The cryonics movement has been dismissed by mainstream scientists as a hopeless, pseudoscientific pipe dream. Even if cryonic freezing is perfected at some point in the future, critics argue that modern techniques are so primitive and toxic, and inflict so much irreversible damage, that resuscitation of people frozen today will likely never be possible. Even Alcor requires clients to sign forms acknowledging that resuscitation may never happen...but that hasn't stopped more than 800 living people from signing up to be cryonically frozen when they die. As of 2007, approximately 80 of them have died and been put into long-term storage at Alcor's facilities in Scottsdale. Scores more have signed up for similar procedures at other cryonic organizations in the United States and Europe. Worldwide, it's estimated that fewer than 500 people have been cryonically frozen so far, but thousands more customers are ready to go the moment their "first life cycle," as cryonics enthusiasts put it, comes to an end.

SON OF A GUN

So how did Ted Williams end up at Alcor? We'll probably never know for certain whether he changed his mind in the final months of his life and opted for cryonic preservation without updating his will, as his son John-Henry Williams claimed, or if John-Henry, acting as his father's power of attorney, had the old man frozen against his wishes.

John-Henry, who was 33 at the time of his father's death, was Ted's middle child and only son, one of two children he fathered with Dolores Wettach, his third wife. For most of John-Henry's life, he and his father had not been close. Ted and Dolores divorced when the boy was only four, and he and his sister Claudia were raised by Dolores on her family's farm in Vermont. Father and son began to grow closer in the early 1990s when John-Henry, fresh out of college, stepped in to manage his father's business affairs after Ted, then in his mid-70s, was swindled out of millions of dollars by a business partner who turned out to be a con man.

WHO'S IN CHARGE?

Over the next few years, John-Henry gradually took control over nearly every aspect of the old ballplayer's life, shutting out many friends, family, and loved ones in the process. He turned his father into a one-man sports memorabilia franchise, badgering him to spend hours a day autographing photos, jerseys, baseballs, bats, and other merchandise—entire cases of the stuff, day in, day out, even after Ted's health began to fail. John-Henry also filled his father's schedule with more paid public appearances at card shows and other events than Ted had ever attended before.

At the time, Ted was one of the biggest names on the card show circuit—photos signed by him routinely sold for $300, baseballs went for $400, bats for $800, and jerseys for $1,000. John-Henry claimed that pushing his father to sign hundreds of signatures a day was therapeutic, and that it kept the old man's mind on baseball. Ted's home-care nurses thought he was being abused, but when they spoke out John-Henry fired them on the spot.

HANDS OFF

When the old slugger was hospitalized in January 2001 for complications from open-heart surgery, John-Henry gave strict instructions that the nurses not insert IVs into his right arm or do anything else that might impair that arm's range of motion.

Then, when Ted was released and began to receive physical therapy at home, "all of the exercises, all of the work, were being done to restore strength and mobility to his right hand," Leigh Montville writes in *Ted Williams: The Biography of an American Hero*. Why focus so much attention on the right hand? "So he'll be able to sign autographs again," John-Henry explained.

ANOTHER BRIGHT IDEA

It was at about this time that Ted Williams's oldest daughter, Barbara Joyce (Bobby-Jo) Ferrell, says that her half brother John-Henry came to her with an idea of how to keep the income flowing in long after their father was no longer able to sign his name. "Have you ever heard of cryonics?" she says John-Henry asked her. "Wouldn't it be neat to sell Dad's DNA? There are lots of people who would pay big bucks to have all these little Ted Williamses running around." Bobby-Jo recoiled at the thought and called John-Henry "insane." Her concerns did not diminish when John-Henry assured her, "We don't have to take Ted's whole body. We can just take the head."

LIKE DAUGHTER, LIKE FATHER

Leigh Montville describes how a home-care nurse overheard John-Henry pitching cryonics to his father more than a year before the old man died. "You're outta your %@#&! mind," Ted reportedly told his son. "What about just your head?" John-Henry asked. Ted's angry response, as he walked back to his room: "%@#& you!" (That nurse was fired in May 2001.)

It isn't clear whether John-Henry really did manage to sell his father on the merits of cryonics in the last year of his life, or if Ted's wish to be cremated and scattered at sea were simply ignored. Ted Williams never met with Alcor representatives, and he never signed their Consent for Cryonic Suspension form, either. John-Henry, acting as power of attorney, signed it for Ted after his death, even though his power of attorney ended when Williams died.

The only written evidence that John-Henry ever presented to support his claim that his father had opted for cryonic freezing was an oil-stained note, handwritten in block letters, that he produced three weeks after Ted's death. The note read:

> 11-2-00 JHW, Claudia and Dad all agree to be put into bio-stasis after we die. This is what we want, to be able to be together in the future, even if it is only a chance.
>
> John-Henry Williams
> Ted Williams
> Claudia Williams

SOMETHING FISHY

John-Henry's detractors were suspicious of the note. While Ted usually signed his autographs as "Ted Williams," he always signed legal documents as "Theodore S. Williams." They didn't doubt it was Williams's signature, only where it came from. Whenever he was getting ready to autograph baseball memorabilia, Ted commonly signed his name on a few blank pieces of paper to warm up. Bobby-Jo and others believe that John-Henry faked the note by writing the text onto a piece of paper that already had one of Ted's warm-up signatures on it. But when Claudia vouched for her signature in an affidavit, the executor of the estate accepted the note as a genuine expression of Ted's wish to be cryonically frozen.

By now Bobby-Jo had spent more than $87,000 from her own retirement fund on lawyers to have her father taken out of deep-freeze and cremated according to the instructions in his will, but with her money running out and Claudia Williams vouching for the authenticity of the note, she gave up the fight. Ted's head and body remain frozen to this day.

Alcor billed John-Henry $136,000 for services rendered; he sent them an initial payment of $25,000 and defaulted on the rest. As of August 2003, he still hadn't paid, though by then it wasn't clear if there was any money left to spend. During the last years of Ted's life, John-Henry had apparently used his power of attorney to raid his father's assets and use them to bankroll an Internet startup company. When the dot-com bubble burst in 2000, the company filed for bankruptcy, nearly $13 million in debt. By the time Ted died, most of his assets had been sold off or mortgaged to the hilt.

THE END?

John-Henry must have worked out some kind of arrangement regarding his father's Alcor bill, because when the younger Williams died from leukemia in 2004 at the age of 35, his body was shipped to Alcor, too. Is he floating in the same tank as his dad? They're big enough to hold four people, but Alcor isn't talking. The only thing that can be said for certain is that if the two men are thawed out and brought back to life, John-Henry will sure have a lot of explaining to do.

To date, only 12 girls have played in a Little League World Series game.

THE TIMELESS SPORT

Baseball, at its best, can stop time...or at least slow it down.

"The strongest thing that baseball has going for it today are its yesterdays."

—Lawrence Ritter

"I believe in the Rip Van Winkle Theory: that a man from 1910 must be able to wake up after being asleep for 70 years, walk into a ballpark and understand baseball perfectly."

—Bowie Kuhn

"Baseball is a beautifully put together pattern of countless little subtleties that finally add up to the big dramatic moment, and you have to be well versed in the game to truly appreciate them."

—Paul Richards

"Poets are like baseball pitchers. Both have their moments. The intervals are the tough things."

—Robert Frost

"Since baseball time is measured only in outs, all you have to do is keep hitting, keep the rally alive, and you have defeated time. You remain forever young."

—Roger Angell

"Baseball is a game dominated by vital ghosts; it's a fraternity, like no other we have of the active and the no longer so, the living and the dead."

—Richard Gilman

"Baseball is the only thing besides the paper clip that hasn't changed."

—Bill Veeck

"Baseball, almost alone among our sports, traffics unashamedly and gloriously in nostalgia, for only baseball understands time and treats it with respect. The history of other sports seems to begin anew with each generation, but baseball, that wondrous myth of 20th-century America, gets passed on like an inheritance."

—Stanley Cohen

"It's designed to break your heart. The game begins in the spring, when everything is new again, and it blossoms in the summer, filling the afternoons and evenings, and then as soon as the chill rains comes, it stops, and leaves you to face the fall alone."

—A. Bartlett Giamatti

Cy Young's real name was Denton True Young. His nickname, Cy, was short for "cyclone."

THE DOCK IS (FAR) OUT, PART II

On page 131, we told you about the controversial career of Pirates pitcher Dock Ellis, but we left out one important chapter: the LSD no-hitter.

MAJOR LEAGUE DRUGS

Substance abuse—from alcohol to steroids—has long been a part of baseball. The peak period for drug abuse, however, seems to have been the 1970s and '80s: Uppers, downers, cocaine, and marijuana were readily available everywhere, from hotel rooms to locker rooms. And, by his own account, Dock Ellis used them all at one time or another.

But few in baseball talked openly about the problem until the 1980s, when the U.S. government's highly publicized "war on drugs" became a part of the national conversation. "Drugs served as tokens of appreciation," pitcher Bill "Spaceman" Lee admitted after he retired in 1982. "While coming off the field after pitching a good game, I would often find my path littered with small packets of hash." And after the Montreal Expos finished third that same year, team president John McHale complained, "We felt we should've won. When we all woke up to what was going on, we found there were at least eight players on our club who were into this thing [cocaine]."

Ellis also came clean about his own extensive drug use. "Some guys I pitched against, we would try to guess which one of us was higher," he said. And then, in 1984, he revealed the secret he'd been keeping for nearly 15 years—when he threw his no-hitter in 1970, he was on LSD. Here's the story he told.

PURPLE HAZE, ALL IN MY BRAIN

It was June 12, 1970, and Ellis thought it was an off-day. Shortly after he dropped a hit of "Purple Haze" in his Los Angeles apartment (supplied by LSD guru Timothy Leary), his girlfriend looked at the newspaper and shouted, "Dock, you're supposed to be pitching in San Diego in a few hours!"

"But that's on Friday, baby," Ellis said. "Today's Thursday."

In 1988 Bill "Spaceman" Lee ran for president. Slogan: "No guns. No butter. Both can kill."

"No," she replied. "You slept through Thursday!"

In a panic, Ellis got a ride to the airport just as the drug was starting to take effect. He caught his short flight to San Diego and barely made it to Jack Murphy Stadium on time, but suited up, downed a few "bennies" (amphetamines), and was ready to go by game time.

"I was zeroed in on the catcher's glove, but I didn't hit the glove too much," Ellis recalled. "I remember hitting a couple of batters and the bases were loaded two or three times. The ball was small sometimes, the ball was large sometimes. Sometimes I saw the catcher, sometimes I didn't. I chewed my gum until it turned to powder. I remember diving out of the way of a ball I thought was a line drive. I jumped, but the ball wasn't hit hard and never reached me." (Ellis claims he even coined a baseball slang term that day: While sitting on the bench after the sixth inning, he looked up at the scoreboard and, much too high to pronounce the word "no-hitter," said, "Hey, I've got a no-no going!")

Although he walked eight batters, Ellis somehow finished the game without allowing a hit en route to a 2–0 victory. He tried to play it cool in postgame interviews, and didn't even realize the magnitude of what he'd accomplished until the next day.

I CAN SEE CLEARLY NOW

Now in his 60s, Ellis has been drug-free since the mid-1980s (the birth of his son, combined with stern warnings from his doctor, convinced him to go straight). Since then, Ellis has taken an active part in trying to curb the use of illegal drugs in baseball and in society. Among other jobs, he's worked with the Pennsylvania Department of Corrections to rehabilitate black prisoners, coordinated an antidrug program for Los Angeles youths, and worked for George Steinbrenner as a minor league drug counselor.

"The biggest misperception about Dock is that he's this untamed, self-destructive wild man," said Brad Corbett, owner of the Rangers when Ellis played for them in 1977. "And part of that is true; he was crazy, but in a good way. Everybody loves to talk about that LSD no-hitter, but come on. Stuff like that was happening all the time. Everybody was doing something. Dock was fun. He had a way of keeping people loose. He had character."

Warren Spahn was the first left-handed pitcher to win a Cy Young Award (1957).

UNIFORMS THROUGH THE AGES, PART III

Here's the final installment of our look at how baseball uniforms have changed over the years. (Part II begins on page 171.)

1920s

• In 1922 the St. Louis Cardinals introduced their famous two-birds-on-a-bat logo. The design has been credited to a Mrs. Allie May Keaton, who was in charge of decorations at a men's group meeting of the local Presbyterian Church on a day when the Cardinals' manager, Branch Rickey, was invited to speak. Mrs. Keaton came up with the design when she happened to look out the window and saw two red birds sitting on a branch of a nearby tree. Rickey liked it so much that he put it on the team uniforms (with a baseball bat replacing the branch). The logo was an immediate hit, and has been in almost continuous use ever since.

• The following year, Rickey tried another idea that was *not a* hit—he added the players' team numbers to the sleeves of their jerseys. When the players took the field wearing the jerseys, fans, sports reporters, and opposing teams showered them with ridicule and abuse. "Because of the continuing embarrassment to the players, the numbers were removed," Rickey later wrote.

• What a difference a few years make: In 1929 both the Cleveland Indians and the New York Yankees added numbers to the backs of their jerseys. Some players worried that fans would assume they were being numbered according to their ability; others thought that numbers on their backs made them look like convicts. No matter—this time, the idea stuck. Over the next three years every major league team added numbers to their uniforms.

1930s

• The V-neck collar, which had been standard on baseball jerseys since the early 1930s, began to lose ground to collarless jerseys as the decade progressed. The last team to wear the V-neck, the Philadelphia A's, switched to collarless jerseys after the 1939 season.

After retiring from baseball in 1939, catcher Moe Berg was a spy for the U.S. in World War II.

- In 1936 the New York Yankees added their famous interlocking "NY" logo to the team's home jerseys for the first time. The look of the team's uniforms has changed very little since then.
- Twenty-seven years after the last lace-up jersey was replaced with a buttoned one, the Chicago Cubs traded in their buttons for professional baseball's first zippered jersey. By the early '40s, about half of all major league teams had at least one jersey that zipped.
- In the late 1930s, a number of major league teams experimented with uniforms made of shiny *satin*. Why satin? Electric lights—and night games—had finally made it to the big leagues, and some teams thought shiny uniforms would show up better under the floodlights. Night games caught on; satin uniforms didn't.
- 1938 was also the year that the Brooklyn Dodgers dumped the block-letter BROOKLYN on the fronts of their jerseys for the script *Dodgers* logo that is still used today.

1940s
- In 1940, three years after introducing the first zippered jersey, the Chicago Cubs struck another blow for modernity by cutting the sleeves off their uniforms—they introduced the first jersey *vest*, worn on top of a shirt with short or long sleeves.
- Last team to wear a baseball cap with no letter or logo identifying the team: the 1945 St. Louis Browns (the cap had brown seams and a brown bill). In 1946 the team switched to caps with a logo of an S superimposed over an L.
- The fabrics used to make baseball uniforms hadn't changed much since 1849: In the mid-1940s, players still suited up in uniforms made entirely of wool flannel or wool-cotton blends. Then in the late 1940s, the first synthetic fibers, including nylon, Dacron, and Orlon, were introduced into baseball uniforms in wool-synthetic blends.

1950s
- Why put player numbers just on the *backs* of jerseys? In 1952 the Brooklyn Dodgers become the first team to add a smaller number onto the front left side of the jersey, just below the logo.
- In 1956, two years after renaming themselves the Redlegs, the Team Formerly Known as the Cincinnati Reds updated their jerseys by removing the word "REDS" from their famous wishbone C

On August 4, 1985, Rod Carew got his 3,000th hit, and Tom Seaver got his 300th win.

logo. (With the anti-communist McCarthy era at its peak, "Reds" had suddenly taken on a more sinister connotation.)

1960s

• As TV made it possible for fans to watch games played all over the country instead of just at local ballparks, keeping track of the players became a bigger challenge than ever. In 1960 the Chicago White Sox made the job a little easier by becoming the first major league team to print the players' *names* on the backs of their jerseys. Many team owners resisted making this change, fearing that it would hurt sales of scorecards in the ballpark.

• From the early days of baseball, uniforms were worn baggy, both for comfort and because the wool in flannel shrinks—a uniform that's too big at the start of the season will still fit at the end of the season. In 1960 Willie Mays helped spark a trend toward more snug-fitting uniforms when he had a tailor cut all the extra material out of his.

• With red-baiting hysteria on the wane, the Cincinnati Redlegs quietly reverted back to their old name and logo in 1961.

• In 1963 the Kansas City Athletics changed from their traditional red-and-blue-trimmed uniforms to a much louder green, gold, and white color combo, a radical departure from the subdued colors of traditional baseball uniforms. A's owner Charlie Finley believed that bold uniforms would look better on color television. Finley rounded out the look with white shoes, the first in major league history to be coordinated with the colors of the uniform (if you can call green, gold, and white "coordinated").

1970s

• Baseball's buttonless, beltless era began with the 1970 season, when the Pittsburgh Pirates "upgraded" to uniforms made of 100% synthetic double-knit fabrics: body-hugging pullover jerseys and pants with built-in elastic waistbands instead of belts. Traditionalists weren't crazy about the new look, but the synthetic fabric proved to be more comfortable, more durable, and easier to clean than traditional wool and cotton blends. Over the next few years every other major league team switched to the new material, too.

• In 1976 Chicago White Sox owner Bill Veeck made a number of unusual updates to his team's look: His players began wearing

pullover jerseys with fake old-style full collars, and they wore them "pajama-style" over the pants instead of tucking them in. The strange-looking jerseys lasted through the 1981 season. An even more unconventional innovation—baseball *shorts*—lasted only one game: the first game of a doubleheader played on August 8. Between games, the Sox changed back to pants.

• On May 19, 1979, in a game against the Montreal Expos, the Philadelphia Phillies introduced an all-burgundy "Saturday Special" uniform—to be worn only during Saturday home games. They lost 10–5…and never wore the Saturday Specials again.

1980s
• In the late 1980s, the belts and buttons "classic look" made a comeback, even as uniforms continued to be made with synthetic double-knit fabrics. The Cincinnati Reds were the last holdouts; they got rid of their last pullover jerseys and beltless pants in 1993.

1990s
• The zippered jersey era ended in 1990 when the Philadelphia Phillies ditched theirs and went back to buttons.

• The biggest change of all during the 1990s: the trend toward much longer baseball pants. A few players experimented with low pant legs in the 1980s, but it wasn't until the early 1990s that the new look began to catch on. Today many players even wear special attachments on the bottoms of their pants to keep them from riding up, so that their stirrup socks—to the extent that they are worn at all—may never see the light of day again.

*　　*　　*

DUMB PREDICTION
"I believe salaries are at their peak. It's quite possible some owners will trade away, or even drop entirely, players who expect $200,000 salaries. There is no way clubs can continue to increase salaries to the level some players are talking about."
—Peter O'Malley, Dodgers president, 1971

Roger Maris is not in the Hall of Fame.

BALLPARK BITES

It's not all hot dogs and beer—a lot of major league stadiums offer local delicacies…as well as some really weird food items.

Ichiroll. Named in honor of Seattle Mariner right fielder (and native of Japan) Ichiro Suzuki, and served at Safeco Field, it's a spicy tuna sushi roll.

Ybor City Cuban Sandwich. The Columbia Restaurant, a landmark in South Florida, has a stand at Tropicana Field in Tampa, where they make this sandwich—a long Cuban roll layered with spicy ham, pork, cheese, pickles, and sweet peppers, then grilled on a Cuban sandwich press known as a *plancha*.

Maryland Crab Cakes. This local favorite and signature dish at Baltimore's Camden Yards is made with fresh crab from Chesapeake Bay and flavored with mustard and Worcestershire sauce.

Boiled Peanuts. Turner Field in Atlanta serves them (they're said to be an acquired taste). Raw green peanuts are boiled in their shells in salty water for hours, until the shells turn soggy. Fans rip off the shells and toss them on the ground. Also available: bison burgers, made from bison raised on Ted Turner's Montana ranch.

Pierogies. Pittsburgh Pirates fans consider pierogies their signature food. They're a sort of ravioli stuffed with potatoes, cheese, and onions, and served topped with butter, salt, and black pepper. You can also get buffalo wings in as many as eight different flavors.

Rocky Mountain Oysters. Okay, they're not really oysters—they're calf testicles halved, battered, and deep-fried. The only ballpark that serves them is Coors Field in Denver.

Wine. AT&T Park in San Francisco is one of the few ballparks where you can get a glass of wine. (San Francisco is near the Sonoma Valley, a major wine-producing region.)

Poutine. Back when the Washington Nationals were the Montreal Expos, Olympic Stadium offered this Canadian fast food item that consisted of french fries topped with cheese curds and gravy. (Nationals Park doesn't offer it.)

Yankee Stadium's 1976 renovations: $167 million. Statue of Liberty's '84 renovations: $62 million.

HALL OF FAME

A quick history of baseball's most hallowed hall.

WHY COOPERSTOWN? It's the small town in central New York where Abner Doubleday supposedly invented baseball in 1839. Although historians disputed that claim, the 1934 discovery of a tattered old baseball in a Cooperstown-area attic convinced many that the origin was true.

• A local businessman named Stephen Clark purchased the ball for $5 and decided to display it, along with some other baseball memorabilia, in an office in town. The response was so strong that Clark decided to open baseball's official "National Museum."

• He approached National League president Ford Frick, who was so enthusiastic about the museum that he convinced Baseball Commissioner Kenesaw Mountain Landis to back the plan.

• They decided to open the museum in 1939, baseball's centennial (according to the Doubleday "origin"). Frick thought it should be more than just a museum filled with bats, balls, and gloves—he felt it should include a "Hall of Fame" to honor the game's greats.

• As contributions of memorabilia came in from across the country, ground was broken for the new building on Cooperstown's Main Street. Meanwhile, the Baseball Writers' Association of America began the arduous task of choosing the first players to be inducted.

• When the "The National Baseball Hall of Fame & Museum" opened on June 12, 1939, a total of 25 players were inducted, 11 of whom were still living, including Cy Young, Honus Wagner, Babe Ruth, Christy Mathewson, and Walter Johnson. They all showed up to the dedication, along with thousands of fans.

• Since then, the Hall of Fame has undergone numerous renovations. Today it houses more than 35,000 artifacts, as well as 130,000 baseball cards. The National Baseball Library, which also opened in 1939, contains over 2.6 million items, including 500,000 photographs that span the history of the game.

• Even though the Doubleday story has long since been debunked, Cooperstown is still considered an important part of baseball history. Each year, more than 350,000 people visit the Hall of Fame.

"Well, a couple of grand slammers and the Brewers are right back in this one." —Bob Uecker

THE UMPIONEERS

The word "umpire" comes from the French noumpere, *meaning "a non-peer, not an equal, one who decides disputes between equals." Or, as veteran ump Ron Luciano once put it, "Umpiring is best described as the profession of standing between two seven-year-olds with one ice-cream cone."*

FROM HONORABLE ARBITRATORS...

Sitting in a rocking chair behind the first-base line, wearing a top hat and Prince Albert coat, an attorney named William Wheaton became baseball's first umpire on October 6, 1845, during a practice game between his fellow teammates on the New York Knickerbockers. The game was much different back then—he didn't call balls and strikes (the pitcher still threw underhand), his job was to judge between "fair and unfair play." Wheaton was typical of baseball's earliest umpires, often a member of one of the teams who volunteered to sit out and officiate. Sometimes a distinguished member of the crowd, perhaps a local judge, would be asked to call the game.

These umpires worked for free and were well respected. But when baseball went professional in the 1870s, the game became much more competitive, increasing the need for neutral observers to keep the peace on the field. The only option: *hire* umpires. Their life as "honorable arbitrators" was about to take an ugly turn.

...TO NO-GOOD BUMS

Calling the first game in National League history in 1876 was Billy McLean, a former bare-knuckle boxer. And he'd need that experience to handle what quickly became the most thankless (and often dangerous) job in baseball. Games were less formal back then: The fans sat much closer to the field, and the parks lacked today's tight security. McLean found himself in the position of single-handedly trying to control rowdy players, corrupt coaching staffs, and unforgiving fans, who often came to the park armed with an arsenal of rotting fruit. Adding even more pressure to umpires, it was their job to set fines for players who broke the rules. If a fine was considered too harsh, it was the ump—not the owners or the league office—who fans and players went after.

While many umpires retaliated, McLean simply strove to do his job and get home safely. But with each passing year he saw the hostility increase. It all came to a head at an exhibition game in Philadelphia in 1884. After a group of fans heckled him all afternoon, McLean walked over and threatened to "clean out the grandstand" if they didn't lay off. They didn't. After a few more taunts, McLean lost it: He picked up a bat and flung it into the seats, reportedly hitting an "innocent" man. A riot nearly ensued and McLean was arrested for assault. But since the fan was uninjured, the charges were dropped. Still, the league pressured McLean into writing an apology to Philadelphia fans. Instead of apologizing, however, he defended himself:

> Goaded by uncalled-for, as well as unexpected taunts, I for a moment—and but for a moment—forgot my position as an umpire and did what any man's nature would prompt if placed in a similar situation.... I urge managers to enforce the strictest order on their grounds, otherwise the death of an honest and manly game is in the near future.

McLean worked the remainder of the season, but quit after that, as fans, players, and coaches became even rowdier...and the owners turned a blind eye.

OUT OF CONTROL

McLean was fortunate to get out of the game when he did—the 1890s were brutal for the umpires. Team owners claimed to be opposed to disorder in the stands and on the field, but secretly supported the anti-umpire sentiment, believing it brought fans to the games...and increased profits. One of the most famous players of the day, Al Spalding, summed it up: "Fans who despise umpires are simply showing their democratic right to protest against tyranny." A popular poem of the time, first printed in the *Chicago Tribune* in 1886, was called "Mother, May I Slug the Umpire":

> Let me clasp his throat, dear mother
> In a dear, delightful grip
> With one hand, and with the other
> Bat him several in the lip.

It's no wonder that the turnover rate for early umpires was so high—despite a good salary of around $5 per game, few were willing to risk their lives. Others, like Richard Higham, tried to supple-

---

Umpire Tom Gorman (1919–86) was buried in his uniform...

ment their incomes by advising gamblers which team to bet on. In 1882 he became the only umpire ever to be banned for life... and provided yet another excuse for fans to jump on the "Kill the Umpire" bandwagon. (No accounts exist of an umpire getting killed by a fan or player, but many did suffer severe beatings.)

THE FATHER OF UMPIRES

The anti-umpire sentiment was so strong that professional baseball may not have survived had it not been not for the efforts of a few key men. The first umpire to start turning things around was "Honest" John Gaffney. A former player who turned umpire in 1883, Gaffney quickly became known as one of the best, which wasn't particularly difficult as most umps were poorly trained and disagreed on many basic rules. Working in more games than any other umpire in the 19th century, he realized that in order for his peers to gain respect, they had to start calling a better game. But to do that, they needed to know the rules...which changed often.

Take home runs—they were still quite rare, and the rules regarding them were murky. Gaffney began ruling that if a fly ball cleared the fence in fair territory, it was a home run even if it landed foul. More importantly, he called it that way consistently. At the end of each season, he sent a list of inconsistencies and proposed rule changes to the National League, many of which were put into play the following year.

Gaffney was also a part of baseball's first two-man umpiring team, which took place in an 1887 postseason game. It didn't become standard practice, though, so Gaffney improvised: He stayed behind the plate until a runner reached base, then he positioned himself behind the pitcher. These innovations and dedication earned Gaffney the title "Father of Umpires." (He was also the first to wear a shirt with an oversize pocket to hold extra balls.)

GET A LITTLE CLOSER

Because there was no set strike zone until 1887 (and even then, no one could agree on it), it fell to the umpire's judgement as to whether a pitched ball was hittable. The same was true for foul balls—they were called strikes only if the umpire thought the batter was attempting to put the ball into play.

Even with a set strike zone, umps still had a difficult time judging it because they positioned themselves a few feet behind the catcher and stood straight up, believing it gave them a better view of the field—as well as an extra split second in which to dodge foul tips. The first umpire to step up, so to speak, was Jack Sheridan, whose 18-year career began in 1890. Referred to by historians as the "prototype of the modern umpire," Sheridan was the first to crouch directly behind the catcher, just above his shoulder, while the pitch was being thrown. He soon became known as the most accurate strike caller in the American League—and umps from both leagues adopted the crouch.

But that led to yet another problem: Foul tips were much harder to dodge from a crouch. Fed up with the bruises, Sheridan came up with a solution. He "borrowed" a leather-bound guest register from a hotel lobby and wore it under his shirt during a game, an innovation that developed into a standard piece of an umpire's equipment—the chest protector.

BRUSH THEM OFF AND BAN THEM

Although Gaffney's and Sheridan's advancements improved the level of play, umpires were still alone out there, with neither the leagues nor the owners stepping in to discipline players. That began to change in 1898, when New York Giants owner John T. Brush introduced his "Brush Rules," which threatened to ban a player for life if he struck an umpire or used "villainously foul language." Did the Brush Rules work? Not really—the rules didn't apply to umpires or coaches. Players complained that they should be held accountable as well. Meanwhile, not a single case ever reached Brush's proposed discipline board.

Those questions were answered definitively by Byron Bancroft "Ban" Johnson, the first president of the American League, which he formed as "cleaner" alternative to the "raucous" N.L. "My determination was to pattern baseball in this new league along the lines of scholastic contests," said Johnson, "to make ability, brains, and honorable play decide the issue—not the swinging of clenched fists, coarse oaths, riots, or assaults on the umpires." Unlike Brush, Johnson tried appease both players *and* umpires:

• Johnson personally recruited player-friendly umps, starting with the highly respected Jack Sheridan as senior umpire, and urged them to stop retaliating against players and managers (such as when umpire Tim Hurst followed New York Highlanders manager Clark Griffith into the tunnel after a game and knocked him out).

• In Johnson's A.L., fines would be imposed by the head office, not the umpires. That alone took a lot of pressure off the umps.

• Johnson made two-man umpiring teams standard for all games. With one calling balls and strikes and the other calling plays in the field, it made their jobs *much* easier. (It also made it a lot harder for players to cheat.) By 1912 both leagues had two-man crews.

In 1902 Johnson made an example of the Baltimore Orioles, notorious for their underhanded tricks, such as hiding extra baseballs in the outfield grass. Johnson attended many Orioles games, keeping tabs on player-manager John McGraw. After several clashes with the league's best umpires, McGraw was suspended indefinitely. Not wanting to play under Johnson's scrutiny, McGraw left Baltimore to play for the N.L. New York Giants, but he soon found that the National League wasn't as rowdy as it used to be. Johnson's efforts were having a profound effect on both leagues: Civility was returning. "His contribution to the game," said Branch Rickey, "is not closely equaled by any other single person or group of persons."

SAFE!

As a result, the new century was looking up for the men in blue. Bill Klem, whose 37-year umpiring career began in 1905, had a big part in that: He won fans over with his larger-than-life personality and legendary stubbornness—he *never* changed a call, even if he knew he blew it. It was Klem, nicknamed "the Old Arbitrator," who successfully lobbied for Sheridan's inside chest protector to be worn throughout the National League. Klem also popularized using arm signals to call balls and strikes. (The jowly Klem did have one major weakness: He hated being called "Catfish." More than a few rookies got tossed from games after seasoned veterans assured them that Klem *loved* the nickname.)

Thanks to Klem—and the pioneering men who came before him—baseball became a safer game, which led to a much better game. The 1930s saw the first umpire schools, the 1960s brought the umpires' union, and today professional baseball umps are among the best paid and most highly trained sports officials in the world...even if they still can't seem to agree on the strike zone.

BASEBALL BY THE NUMBERS

*Why bother with earned-run averages or RBIs
when you can compile stats like these?*

5 Players who Chewed Something Besides Tobacco

1. Harry Coveleski: bologna

2. Greg Swindell: a fingernail (he was afraid he'd swallow tobacco, and he didn't like gum)

3. Todd Welborn: dirt ("Dirt is free and nobody bums it off you")

4. Joe Horlen: Toilet paper (tobacco made him sick)

5. Enos Slaughter: bubble gum and chewing tobacco *together* (smoother than plain tobacco)

5 Players Put on the Disabled List for Injuries Due to "Violent Sneezing"

1. Sammy Sosa

2. Juan Gonzalez

3. Russ Springer

4. Marc Valdes

5. Goose Gossage

3 Players with the Same Name as a U.S. President

1. John Kennedy

2. "Ike" Eisenhower

3. Grover Cleveland Alexander

9 Illnesses of Luke "Old Aches & Pains" Appling

1. Astigmatism

2. Fallen arches

3. Sore kneecaps

4. Dizzy spells

5. Insomnia

6. Sore throat

7. Seasickness

8. Gout

9. Not sick enough (his explanation for letting his batting average drop below .300 after 9 seasons)

2 Players with the Same Name as a Department Store

1. Ken Sears

2. John Montgomery Ward

6 Players with Unusual Nicknames

1. Putsy Caballero

2. Togie Pittinger

3. Bots Nekola

4. Pid Purdy

5. Twink Twining

6. Waddy MacPhee

4 Players who Were Amputees

1. Pete Gray, outfielder (one arm)

2. Hugh "One Arm" Daily, pitcher (lost his left hand in a gun accident)

3. Mordecai "Three Finger" Brown, pitcher (lost parts of two fingers on his right hand)

4. Bert Shepard, pitcher (one leg)

3 Pitches Thrown by Satchel Paige

1. The "Bee Ball"

2. The "Hurry Up" Ball

3. The "Bat Dodger" Pitch

Lowest-paid major league contract player: Chicken Wolf. (In 1882 he earned $9 per week.)

THE BAD NEWS BEARS GO TO JAPAN

Hooray for Hollywood! There are some great baseball movies, like Field of Dreams, The Natural, *and* Major League...*and then there are these.*

THE SLUGGER'S WIFE (1985) "One of the most disappointing, least credible films about baseball in recent memory. Michael O'Keefe plays a power hitter closing in on the single-season home run record. It might not have mattered that O'Keefe looks like anything but a long-ball hitter—if he or the film had anything else to offer." (*TV Guide's Movie Guide*)

STEALING HOME (1988) "Down-on-his-luck baseball pro Mark Harmon returns home when he learns that his childhood sweetheart (Jodie Foster) has killed herself. Lame melodrama which comes complete with syrupy music and excruciating flashback sequences. The baseball references are hardly part of the story—they seem to have been tagged on to justify the punchy title." (*Time Out Film Guide*)

THE SCOUT (1994) "Besides the fact that we have trouble seeing the Yankees as an underdog, we have to wonder why a scout (Albert Brooks) who consistently finds talented but neurotic pitchers (in this case, Brendan Fraser) who freak out at the thought of pitching in the majors hasn't been fired." (*The Bakersfield Californian*)

HARD BALL (2001) "The story of a compulsive gambler whose life is turned around by coaching an inner-city baseball team. That sounds like a winning formula for a movie, and it might be, if the story told us more about gambling, more about the inner city, and more about coaching baseball. Dialogue consists of the announcement of plot points. There is not a single scene in which the gambler tells a kid anything specific about baseball strategy. Does he know anything about baseball?" (*Roger Ebert's Movie Yearbook*)

ED (1996) "A chimp plays third base and teaches a pitcher with a bad case of stage fright (Matt LeBlanc) how to be the best he can be. The only thing that could've saved this movie would be if the monkey threw a pile of his own feces instead of the baseball." (*BravesBeat.com*)

THE BABE (1992) "Loosely based on Babe Ruth's life, this shallow, soap-opera treatment makes the man fit the myth. Like the Babe himself, John Goodman never seems challenged by the demands of his role or the rigors of the game. Baseball cards are deeper." (*Washington Post*)

THE BABE RUTH STORY (1948) "*The Babe* was pretty bad, but an improvement over this one. Let's just call it sentimental tripe of Ruthian proportions. Sometimes the movie even throws in a little baseball. Most of Ruth's feats are depicted in close-ups in the batter's box, with newpaper headlines that tell us what the decidedly dumpy star William Bendix couldn't demonstrate." (*The Worst Movies of All Time*)

NIGHT GAME (1989) "A cop (Roy Scheider) links a string of serial killings to the night games won by the Houston Astros. The brave cast tries hard, but is retired without a hit." (*Videohound's Golden Movie Retriever*)

THE BAD NEWS BEARS GO TO JAPAN (1978) "The movie features Tony Curtis and a bunch of kids wandering around Japan for two hours doing nothing. We don't mean that they get in unexciting or flat comic situations—they do *nothing*. It doesn't have a climax, and the final baseball game is played off-screen in a hotel parking lot." (*Apollo Movie Guide*)

THE WINNING TEAM (1952) "This biography of pitcher Grover Cleveland Alexander would have worked better with a different cast. Ronald Reagan's inept acting is a distraction." (*Video Movie Guide*)

THE FIX IS IN

The biggest scandal in sports history took place in 1919: Promised a fortune by a group of gamblers, seven members of the Chicago White Sox agreed to lose the World Series. Here's the story of the "Black Sox."

MONEYBALL

The 1919 Chicago White Sox were one of the best teams in baseball, compiling a league-leading .287 team batting average, posting an 88–52 record en route to winning the American League pennant. They also had one of the lowest payrolls in the league: Owner Charles Comiskey was notoriously "thrifty," paying his players an average salary of about $4,000 a year—about half of what players on other teams made.

To make some extra money, first baseman Chick Gandil had a sideline: He sold insider information on the team (such as what hitters and pitchers were sick or slumping) to Chicago gambler Joseph Sullivan.

As the season wound down and the White Sox prepared for the World Series against the Cincinnati Reds, the 33-year-old Gandil was looking for one last chunk of extra cash before he retired. So he approached Sullivan with a provocative idea: Instead of passing on player information, he and his teammates would lose the World Series on purpose. What did he want in return? A hundred thousand dollars (the equivalent of $1.3 million today), which he would split among any players who were willing to go in on the fix with him. Sullivan enthusiastically agreed.

SEVEN MEN OUT

One small problem: Sullivan didn't have anywhere near enough cash to pay a bunch of guys $100,000. So he got some other professional gamblers and underworld figures in on the deal: boxing champion and bookie Abe Atell, one-time White Sox pitcher Bill Burns, avid gambler and New York Giants first baseman Hal Chase, and Arnold Rothstein, who was well known in New York for fixing sporting events and then betting on them.

Now Gandil had to sign up as many of his teammates as possible, but with a promise of $100,000, it wasn't difficult. First he

---

In the 1919 World Series, "Shoeless" Joe Jackson hit 3 doubles and 1 HR, and scored 5 runs.

approached Eddie Cicotte and Lefty Williams, two of the league's best pitchers (Cicotte won 29 games that year and Williams won 23). Both agreed, as did centerfielder Oscar Felsch and shortstop Charles Risberg. Utility infielder Fred McMullin overheard Gandil soliciting Risberg and demanded to be included, too. Third baseman Buck Weaver overheard his teammates discussing the fix and knew what they were up to, but he refused to throw any games and wouldn't take any money. The hardest sell: Outfielder "Shoeless" Joe Jackson. Jackson, the team's best hitter that year with a .351 average, adamantly refused Gandil's offer to participate in the fix. His skills with the bat could make or break the plan, so when Sullivan got word that Jackson wouldn't go along, he reportedly threatened to kill Jackson and his family if he didn't. Jackson relented and the fix was in: Seven White Sox players would play badly, lose the World Series, and earn a *lot* of money.

PUT ALL YOUR MONEY ON RED(S)

Game 1 of the World Series (which followed the era's best-of-nine format) was set to take place on October 1, 1919. By game time, rumors were already swirling among fans and gamblers that the Sox might be planning to throw the Series. A few days before the game, the White Sox were 7–1 favorites to win. By game time, the odds were even.

To show good faith, Sullivan gave Cicotte, Game 1's starting pitcher, $10,000 before he took the mound. As a prearranged signal to his partners, Cicotte let the gamblers know the fix was still on by beaning lead-off batter Morrie Roth. Final score of Game 1: Reds 9, White Sox 1. Since the White Sox would have to lose five games in all, the seven fixers demanded that they receive one-fifth of the $100,000 payout—$20,000—after each loss. Sullivan and the other gamblers didn't have enough money to pay up after Game 1, but promised them $40,000 to split when they lost Game 2. The White Sox lost Game 2, but the money still didn't come. Instead, Sullivan gave Gandil $10,000, which he split with his co-conspirators.

THOSE CHEATERS CHEATED!

The seven players, now owed a total of $80,000, were beginning to feel like they'd been swindled. As a protest against the gamblers, the White Sox played hard in Game 3 and won it 3–0. But that made Abe Atell think the players were reneging on the deal, so he refused to pay them any more money. To appease both parties and keep the fix alive, Sullivan scraped together $20,000 and split it up among the players, who then lost Game 4 and Game 5. But Jackson still felt betrayed and was getting increasingly angry. He hadn't wanted to be in on the plot to begin with, and now he wasn't even getting paid. After Game 4, Williams gave Jackson $5,000—out of his own pocket—as hush money.

KEEPING SCORE

After Game 5, the White Sox were down four games to one. They were losing as they'd agreed to, but they hadn't been paid what they'd been promised: They should have received $80,000, but so far had gotten only a total of $40,000 from the gamblers, and more than a quarter of that had gone to Cicotte. They decided to chuck the fix, play hard, and try to come from behind to win the World Series...after they realized that winning came with a $5,000 bonus from Major League Baseball. The White Sox won Game 6 and Game 7, putting the series at Cincinnati 4, Chicago 3.

While the rest of the gambling contingent bet on the individual games of the World Series, Arnold Rothstein had made only one bet: for Cincinnati to win the Series. Standing to lose an estimated $270,000 ($3.5 million today), Rothstein sent a couple of thugs to visit Williams, the starting pitcher for Game 8. They warned Williams that if he didn't lose the game, he and his wife would be murdered. Williams threw the ball straight down the middle and gave up three runs in the first inning. And despite a home run from an angry and defiant Jackson, the Reds won the game 10–5. The World Series was over—Cincinnati had won it, five games to three. Did the players get the money they were promised? No. Gandil, Cicotte, and Jackson received a total of $25,000; the rest got about $4,000 each.

IT HITS THE FAN

The White Sox had played so badly that rumors of a fix floated around throughout the 1920 season. That summer *Chicago Herald Examiner* sportswriter Hugh Fullerton published a series of articles called "Is Big League Baseball Being Run by Gamblers, With Ball Players in the Deal?" In these articles, Fullerton uncovered evi-

dence that a Detroit gambling syndicate had fixed a game between the Chicago Cubs and the Philadelphia Phillies. Fullerton also strongly suggested that the White Sox played so badly in the World Series that they could only have done it on purpose.

THE PLOT THICKENS

With both Chicago ball clubs linked to gambling scandals, Cook County, Illinois, convened a grand jury on September 7, 1920. As more and more ballplayers and gamblers testified, the focus of the hearings started to shift to the 1919 World Series. On September 27, Eddie Cicotte confessed. "I've lived a thousand years in the last twelve months," Cicotte testified, through sobs. "Now I've lost everything—job, reputation, everything." Joe Jackson and Lefty Williams confessed next, corroborating Cicotte's testimony that the fix was Chick Gandil's idea. Ultimately, the hearings revealed the identities of all seven White Sox players who participated in the plot, along with the information that nonconspirator Buck Weaver knew about the fix but didn't report it.

DOWN FROM THE MOUNTAIN

In June 1921, the eight indicted players went on trial along with gamblers Atell, Sullivan, Burns, Chase, and two of Rothstein's thugs. (Rothstein himself avoided charges, only to be murdered seven years later after being accused of fixing a poker game.) But a few days before the trial began, key evidence disappeared from the Cook County courthouse, including signed confessions from Williams, Cicotte, and Jackson. With the proof gone, all three recanted their confessions. After a month of testimony, the jury convened for just under three hours and returned not-guilty verdicts for all defendants.

But they weren't off the hook. The day after the acquittal, baseball commissioner Kenesaw Mountain Landis delivered his own verdict. Chick Gandil, Eddie Cicotte, "Shoeless" Joe Jackson, Lefty Williams, Fred McMullin, Charles Risberg, and Oscar Felsch were all banned from Major League Baseball for life. Also banned was Buck Weaver, for failing to blow the whistle. St. Louis Browns second baseman Joe Gedeon also received a lifetime ban because he was a friend of Risberg, knew of the plot, and remained silent.

The first All-Star Game, held at Comiskey Park, was part of the 1933 Chicago World's Fair.

Said Landis: "Regardless of the verdict of juries, no player who throws a ball game, no player who undertakes or promises to throw a ball game, no player who sits in confidence with a bunch of crooked ballplayers and gamblers, where the ways and means of throwing a game are discussed and does not promptly tell his club about it, will ever play professional baseball."

As for the missing confessions, they turned up five years later...in the office of George Hudnall, the attorney for White Sox owner Charles Comiskey. Hudnall offered no explanation for their sudden reappearance.

*   *   *

MYTH CONCEPTIONS

Myth: *The tie goes to the runner.*
Fact: Actually, the opposite is true, according to major league umpire Tim McClelland. "There is no rule that says the tie goes to the runner. But the rule book does say that the runner must beat the ball to first base, and so if he doesn't *beat* the ball, then he is out."

Myth: *A player must touch the ball to be charged with an error.*
Fact: It's false, although you wouldn't know it by listening to most baseball analysts during game broadcasts. For some reason, this myth begins in Little League and sticks with players all the way up to the bigs. However, it says clearly near the beginning of rule 10.13: "It is not necessary that the fielder touch the ball to be charged with an error."

Myth: *Minor leaguers refer to the majors as "The Show."*
Fact: This term was popularized by the 1988 film *Bull Durham*. But ESPN analyst Bob Halloran says the screenwriter simply made it up. (He doesn't like the rest of the movie, either.) In his experience, Halloran never heard anyone call the big leagues "The Show," and after asking around, found that no one else had heard them called that, either...although Arkansas Travelers owner Bert Parke said that some minor leaguers refer to the majors as "The Big Club."

Tom Seaver wrote a crime novel in 1991 called *Beanball: Murder at the World Series.*

WHY IS IT CALLED "HOME PLATE"?

And other vitally important questions about life on Earth.

Q: *Why is a bunt with two strikes an out if it goes foul, but a full-swing foul ball with two strikes is not?*
A: Because it's much easier to make contact with the ball when bunting than when swinging, and a player could hit foul bunts all day long and tire a pitcher out unfairly if it were allowed. On a full swing there is a much greater chance of the batter striking out.

Q: *Why are there no left-handed catchers?*
A: There actually have been some, but very few. The reason is that one of a catcher's most important duties is throwing out runners attempting to steal a base. Since most players bat right-handed, a left-handed catcher would have to move to his right to throw past a batter in the batter's box, wasting valuable time. For that reason, lefties are seldom picked for the position. Over the course of major league history, there have been just 33 left-handed catchers to catch at least one inning of play, only five who played more than 100 games, and only one who played more than 1,000: Jack Clements, who started out with the Philadelphia Keystones in 1884. (Records say that batters learned to duck when someone tried to steal second...because Clements would try to throw right through them.)

Q: *Why is home plate shaped differently than the other bases?*
A: Before 1900 it wasn't. From 1869 to 1900, it was a 16" square (the other bases are 15" squares), positioned with one corner pointed at the pitcher. That made it hard for both the pitcher and the umpire to pinpoint the strike zone, so in 1900 the baseball rules committee changed it to the pentagon shape that's still used today, with its square bottom, 17" across, and the bottom, or flat part pointing at the pitcher. Before 1869, home plate was circular and 12" in diameter, and made from wood, cast iron, marble—or a dinner plate...hence the name.

Bobby Richardson of the New York Yankees is the only player...

WHAT'S IN A BASEBALL?

*On page 68 we told you the story of how the baseball grew from
its homemade origins into the ball we're all familiar with today.
Here's a look at how the modern professional ball is made.*

SHHHH!

One of the drawbacks associated with manufacturing a product like baseballs, which have been around for more than a century and haven't changed significantly since the 1930s, is that whatever patents existed on them expired long ago. The Rawlings Sporting Goods company has been the exclusive supplier of baseballs to the major leagues for more than 30 years, but because the design of the baseball is in the public domain, other companies are free to make them, too.

The only way that Rawlings can protect itself is to keep its manufacturing processes a secret—if competitors don't know *how* the company makes the balls, it's harder for them to match Rawlings on quality or price. Because of this, the company's manufacturing process is shrouded in mystery. They don't allow the public into their factory in Turrialba, Costa Rica, where the balls are made. What little we do know comes from those rare occasions when they allow a reporter to tour the facility, always on the condition that the reporter not photograph sensitive equipment or reveal any of the company's trade secrets. Here's what *is* known about how major league baseballs are manufactured.

THE INGREDIENTS
1. The "Pill"

The spheres at the center of major league baseballs have been made by the Muscle Shoals Rubber Company using the same methods and ingredients since 1949. Ground cork imported from Spain and Portugal is mixed with Indonesian rubber and five other secret ingredients, then compressed molded into a round, dark brown pellet. The pellet, in turn, is covered with two layers of rubber. (Even Major League Baseball officials don't know what the five secret ingredients are—they've repeatedly asked owner Cowles Horton for the formula, but he won't give it to them for

fear they'll switch to a lower-cost supplier. "I'm not going to give you the bullets to shoot me in the back of the head with," he told a Memphis newspaper in 2002.)

2. The Yarn

A baseball gets most of its volume and weight from the 900 feet of yarn that's wound around the pill. In the past the yarn was 100% wool, but today it's allowed to contain up to 15% synthetic fibers. It also used to be recycled from old wool carpeting, but now that so much American carpet is made from synthetic fibers, the wool comes from old sweaters. Wool is used because it has good "memory"—it returns to its original shape quickly after being hit by a bat.

3. The Thread

After the yarn is wound around the pill, a thin layer of white polyester-cotton thread is wound on top of it. This creates a smooth surface that prevents the coarse wool yarn from showing through the baseball's leather cover.

4. The Cover

The covers on major league balls are made from the hides of Holstein milk cows that come from farms in New York, Michigan, Pennsylvania, and Ohio. The tanned hides are shipped whole to the factory in Costa Rica, where they are cut into baseball covers. One hide supplies enough leather for between 95 and 120 baseballs, depending on the quality of the leather.

THE ASSEMBLY PROCESS

1. Winding the Yarn

A thin layer of latex adhesive is applied to the pill so that the yarn will stick to it. A worker winds the yarn by hand to get it started, then places the pill on the first of four winding machines. The details of the machines are a closely guarded secret; what is known is that they maintain a constant tension on the yarn. This eliminates dead spots and gives the ball a uniformly round shape.

The first three winding machines apply yarn, and the last machine adds the white finishing thread. After each wind, the ball is carefully measured and weighed; if it's more than .03 inches or .03 ounces off at any stage, that part of the yarn is unravelled and wound again. After the four stages of winding are completed, the balls are rolled in latex glue (it stays a little tacky, which helps the covers stick to the yarn), then left to dry overnight.

2. Cutting the Covers
Each cowhide is carefully examined for softness, porosity, and other features to make certain that it's good enough to be made into baseballs. Hides that pass the test are then cut into figure-eight-shaped pieces, and 108 holes are stamped into each piece to hold the stitching. The pieces are then inspected, sorted, and soaked for 30 to 90 minutes to make them soft enough to be stitched together easily.

3. Stitching the Covers onto the Ball
While still moist, the cover pieces are applied to the ball, which is placed into a special vise with cupped holders that secure it while a worker hand sews each of the 108 V-shaped lock stitches, using a single piece of waxed red thread 7'4" long. A skilled worker can sew a cover onto a baseball in as little as eight minutes.

Once the cover has been stitched, the ball is placed into a rolling machine and rolled under 60 lbs. of pressure for about 20 seconds. This flattens out the seams, making the overall surface smoother…which makes it harder for pitchers to throw curveballs. The ball is then cleaned by hand and left to dry in a climate-controlled room (72°F, 45% humidity) for 24 hours.

TESTING, TESTING, 1-2-3
Each finished baseball undergoes a series of tests to ensure that it's good enough to be used in the major leagues:
• It's weighed and measured to see if it conforms to major league specifications (5 to 5 ¼ ounces in weight, and 9" to 9 ¼" in circumference). If a ball is a little too heavy, it goes back into the drying room to see if there's any more moisture to be removed. If not, or if the ball is too light, it's rejected.
• The baseball is shot through an air cannon at a backboard made of white ash—the same wood used to make baseball bats—to see if it rebounds at the proper velocity. If a ball doesn't rebound at 54.6% of that velocity, it's rejected.
• Each ball is squeezed with 65 psi of pressure and pounded 200

times to see if it distorts under pressure. If it distorts more than .08", it's rejected.

The balls must pass a battery of other tests as well before they can be stamped with the seal of Major League Baseball and the signature of the Commissioner of Baseball. Ninety percent of the baseballs made at the Rawlings factory will be accepted for use in major league games. What happens to the rejects depends on how bad they are. The worst balls are destroyed to salvage any reusable parts; the ones that aren't quite as bad are sold at a discount for use in batting practice. Balls that have only minor flaws are sold commercially.

¿QUE?

The Rawlings plant in Costa Rica employs 300 people who produce 3,400 *dozen* major league baseballs per week. It takes a stitcher three years to develop the skills necessary to make major league baseballs; they learn their trade making baseballs that will be sold to the minor leagues, colleges, and high schools. Three years in the minors before making it to the big leagues—that's a long time to learn how to make a baseball that has a life expectancy of just *six pitches* at the major league level.

And, ironically, Costa Ricans don't play baseball: At last report this nation of four million people had exactly 15 baseball fields, only *two* of which had spectator stands. The Rawlings plant doesn't have a softball team. Many people who earn their living making baseballs have never even seen a game on TV; if they ever got a chance to watch one, it's not clear that they'd understand what was going on. As Francisco Bermudez, the plant's manufacturing manager, put it to the *Chicago Tribune* in 2003, "We know how to make this toy, but we don't know to play with it."

*   *   *

ACTUAL NEWSPAPER ANNOUNCEMENT

"The Volusia County Umpires Association, which provides baseball and softball umpires for the city recreation department, is meeting Sunday at 7 p.m. at the Florida Regional Library for the Blind."

1970s pitcher Mark Fidrych (Detroit Tigers) shook hands with his infielders after good plays.

PITCHING ZINGERS

Pitchers always look so serious on the mound. But off the mound…

"The way to make coaches think you're in shape in the spring is to get a tan."

—Whitey Ford

"I'd always keep it in at least two places, in case the umpire would ask me to wipe off one. I never wanted to be caught out there without anything. It wouldn't be professional."

—Gaylord Perry, on using foreign substances

"I've never seen anyone on the disabled list with pulled fat."

—Rod Beck, on his weight

"I told him I wasn't tired. He told me, 'No, but the outfielders sure are.'"

—Jim Kern, Rangers, on being removed from a game

"How can a guy win a game if you don't give him any runs?"

—Bo Belinsky, after losing a game 15–0

"When they operated on my arm, I told them to put in a Koufax fastball. They did—but it was Mrs. Koufax's."

—Tommy John

"I'm throwing twice as hard as I ever did. It's just not getting there as fast."

—Lefty Gomez

"Don't tell me I don't know where to play the hitters!"

—Ray Culp, after a hit ricocheted off his head and was caught by the centerfielder

"Scenario games, like, 'Would you rather open-mouth kiss a bum or get into a sleeping bag with your manager?'"

—Brian Fuentes, reliever, on what goes on in the bullpen

"Baseball's a very simple game. All you have to do is sit on your ass, spit tobacco, and nod at the stupid things your manager says."

—Bill "Spaceman" Lee

"I never throwed an illegal pitch—just once in a while I used to toss one that ain't never been seen by this generation."

—Satchel Paige

"I'm working on a new pitch. It's called a strike."

—Jim Kern

Youngest Hall of Fame inductee: Sandy Koufax, age 36.

THE IRON HORSE, PART II

Lou Gehrig's body began to break down in 1938, forcing him into early retirement (see page 109). But even though he had less than three years to live, Gehrig still had a lot of work to do.

ON PAROLE
In late 1939, Mayor LaGuardia presented Lou Gehrig with an offer to serve on the New York City Parole Commission. He told Gehrig that, as the most respected man in the city, he could inspire troubled kids to choose a better path. Gehrig agreed to take on the job and signed an optimistic 10-year contract (only Gehrig's family knew that his life expectancy was much shorter). Taking his typical workmanlike approach, Gehrig took a crash course in the law and read countless books about criminology and psychology.

On January 2, 1940, Gehrig drove himself to work on the first day of his second career. (His wife, Eleanor, would soon take over the driving when he became too weak.) The caseload was heavy, and he was immediately put to work judging whether or not prisoners should be released. He met with each of them personally; they talked about the decisions a man can make in life. One of Gehrig's strengths had always been to see the good in people and situations, and he tried to get them to see it, too. "Only a small percentage of these men have to go back to prison," he told LaGuardia. "I think that many convicted fellows deserve another chance. However, we not only have to play fair with the fellow who's gotten bad breaks, but we must also consider the rights of taxpayers and our duties towards them. We don't want anyone in jail who can make good."

SLOWING DOWN
It was a good year for the Gehrigs. Lou loved the work—it fulfilled him in a way that baseball never had. And even though he grew more and more frail, he never lost his optimism. "You have to get knocked down to realize how people really feel about you," he said in an interview. "I've realized that more than ever lately. The other day, I was on my way to the car. It was hailing, the streets

---

After pitcher Buck O'Brien gave up five runs in the first inning of a 1912 World Series game...

were slippery and I was having a tough time of it. I came to a corner and started to slip. But before I could fall, four people jumped out of nowhere to help me. When I thanked them, they all said they knew about my illness and had been keeping an eye on me."

By the spring of 1941, the daily commute became too much for Gehrig to handle (he could barely even sign his own name anymore). So he asked the mayor for a temporary leave of absence. LaGuardia gave him the same answer that Joe McCarthy had in 1939: "The job's here for you when you're ready to come back." But Gehrig never did.

OUT LIKE A LAMB

His final days were quiet. While the talk outside was of the growing war in Europe, Lou and Eleanor stayed inside their Bronx home most of the time listening to opera (Eleanor had introduced him to it years earlier) and hosting visitors. Lou entertained his guests with stories from his baseball days and from his childhood (he loved to tell about the time he swam across the Hudson River to New Jersey and back). Lou knew his death was imminent; his wife and parents knew it, too, and saw to it that he was kept comfortable.

The month of June had always figured heavily in Gehrig's life: He was born in June 1903, played in his first big-league game in June 1923, started his consecutive-games streak in June 1925, and ended the streak—and his baseball career—in June 1939. And on June 2, 1942, sixteen years to the day after he replaced Wally Pipp at first base, Gehrig died in his bed at 10:10 p.m.

The next morning, Babe Ruth and his wife came to the house to comfort Eleanor. Mayor LaGuardia ordered all of the flags in New York to be flown at half-mast. The 1941 baseball season was in full swing, and as the news of Gehrig's death spread, ballparks all over the nation held their own tributes.

LOU GEHRIG'S DISEASE

People began referring to ALS as "Lou Gehrig's Disease" even before he died. That was because hardly anyone had heard of it. Yet as tragic as it was for the Gehrigs, the fact that it happened to him—such a well-known and respected figure—gave a face to a little-known disease. First identified in France in 1869, ALS was

still a mystery to doctors, who knew almost nothing about its cause...or its cure. Gehrig was treated with experimental procedures, such as histamine injections and vitamin E, but none of them had any effect.

The public knew even less than the doctors. Some press reports erroneously referred to ALS as being similar to polio, the disease that had afflicted President Franklin Roosevelt. Others claimed ALS was contagious, and pointed to it as an explanation for the dismal season the Yankees suffered in 1940.

Gehrig himself helped put these myths to rest: Ever the student, he assisted his doctors by keeping detailed notes on his condition. After her husband's death, Eleanor Gehrig dedicated her life to finding a cure. But, sadly, ALS still affects approximately 5,600 people per year in the United States, and the cure still eludes researchers.

POSTSCRIPT

Eleanor Gehrig lived until 1984, when she died on her 80th birthday, having never remarried. The best years of her life, she insisted, were the 10 she spent with Lou. "I would not have traded two minutes of the joy and the grief with that man for two decades of anything with another," she once said. Gehrig's influence on baseball is still huge: In 1999 Major League Baseball asked fans from across the nation to pick the 100 greatest players of the 20th century—the All-Century Team. The top vote getter: Lou Gehrig, with more than 1.2 million votes.

Gehrig's teammate, Sam Jones, said of him: "Lou was the kind of boy that if you had a son, he's the kind of person you'd like your son to be."

*   *   *

ON HITTING A HOME RUN

"No one can stop a home run. No one can understand what it really is, unless you have felt it in your own hands and body. As the ball makes its high, long arc beyond the playing field, the diamond and the stands suddenly belong to one man. In that brief, brief time, you are free of all demands and complications."

—**Sadaharu Oh, world all-time home run leader, with 868**

George Washington played a version of baseball with his men at Valley Forge.

THE SCHOOL OF HARD KNOCKS

It stands to reason that for as long as baseball players have been "beaned" in the skull by errant—or deliberate—pitches to their heads, they've also thought about how to protect their noggins from being hit again. Even so, it took more than a century to find a solution players could live with.

DÉJÀ VU

In 1907 Roger Bresnahan, a catcher for the New York Giants, was knocked unconscious when he was hit in the head by a pitch thrown by Andy Coakley of the Cincinnati Reds. The pitch nearly killed him, and it was a month before he was well enough to get back in the game. When he finally suited up again and stepped up to the plate, the pitcher he faced was...Andy Coakley, the guy who'd put him in the hospital in the first place.

Why risk repeating the previous incident? Bresnahan already had a reputation for experimenting with safety equipment—a year earlier he'd braved the catcalls of fans and players alike when he became the first catcher to openly wear shin guards in a major league game (see page 181). This time, when he stepped up to the plate half of his head was concealed by an inflatable device called a Pneumatic Head Protector.

HEY BUDDY, CAN YOU DO ME A FAVOR?

The bizarre device, sold by the A. J. Reach sporting goods company (cost: $5), looked a little like a two-fingered catcher's mitt. The wearer strapped it to the side of his head that faced the pitcher: The top finger wrapped around the forehead to protect the temple, the bottom finger protected the cheek and jaw, and the space between the two fingers provided just enough room for the wearer to peek out and see the pitches coming his way.

Bresnahan had tried out the Pneumatic Head Protector during spring training in 1905, but had rejected it because it was too bulky. Getting smashed in the head with a 90 mph baseball has a way of clarifying the thought process, however, and now Bresna-

---

han was a believer. He wanted the Giants to buy left- and right-faced versions so that everyone on the team could wear them.

HEAD GAMES

The Giants never did buy Pneumatic Head Protectors; the contraptions never caught on anywhere else, either. As if its frightening appearance wasn't bad enough, the wearer couldn't even inflate it himself. After strapping it to his face he was supposed to find someone to blow into the little rubber tube at the back of his head. (How many players would have been willing to do *that*?) It probably didn't offer any real protection against baseballs to the head, either. Even Bresnahan stopped wearing his after a few games. If protective headgear was ever going to win acceptance, it was going to have to be designed in a way that didn't make the wearer look (or feel) foolish.

But "beanballs" were a part of baseball. Some were accidental, but as baseball evolved into an ever-more-competitive game, some pitchers (known as "headhunters") had taken to deliberately firing pitches right at the batters' heads, sometimes just to intimidate, but sometimes with a genuine desire to cause harm. What was a batter to do? Few were willing to don the silly-looking Pneumatic Head Protector, and there were few other options to choose from. Some players had taken to pouring plaster over ordinary baseball caps to make them more rigid, but that wasn't very effective, either.

THE INJURED LIST

By 1917 "beanball wars" were such a serious problem that baseball's National Commission tried—unsuccessfully—to institute a five-year ban on any player found to have deliberately thrown a beanball. Then, in 1920, Cleveland Indians shortstop Ray Chapman became the first and (so far) only major league player to be killed in a game when he was beaned by a pitch thrown by Yankees pitcher Carl Mays (see page 63). In the minor leagues, where the pitching was wilder and the batters less adept at getting out of the way of bad pitches, the problem was even worse: At least four players were killed by beanballs between 1910 and 1920.

Chapman's death led to a number of reforms designed to prevent such an incident from happening again, but none of them had anything to do with protective headgear. The issue faded away, only to resurface briefly whenever another big-name player was struck down by a beanball. Some players recovered fully, but many did not. Frank Chance, who played for the Chicago Cubs from 1898 to 1912, was hit by so many beanballs that he went permanently deaf in one ear. More than a few promising careers were ended by beanballs.

TWO OUTS

The next step toward finding a solution didn't come until 1940, after two Brooklyn Dodgers players, shortstop Pee Wee Reese and outfielder Joe Medwick, were hit with beanballs three weeks apart. Reese was out for 18 days but made a full recovery; Medwick nearly died and was never the same again. Two players in three weeks? Dodgers chief Larry MacPhail decided he'd had enough. He looked around for some kind of head protection for his players, but in the 20 years since Ray Chapman's death nothing had come along to solve the problem. Spalding sold a head protector that looked like a pair of ear muffs, and some players had taken to wearing cork-lined polo helmets. Neither item was very effective.

MacPhail asked a Johns Hopkins neurosurgeon named Dr. George Dandy to come up with some kind of headgear that provided true protection without looking so ridiculous that players would refuse to wear it. The solution he came up with was surprisingly simple: an ordinary cloth baseball cap with zippered compartments on either side, into which players could insert form-fitting pieces of protective plastic when they went up to bat.

MacPhail was impressed by Dandy's hat and had some made for the team. "Now they can throw at us all they want," he told his players. The investment paid off later that season when outfielder Pete Reiser was hit by a beanball while wearing one of the caps. He had a *terrible* headache afterward, but wasn't seriously injured.

HEAVY METAL

Dr. Dandy's reinforced baseball caps were a big improvement over no protection at all, but they still left a lot to be desired. They didn't provide much protection to the temple, one of the most vulnerable parts of the skull, the way a military helmet or construction hardhat would. So why didn't players just wear helmets or hardhats when they went up to bat? At least one player did—a

Negro League player named Willie Wells. After he was hit by a beanball in a game in 1942, he borrowed a hardhat from a construction site and wore it when he went up to bat.

But in those days, hardhats were made of steel—and heavy enough to impede a player's performance. It wasn't until the development of strong, lightweight plastics in the late 1940s that helmets specifically designed for baseball players became practical for the first time. And because plastic can be molded into just about any shape, designing one that resembled an ordinary baseball cap—so that players wouldn't feel foolish wearing them— was no problem.

HARDHEADED MAN

If you're familiar with baseball history, you may already know that Branch Rickey is the guy who broke major league baseball's color barrier by signing Jackie Robinson to the Brooklyn Dodgers. Did you know he's also credited with creating the first baseball helmet? Rickey, who became general manager of the Pittsburgh Pirates in 1950, knew of several cases over the years where minor leaguers and amateur baseball players had been killed by beanballs. (He also happened to be president of the American Baseball Cap Company.) In 1952 he had the company develop a baseball helmet made of fiberglass and polyester resin, the same materials what were used to make body armor for the military. On September 15, 1952, the Pirates took to the field wearing his helmets for the first time. Not that they had any choice: Rickey ordered his players to wear them, and not just when they were up at bat, either. He wanted them to wear their helmets the entire game.

FEELING IS BELIEVING

It took a while for Rickey's helmets to catch on. Sure, they were lighter than steel helmets, but they were still much heavier than the cloth caps the players were used to. They also trapped a lot of heat, and when the players sweated, the foam rubber padding inside the helmet soaked up the perspiration until it dripped into their eyes.

The Pirates players didn't come to appreciate the helmet until later in the season when they were playing the Chicago Cubs. While pitcher Paul Pettit was running to second base, the Cubs shortstop fired the ball to the second baseman but hit Pettit in the head by accident. Was Pettit killed? Did he lose his eyesight or his ability to speak? Did he need a metal plate in his head? All of these things had happened to players in the past, but Pettit was fine. He didn't even get a headache, didn't even have to leave the game. "All it did was dent the helmet," Pirates catcher Joe Garagiola told *Sports Illustrated* in 1997. "He stayed in the game. Made believers out of everybody."

JOIN THE TEAM

Rickey's helmet had worked, and, just as important, it wasn't embarrassing to wear (at least not at home plate, and Rickey soon relented and let his players wear ordinary baseball caps when they were in the field). So, given the protection they offered, all of baseball immediately adopted the use of batting helmets, right? Not quite. By 1955, 14 of the 16 major league teams supplied batting helmets to any hitters who wanted them…although many didn't. In 1958 some form of head protection, either a cloth cap with inserts or a batting helmet, finally became mandatory for all teams in both the National and American Leagues. Caps with plastic inserts weren't phased out until 1971, and batting helmets with at least one ear flap didn't become mandatory until 1994.

*   *   *

HOW TO STAY YOUNG

1. Avoid fried meats which angry up the blood.

2. If your stomach disputes you, lay down and pacify it with cool thoughts.

3. Keep the juices flowing by jangling around gently as you move.

4. Go very light on the vices, such as carrying on in society. The social ramble ain't restful.

5. Avoid running at all times.

6. Don't look back. Something might be gaining on you.

—Satchel Paige

Satchel Paige was the first Negro Leaguer inducted into the MLB Hall of Fame, in 1971.

HILDA IS HERE

She's been described as the most famous baseball fan in history.

LARGER THAN LIFE

Her name was Hilda Chester, also known as "Howling Hilda" and "the Queen of Flatbush," and she was Brooklyn Dodger Fan #1. Legend has it that her voice could be heard above all others at Ebbets Field in the 1930s. But after she suffered a heart attack, Chester's doctor told her to stop the yelling. So, perched in her seat in the center field bleachers, she came equipped with a barrage of noisemakers—a truck horn, a cowbell, and a frying pan that she pounded with an iron ladle—and a big white banner that read "HILDA IS HERE." Dodgers manager Leo Durocher loved Chester so much that he gave her a lifetime pass to the grandstands (she preferred the outfield bleachers), but sometimes she went too far.

DULY NOTED

During the seventh inning of a game in 1941, Chester beckoned to Dodgers center fielder Pete Reiser. When he came over to her, she handed him a folded-up note and said, "Give this to Leo." At the end of the inning, Reiser ran to the dugout, and as he did, he passed Dodgers team president Larry MacPhail, who was sitting in a nearby box seat. MacPhail waved and Reiser said, "Hi, Larry." Then Reiser took a seat in the dugout next to Durocher and handed him the note, which read "Get Casey hot. Wyatt's losing it." Durocher was livid. He immediately sent a message to the bullpen to start warming up reliever Hugh Casey. The next inning, after Dodgers starter Whit Wyatt gave up a base hit, Durocher pulled him out and brought in Casey. It was an odd move; Wyatt had been pitching a pretty good game. But although Casey gave up some runs, the Dodgers (barely) eked out a win.

After the game, Durocher approached Reiser in the locker room and told him, "Don't you ever hand me a note from MacPhail again!" Reiser told him the note wasn't from MacPhail. "That was from Hilda." It was then that Durocher realized he had just made his first managing decision at the insistence of a fan.

The Reggie Bar (named for Reggie Jackson) was a round version of the Baby Ruth bar.

A LEAGUE APART

If you look at almost any professional sport today, you'll see players from a wide range of ethnic groups: black, white, Asian, Hispanic. But not long ago, professional sports in America was a whites-only world. Here's the story of the black baseball players who fought for almost a century to cross the color line—and finally did.

AMERICA'S GAME?

Every baseball fan knows that Jackie Robinson changed the face of baseball in 1947, when he became the first African American to play in the modern major leagues. But he wasn't the first black ballplayer to play the game for a living—not by a long shot. Black baseball players had been around nearly since the invention of the game.

The first recorded game between all-black teams took place on September 28, 1860, in Hoboken, New Jersey. The Civil War would break out the following year, and would eventually end slavery and help spread the popularity of the relatively new game of baseball. A favorite pastime in Union army camps, baseball came home with returning soldiers, who founded amateur ball clubs throughout the industrial cities of the North. Emancipated slaves settled into these same cities in droves, and, by the late 1860s, black athletic clubs in towns like Philadelphia, New York, and Washington were sending baseball teams from city to city to stage contests.

In 1867 the all-black Pythians of Philadelphia applied for membership in the 400-club National Association of Base Ball Players, baseball's first governing body. The association flatly rejected the Pythians on the basis of race and drafted a resolution that barred membership for "any club which may be composed of one or more colored players."

A HARDER ROAD THAN MOST

Nevertheless, blacks continued to play what was quickly becoming America's national pastime. In 1870, as professional teams began to replace amateur ones, the National Association of *Professional* Base Ball Players replaced the older governing body. But unlike

---

The Negro League's Josh Gibson is the only player ever to hit a ball *out* of Yankee Stadium.

the previous organization, the NAPBBP didn't explicitly prohibit black players. Most teams were still white-only, but no rule said they had to be.

In 1878 a black barber named Bud Fowler joined an otherwise all-white professional team based in Chelsea, Massachusetts. This makes Fowler the first black man to ever play on a professional squad. Another pioneer was catcher Moses Fleetwood Walker, who signed with the Toledo Blue Stockings of the minor Northwestern League in 1883. In 1884 the Blue Stockings moved up to the American Association, one of the major leagues—technically making Walker the first black player in the majors. Walker got injured halfway through his first season, and the Blue Stockings went out of business shortly after, prematurely ending Walker's pro career.

Walker went on to play in the minor International League for five years for the Newark Giants, a team that employed a handful of black players (the spotty records of the time make it hard to say how many). But in 1887, International League owners made an unofficial "gentlemen's agreement" to get rid of all their current black players and not sign any more. Now black ballplayers weren't welcome in the minor leagues, which effectively blocked them from ever rising into the majors.

INDEPENDENT BASEBALL

In the early 1880s, black players began to develop their own baseball community. Within a few years, there were more than 200 all-black teams around the country. All were "independent" teams, meaning they scheduled their own games against each other (and sometimes against all-white or college teams), or they toured from ballpark to ballpark as "barnstorming" teams.

The first serious attempt at forming an all-black *professional* league came in May 1887, with the National Colored League of Base Ball Players. The league consisted of eight all-black teams from Baltimore, Boston, Cincinnati, Louisville, New York, Philadelphia, Pittsburgh, and Washington. But the league was a financial disaster—half the teams ran out of money and folded within three weeks, and the league folded with them. But the mold had been cast for the future of black baseball. Players returned to the barnstorming circuits and joined popular city

leagues, attracting audiences and biding their time until another black league organization could be formed.

FOSTER FATHER

In 1907 a Texas native named Rube Foster arrived in Chicago to pitch for the all-black Leland Giants. He was already a star attraction on the barnstorming circuit, where he had played in exhibitions against big-leaguers and reportedly taught legendary pitcher Christy Mathewson how to throw his signature pitch—the screwball. In 1909, while still an active player, Foster bought the team and renamed it the Chicago American Giants.

Foster believed his team played at a major league level, even if the majors weren't interested in him or his players. By 1919 Foster believed that there were enough well-run professional black ball clubs in the Midwest to form a separate black "big league." Foster convened a meeting of the owners of these teams at a Kansas City YMCA in February 1920, where they agreed to play a set schedule of league games, with a playoff after the regular season. They called themselves the Negro National League, with a roster of eight teams: the Chicago American Giants, the Chicago Giants, the Cuban Stars (a traveling team), the Dayton Marcos, the Detroit Stars, the Indianapolis ABCs, the St. Louis Giants, and the Kansas City Monarchs. The Hilldale (Penn.) Daisies and the Atlantic City Giants later joined the league.

ROOKIE SEASON

The league got off to a shaky start in the spring of 1920. Teams had a hard time convincing their top players to stay, since they could make more money barnstorming than they could playing for an upstart league. But enough of them stuck around that by 1921, the NNL was turning a profit.

In fact, it was turning enough profit that it spawned imitators—a Southern Negro League formed in 1922, and more offshoots soon began to grow. In 1923 the Hilldale Daisies and Atlantic City Giants broke off from the NNL to form a new league with four other teams—the Baltimore Black Sox, the Brooklyn Royal Giants, a different Cuban Stars squad, and the Lincoln Giants (New York). The new league, organized by white sports promoter Nat Strong, was called the Eastern Colored League.

In the 1930s, to attract white fans, some black baseball games included vaudeville-style skits.

The ECL raided the rosters of the NNL for top talent. In 1924 the two leagues called a truce and arranged for each league's regular-season champion to meet in an annual Negro League World Series. In the first NLWS, the Kansas City Monarchs of the NNL beat the Darby Daisies, five games to four.

Rube Foster, who'd been running the National Negro League almost single-handedly, suffered a mental breakdown in 1926 and was institutionalized. Without him, the NNL began to unravel. So did the ECL, which folded in the middle of the 1928 season. The NNL fell apart for good in 1931.

THE GLORY YEARS

In 1933 a black bar owner named Gus Greenlee revived the Negro National League, incorporating teams from both the old ECL and NNL as well as new teams. The league had teams in Baltimore, Chicago, Brooklyn, Detroit, Columbus, Indianapolis, Nashville, and Pittsburgh.

Greenlee's own team, the Pittsburgh Crawfords, fielded one of the most remarkable lineups in baseball history. The team featured five future Hall of Famers, including Cool Papa Bell, Josh Gibson, and Satchel Paige, and won the first two NNL titles. Their chief rival was the Homestead (Penn.) Grays, a team that joined the NNL in 1935 led by star first baseman Buck Leonard (Bell and Gibson would later play for the Grays as well). From 1937 to 1945, the Grays won nine straight championships.

Meanwhile, to rival the mostly east coast NNL, eight teams in the Midwest formed the Negro American League in 1937. The NAL was dominated by the Kansas City Monarchs, who won five championships between 1937 and 1942. Champions of each league met in 1942 for a revived Negro League World Series. (The Monarchs beat the Grays, four games to none.) An even bigger event than the championship was the annual East-West All-Star Game held in Comiskey Park in Chicago—which sometimes drew as many as 50,000 fans. Many Negro League games were held in big-league stadiums—and attracted black and white audiences.

JUST A MATTER OF TIME

The talent pool in the Negro Leagues was deep by the late 1930s, and white Americans' attitudes about racial equality were begin-

---

The last *legal* spitball was thrown by Burleigh Grimes on September 10, 1934.

ning to change. In 1938 Clark Griffith, owner of the major league Washington Senators, publicly stated that "the time is not far off when colored players will take their places beside those of other races in the major leagues." And in 1942, baseball commissioner Kenesaw Mountain Landis, a Southerner and "traditionalist," reluctantly admitted that integration was around the corner: "There is no rule, formal or informal, no understanding, subterranean or otherwise, against hiring Negro players."

But behind the scenes, Landis helped kill a 1944 bid by Bill Veeck to buy the Philadelphia Phillies after Veeck announced his intention of hiring star players from the Negro Leagues. When Landis died of a heart attack later that year, one of the last hurdles facing baseball integration went with him.

HERE'S TO YOU, MR. ROBINSON

In August 1945, Brooklyn Dodgers general manager Branch Rickey, who had once referred to African Americans as "the greatest untapped reservoir of raw material in the history of the game," made history himself when he signed a promising young player named Jackie Robinson to a minor league contract. It was the first time a major league GM had reached across the color line to sign a black player into his team's farm system.

Robinson was a 26-year-old World War II veteran who'd been an All-American football player at UCLA. He'd played only one season with the Kansas City Monarchs in the Negro American League, but Rickey's scouts recognized his talent, as well as something else Rickey wanted—self-discipline and a calm temperament. Rickey believed that the first African American in the big leagues would become the standard-bearer for integration, and would need to be an above-average player who could also handle the pressure and prejudice he was sure to face.

After a standout 1946 season with the Dodgers Triple-A team in Montreal, Robinson broke into the big leagues with Brooklyn in 1947, winning the National League Rookie of the Year award that same year and leading the Dodgers to the World Series in 1955. But he became perhaps more famous for doing just what Branch Rickey had hoped: He remained a focused and dedicated player in spite of the constant barrage of racist taunts hurled at him by spectators and opponents.

September 1, 1974: The Pirates fielded MLB's first all African-American starting lineup.

THE BEGINNING AND THE END

The other handful of players who were among the first to break the color barrier have been somewhat overshadowed by Robinson's accomplishments. During that first integrated season of 1947, the Cleveland Indians—now owned by the same Bill Veeck who had attempted to integrate the Phillies three years earlier—brought Larry Doby from the NNL Newark Eagles to the big leagues. Two other former Negro Leaguers, Willard Brown and Hank Thompson, saw playing time with the St. Louis Browns that year, and the Dodgers brought a black pitcher, Dan Bankhead, up from the minors before the season was out.

In 1948 the Dodgers added another African American to their lineup: future Hall of Fame catcher Roy Campanella, who was followed the next year by pitcher Don Newcombe. Also in 1948, the Indians signed the great Satchel Paige, who became the first black pitcher to appear in a World Series game when Cleveland won the championship that fall.

Once major league teams started signing the best black players, Negro League teams found themselves in financial trouble. The NNL shut down for good after the 1948 season; the NAL hung on until 1957. For a while, what remained of the Negro Leagues still served as a source of black talent for major league clubs, a sort of independent farm system. Willie Mays, Hank Aaron, and Ernie Banks were among the crop of young players who made brief appearances in the post-Jackie Robinson Negro Leagues on their way to big-league careers.

LASTING IMPACT

In the first seven years of integrated baseball, six National League Rookie of the Year winners were African American: Robinson, Newcombe, Sam Jethroe, Mays, Joe Black, and Joe Gilliam. Beginning with Jackie Robinson's first trip to the postseason in 1947, 11 of the next 13 World Series would feature former Negro League players. Jackie Robinson retired in 1956, and in 1961 he became the first African American inducted into the Hall of Fame. In 1997, the 50th anniversary of the year he broke the color line, Jackie Robinson's #42 was retired by every team in the major leagues.

Only player to win the Rookie of the Year, MVP, and Cy Young awards: Don Newcombe.

OH, NO! NO NO-NO!

*It's heartbreaking when a pitcher comes oh-so-close to throwing a
no-hitter—only to have some lucky batter...or a clueless
Hollywood actor...or even himself, mess it all up.*

RULE #1

During a Rockies home game, baseball fan and actor Kurt-
wood Smith (he played the father on *That '70s Show*)
dropped by the radio booth for an interview. Apparently he had
never heard the first rule of a possible no-hitter: *You do not talk
about the possible no-hitter!* Whatever Smith said before or after the
phrase "Shawn Chacon's got a no-hitter going" has been lost to
history, because on the very next pitch, Chacon gave up a single
to right-center.

WHAT'S THAT RULE AGAIN?

Apparently Yahoo! Sports wasn't concerned about jinxing Boston's
Curt Schilling's amazing performance, as the site kept posting
updated headlines during his outing against the A's on June 7, 2007:

SCHILLING HAS A NO-HITTER THROUGH SIX INNINGS.

SCHILLING HAS A NO-HITTER THROUGH SEVEN INNINGS.

SCHILLING HAS A NO-HITTER THROUGH EIGHT INNINGS.

SCHILLING HAS A NO-HITTER THROUGH 8 ⅓ INNINGS.

SCHILLING HAS A NO-HITTER THROUGH 8 ⅔ INNINGS.

SINGLE BY OAKLAND'S SHANNON STEWART WITH TWO OUTS
IN THE NINTH INNING ENDS SCHILLING'S NO-HITTER.

Don't blame Yahoo!, though—blame Schilling. With one out to
go, catcher Jason Varitek called for a slider to Shannon Stewart,
but Schilling shook him off and threw a fastball instead. "I was
sure he was taking, and Tek was sure he was swinging," Schilling
said. "And I was wrong." (The exact same thing had happened in
Pedro Martinez's brush with a no-hitter seven years earlier: 8 ⅔
innings, no hits. Varitek called for a curve; Martinez wanted to
throw a fastball. Tampa Bay's John Flaherty wanted a fastball,
too...and hit it for a single.)

Harvey Haddix was the first pitcher to throw 12 perfect innings—then lose the game in the 13th.

LAYING DOWN A BUNT? THAT'S A BEAMIN'

If there's anything a pitcher can't stand when he has a no-hitter going in the late innings, it's when the batter tries to bunt for a base hit. During one game in 1986, Royals pitcher Danny Jackson hadn't given up a hit to the Angels through seven innings. Angels outfielder Devon White tried to lay down a bunt, but missed. Jackson showed his disapproval by hurling the next pitch high and inside, nearly beaning White and sending him crumpling to the ground. Ironically, that pitch may have upset the thrower more than the batter—Jackson seemed off his game after that, and he ended up giving up two hits. (But he still won).

HORACE CLARK: NO-HITTER KILLER

During one month in 1970, three American League teams came within one inning of throwing a no-hitter. The pitchers: Jim Rooker of the Kansas City Royals, Sonny Siebert of the Boston Red Sox, and Joe Niekro of the Detroit Tigers. The batter who ended them all: Yankees second baseman Horace Clark, who broke up all three no-hitters with a hit in the ninth inning.

BUTTERFINGERS

On June 13, 1994, Expos pitcher Jeff Fassero was one out away from a no-hitter when he threw a fastball to the Pirates' Carlos Garcia. Garcia lined a waist-high shot right back to Fassero, who quickly reached across his body and speared the ball. Thinking he'd caught it, Fassero looked into his glove. The baseball wasn't there—it was rolling toward third base. After a moment's confusion (and what must have seemed like an eternity), Fassero lunged at the ball, grabbed it, and fired it to first base. Garcia slid head-first, but because of Fassero's hesitation, he barely beat out the throw and was called safe. The official scorer's ruling: infield hit. "I really thought I had it," said a stunned Fassero after the game.

HINDSIGHT IS 20-20

It was 1934 when the St. Louis Cardinals' two best pitchers, brothers Dizzy and Paul Dean, combined for 49 wins. In game one of a doubleheader against the Brooklyn Dodgers, Dizzy took a no-hitter into the eighth inning but had to "settle" for a three-hit shutout. In game two, Paul went out and pitched a gem, not

---

allowing a single hit. Afterward, in the locker room, Dizzy famously said, "Shucks! If'n Paul had told me he was gonna pitch a no-hitter, I'd-a throwed one, too."

DATES WITH DESTINY

September 24, 1988: Toronto's Dave Stieb was one out away from throwing the first no-hitter in Blue Jays history. Cleveland's Julio Franco hit a grounder toward second base…but it took a bad hop and went over the second baseman's head, and Franco reached first safely.

September 30, 1988: On Stieb's very next start, he no-hit the Orioles through 8 ⅔ innings…and then gave up a bloop single to Jim Traber.

August 4, 1989: This time, Stieb was one out away from a perfect game when the Yankees' Roberto Kelly hit a double. That made three no-hitters lost with one out to go.

September 2, 1990: The Jays were playing in Cleveland, and Stieb found himself in familiar territory: no hits through the bottom of the ninth—one more out and he'd have his (and Toronto's) first no-hitter. Alex Cole came to the plate and Stieb walked him on four pitches…but the no-hitter was still intact. Then Jerry Browne came up. Stieb's first pitch missed badly. Had Stieb lost his control? The next pitch was right down the middle. Browne made contact, but didn't get all of it. It was an easy fly-out to right field and Stieb had finally done it. The Indians' fans cheered the visiting pitcher's accomplishment while the Blue Jays hoisted Stieb on their shoulders for a victory lap around the infield. (As of 2007, it is still the only no-hitter in Blue Jays history.)

*   *   *

I'VE GOT A SECRET

In 1956 Yankees outfielder Bob Cerv was sitting on the bench in the dugout when manager Casey Stengel sat down next to him. The two sat quietly for a few moments. Then Stengel leaned in and said, "Nobody knows this, but one of us has just been traded to Kansas City."

FINAL THOUGHTS

We leave you with some wise words about this wonderful game.

"Baseball, it is said, is only a game. True. And the Grand Canyon is only a hole in Arizona."
—George Will

"Ninety feet between home plate and first base may be the closest man has ever come to perfection."
—Red Smith

"The greatest thrill in the world is to end the game with a home run and watch everybody else walk off the field while you're running the bases on air."
—Al Rosen

"You can't sit on a lead and run a few plays into the line and just kill the clock. You've got to throw the ball over the plate and give the other man his chance. That's why baseball is the greatest game of them all."
—Earl Weaver

"You gotta be a man to play baseball for a living, but you gotta have a lot of little boy in you, too."
—Roy Campanella

"There are only three things America will be known for 2,000 years from now when they study this civilization: the Constitution, jazz music, and baseball."
—Gerald Early

"The other sports are just sports. Baseball is a love."
—Bryant Gumbel

"Love is the most important thing in the world, but baseball is pretty good, too."
—Yogi Berra

"People ask me what I do in winter when there's no baseball. I'll tell you what I do. I stare out the window and wait for spring."
—Rogers Hornsby

"When I put on my uniform, I am the proudest man on Earth."
—Roberto Clemente

"You spend a good piece of your life gripping a baseball, and it turns out it was the other way around all the time."
—Jim Bouton

ANSWER PAGES

BASEBALL 101
(Answers for page 81)

1. c) If such a game is called on account of inclement weather or any other reason, it is considered a complete game. So what happens if the score is *tied* when a regulation game is called? The game is suspended and, depending on scheduling and other circumstances, can be completed at a later date or replayed in its entirety. If the game isn't going to affect the league championship, it may not be rescheduled at all.

2. b) Okay, that was a pretty easy question…but do you know how the strike zone is defined? The upper limit of the rectangle is a horizontal line midway between the top of the batter's shoulders and the top of his uniform pants when he is crouching in his batting stance. The lower limit is a horizontal line at the hollow below the batter's kneecap. The left and right boundaries correspond to the left and right edges of home plate.

3. b) The game ends immediately after a walk-off home run because the losing team does not have another turn at bat and thus has no chance of tying the game or taking the lead.

4. a) Did you know that a sacrifice fly is not counted as a turn at bat? The thinking behind this is that a tactical move should not be allowed to impact a player's batting statistics, which are supposed to reflect only their batting skill and nothing else. Sacrifice bunts aren't counted as at-bats, either, for the same reason.

5. b) The infield fly rule applies only when there are fewer than two outs (with two outs, only one more out is possible, so the rule is not necessary), and when there are runners on first and second or the bases are loaded.

6. b)

7. c)

TEST YOUR UMPIRE I.Q.
(Answers for page 148)

1. a) The umpire-in-chief decides whether games already in play

---

Roger Clemens has won the Cy Young Award seven times, and in three different decades.

should be called due to weather or field conditions, but if the game hasn't started yet, it's the home team's manager who makes the call. (Note: this rule does not apply to the second game of a doubleheader. The umpire-in-chief of the first game is the one who decides whether the second game should start.)

2. a) Foul territory begins on the foul side of the pole, so by definition, if the ball strikes the foul pole it is in fair territory.

3. b)

4. False. If the ball passes over the fence or into the stands at a distance of 250 feet or greater, it counts as a home run. If the distance is less than 250 feet, it counts as a double and the batter and any runners on base can only advance two bases.

5. c) If the fly is deflected at a point less than 250 feet from home plate, the batter advances two bases. If it's deflected at a point more than 250 from home plate, it counts as a home run. (If it's deflected into *foul* territory, the batter advances two bases no matter how far it is from home plate.)

6. c) If the umpire determines that a runner on third base would have scored after the catch if the spectator had not interfered with the fielder, the umpire can permit the runner to score.

7. c)

8. b)

9. a)

10. b)

11. c)

12. a) If the batter still refuses to step up after the first strike is called, the umpire can call two or even three strikes.

TEST YOUR UMPIRE I.Q.
(Answers for page 212)

1. b) "The umpire shall not direct the attention of any person to the presence in the batter's box of an improper batter. This rule is designed to require constant vigilance by the players and managers of both teams."

2. c) The same rule applies whenever a fielder steps foot in any out-of-play area. (Note: If the fielder falls into the dugout after

According to the movie *Total Recall* (1990), the Tokyo Samurais will win the 2070 World Series.

catching the ball outside the dugout, the ball is dead and each runner may advance one base.)

3. b) He's also out if he moves from one side of home plate to the other while the pitcher is in position ready to pitch.

4. c) As soon as he steps into the batter's box, he is called out, ejected from the game, and referred to the league president for further punishment.

5. a) "The run would score on the theory that the run was forced home by the base on balls and that all the runners needed to do was proceed and touch the next base."

6. b) These penalties apply only if the umpire determines that the thrown glove or the other items actually did touch the ball. There is no penalty if the ball is untouched.

7. c)

8. b) The first runner is considered to have been put out *before* the second runner scored. Since there are already two outs, this counts as the third out and there is no further scoring. Had there been fewer than two outs when the first runner was put out, the run would have counted.

9. b) The countdown begins as soon as the pitcher has the ball and the batter is in the batter's box. Every time the pitcher delays more than 12 seconds, the umpire must call a ball.

10. a)

*   *   *

YOU'VE URNED IT

Want to take your fanataicism with you to the grave? Thanks to Eternal Images, maker of "brand name funerary products that celebrate the passions in life," you can choose from their Major League Baseball™ line of caskets, complete with your favorite team's logo. Can't afford the casket? Then have yourself cremated and spend eternity in your team's official urn, each one "hand-designed" made of die-cast aluminum sealed with a long-lasting clear-coat finish. "Each urn sits on a 'home plate' base outlined in black. Each also features a baseball display dome at the top in which a favorite collectible baseball can be displayed."

"Baseball isn't statistics. Baseball is DiMaggio rounding second." —Jimmy Cannon

UNCLE JOHN'S BATHROOM READER CLASSIC SERIES